Health and Globalization

Health and Globalization

GEOFFREY B. COCKERHAM

AND

WILLIAM C. COCKERHAM

polity

First published in 2010 by Polity Press

Polity Press
65 Bridge Street
Cambridge CB2 1UR, UK

Polity Press
350 Main Street
Malden, MA 02148, USA

ISBN-13: 978-0-7456-4512-4
ISBN-13: 978-0-7456-4513-1 (pb)

A catalogue record for this book is available from the British Library.

Typeset in 11 on 13 pt Berling
by Toppan Best-set Premedia Limited
Printed and bound in Great Britain by MPG Books Group Limited, Bodmin, Cornwall

The publisher has used its best endeavours to ensure that the URLs for external websites referred to in this book are correct and active at the time of going to press. However, the publisher has no responsibility for the websites and can make no guarantee that a site will remain live or that the content is or will remain appropriate.

Every effort has been made to trace all copyright holders, but if any have been inadvertently overlooked the publisher will be pleased to include any necessary credits in any subsequent reprint or edition.

For further information on Polity, visit our website: www.politybooks.com

Contents

Abbreviations   vii

1   Defining Globalization   1

2   Globalization: Health Benefits and Risks   24

3   Globalization and Disease   42

4   Globalization and Health Care: the United States   63

5   Globalization and Health Care in
    Selected Countries   85

6   Actors in Global Health Governance   119

7   Global Health Governance: Public Goods and
    Collective Action   148

Concluding Remarks   185
References   188
Author Index   206
Subject Index   211

Abbreviations

AIDS	acquired immune deficiency syndrome
AMA	American Medical Association
ARV	antiretroviral drug
BAT	British American Tobacco
BMA	British Medical Association
CDC	Centers for Disease Control and Prevention
CFC	chlorofluorocarbon
DHA	district health authority
DRG	diagnostic related group
EC	European Community
FBO	faith-based organization
FCTC	Framework Convention on Tobacco Control
FDA	Food and Drug Administration
GATS	General Agreement on Trade in Services
GATT	General Agreement on Tariffs and Trade
GDP	gross domestic product
GM	genetically modified
GP	general practitioner
GPA	Global Program on AIDS
GSDPAH	Global Strategy on Diet, Physical Activity, and Health
HIV	human immunodeficiency virus
HMO	health maintenance organization
HSU	Human Security Unit
IGO	intergovernmental organization

IHR	International Health Regulations
IMF	International Monetary Fund
IPCC	Intergovernmental Panel on Climate Change
ITO	International Trade Organization
IV	intravenous
MNC	multinational corporation
MSF	Médecins Sans Frontières
NAFTA	North American Free Trade Agreement
NATO	North Atlantic Treaty Organization
NGO	non-governmental organization
NHS	National Health Service
PPO	preferred provider organization
PPP	public–private partnership
SAP	structural adjustment program
SARS	severe acute respiratory syndrome
SPS	Agreement on Sanitary and Phytosanitary Measures
STD	sexually transmitted disease
TFI	Tobacco Free Initiative
TRIPS	Agreement on Trade-Related Aspects of Intellectual Property Rights
UN	United Nations
UNDP	United Nations Development Program
WHA	World Health Assembly
WHO	World Health Organization
WTO	World Trade Organization

1

Defining Globalization

Health and disease are connected globally. Take, for example, the case of the Ebola virus (hemorrhagic fever), which typically kills 90 percent of those infected. Two decades ago the virus showed up in the United States by way of the Philippines after being first identified in 1976 in central Africa. It is transmitted by close contact with infected people and monkeys through blood and other bodily fluids, as well as by the use of contaminated needles and sexual activity. In 1989, two shipments of monkeys infected with the virus arrived at a medical laboratory in Reston, Virginia, from a facility in the Philippines. In a dramatic series of events, a team of medical scientists and army personnel contained the virus within the lab facility before it was able to spread to humans in the greater metropolitan area of Washington, DC (Preston 1994). The monkeys in the first shipment, including one that temporarily escaped within the building, were killed by lethal injection by a team dressed in space suits to protect them from infection. Those in the second shipment were simply allowed to die of the disease in their cages. Four human caretakers tested positive for Ebola but did not become sick, and eventually the virus cleared from their blood. They are among the very few humans ever to survive Ebola.

Ebola's existence in the United States was short-lived and its potentially deadly effects were eliminated quickly before widespread harm was done. The fact that a deadly African disease could suddenly surface in the vicinity of the nation's capital was an unpleasant surprise. However, the process of globalization brings people and disease agents into closer contact with one another today more so than in any other period of human history. The purpose of this book, accordingly, is to examine the effects of globalization on health. This is an important topic because neither health nor disease in modern society is simply a local phenomenon. Diseases now jump rapidly from continent to continent and efforts to contain them function on a global level; markets for drugs and other health care commodities and the corporations that produce them span the globe; and global processes such as pollution, modernization, and technological change impact on local environments to affect the health of the residents. We will begin, in this chapter, by defining globalization and discussing the broad contours of its influence on health before turning in subsequent chapters to a more detailed examination of the relationship.

What Is Globalization?

Globalization is a widely used term that emerged in the late 1980s as a buzz-word to refer to the increased trade and investment flows taking place among different countries following the end of the Cold War and the collapse of the communist governments in the former Soviet Union and Eastern Europe. The closing stages of the Cold War in 1989 became the turning point in the maturing of globalization because it became possible at that time to visualize a "borderless" world, in which people, goods, ideas, and images would flow with relative ease across national boundaries. The major global division between the West (capitalism) and the East (state socialism) was gone (Ray 2007a, 2007b). Capitalism was now the dominant economic and social system in the world. "With the collapse of the Soviet system," states Larry Ray (2007b: 3), "so also fell the belief that [the] state could control and manage the affairs of society for maximum well-being and exclude the rest of the world." The demise of state socialism had also coincided with the development and explosion in worldwide wireless digital communication systems, dramatically easing the capability of people to communicate not only locally, but across borders.

The use of e-mail, cell phones, and text messaging became commonplace, as did the rapid provision of news and information via television, radio, computers, and cell phones. "A globalized world," says Ray (2007a: 1956), "is one of increasing instantaneity, where events are experienced instantly even by people in spatially distant locations through access to digital communicative technologies."

However, as the restructuring of economic, political, and social relationships has taken place on a global scale, the term "globalization" itself remains fairly vague and without a universally accepted definition. Part of the imprecision can be attributed to the modern media, which have used the term frequently and in many different ways to describe the complexities of the global economy. Another reason for its vagueness has to do with the increased use of the term beyond its economic origins to include political, social, cultural, environmental, and even security connotations. The result is a wide range of perspectives concerning globalization.

Many definitions of globalization focus on its economic context. Such definitions see it as the increasing internationalization of markets for goods and services, means of production, financial systems, business corporations, technology, and competition (Frieden 2006; Gilpin 2002). Other definitions have stressed both the economic and the social aspects of globalization. For example, Joseph Stiglitz (2003: 9) defines globalization as "the closer integration of the countries and peoples of the world which has been brought about by the enormous reduction of costs of transportation and communication, and the breaking down of artificial barriers to the flows of goods, services, capital, knowledge, and (to a lesser extent) people across borders."

Roland Robertson (1992: 8) was one of the first sociologists to discuss globalization, which he defined as "the compression of the world and the consciousness of the world as a whole." He suggests that awareness of the world as a single place promotes a global consciousness in the minds of people. Robertson credited globalization by the end of the twentieth century, if not sooner, with transforming the view people have of the world and their situation in it. This does not mean that everyone has the same perspective, but that their view is influenced by their particular place in the world in relation to people in other places. This makes the world seem smaller to all concerned. In such a compressed world, however, differing views can be expected to produce new conflicts and stimulate old, unresolved ones.

Another sociologist, Anthony Giddens (2002: 60), focuses on the social aspect of globalization by defining it as "the intensification of worldwide social relations which link distant localities in such a way that local happenings are shaped by events occurring many miles away and vice versa." As Giddens explains, anyone who studies cities today is likely to recognize that what happens in local neighborhoods is influenced by factors such as money and commodity markets operating at an indefinite distance away from the neighborhood itself. We see this when the price of oil rises and worldwide demand drives up the costs of food and other commodities in local markets. Since most areas of the world are connected economically, Giddens suggests that capitalism is a more fundamental globalizing influence than politics. This is because he finds that economic practices inherent in capitalism have been able to penetrate far-flung regions of the world more effectively than political concepts. China, for example, has adopted capitalism as an economic model, but politically remains communist.

In contrast to Giddens, Ethan Kapstein (1999) emphasizes the political nature of globalization. He claims that globalization is fundamentally a political phenomenon that did not arise "naturally." Rather, it was the result of policy decisions taken after World War II among the Western allies that established more extensive global relationships in comparison to the past. These relationships continue to spread and evolve today.

In addition to these perspectives, which emphasize particular aspects of globalization, some views suggest that globalization defines a new international system. In fact, journalist Thomas Friedman (2000) has described globalization as the international system that replaced the old Cold War arrangement of states. He views this system as the integration of markets, states, and technologies, creating a world that is faster, deeper, less expensive, and more global than ever before. Friedman (2005) describes, for example, playing golf in Bangalore, India. As he was about to tee off, he was told to aim at two buildings in the distance. One was the offices of Microsoft and the other of IBM:

I was standing on the first tee at the KGA Golf Club in downtown Bangalore, in southern India, when my playing partner pointed at two shiny glass-and-steel buildings off in the distance, just behind the first green. The Goldman Sachs building wasn't done yet; otherwise he could have pointed that out and made it a threesome.

HP and Texas Instruments had their offices on the back nine, along the tenth hole. That wasn't all. The tee markers were from Epson, the printer company, and one of our caddies was wearing a hat from 3M. Outside, some of the traffic signs were also sponsored by Texas Instruments, and the Pizza Hut billboard on the way over showed a steaming pizza, under the headline: "Gigabytes of Taste!"

No, this definitely wasn't Kansas. It didn't even seem like India. Was this the New World, the Old World, or the Next World? (Friedman 2005: 3)

Friedman (2005) says there have been three periods of globalization. The first period, what he calls Globalization 1.0, began in 1492, when Columbus opened up the New World to trade with the Old World, and lasted to around 1800. Friedman states that this period shrank the world from a large to a medium size. The key agent of change in his view during this era was inanimate brawn, namely how much power – harnessed from horses, the wind, or steam – a country could employ in integrating the world. The second period, Globalization 2.0, lasted from 1800 to 2000 and included the twentieth-century interruptions of the Great Depression and two world wars. It shrank the world from a size medium to a size small. The key agent of change was multinational corporations, whose markets and labor became global. Beginning with steamships and railroads, the period was marked by a transition to telephones and mainframe computers. During this era we see the birth and maturing of a true global economy.

Globalization 3.0 began around 2000 and shrank the world from size small to size tiny. Friedman (2005: 10) observes that "while the dynamic force in Globalization 1.0 was countries globalizing and the dynamic force in Globalization 2.0 was companies globalizing, the dynamic force in Globalization 3.0 – the force that gives it its unique character – is the newfound power for *individuals* to collaborate and compete globally." What allowed individuals and small groups to globalize easily, and large and small companies to join them in this process, is essentially the Internet (or what Friedman calls a flat-world platform):

> The flat-world platform is the product of a convergence of the personal computer (which allowed every individual suddenly to become the author of his or her own content in digital form) with fiber-optic cable (which suddenly allowed all those individuals to access more and more digital content around the world for next to nothing) with the rise of work flow software (which enabled individuals all over the world to collaborate on that same digital content from anywhere, regardless of the distances between them). No one anticipated this convergence. It just happened – right around the year 2000. And when it did, people all over the world started waking up and realizing that they had more power than ever to go global as *individuals*...(Friedman 2005: 10–11)

Therefore, one aspect of globalization is the connecting of individuals into a global network of contact and information exchange, including commercial activities such as E-Bay and cyber-based social relationships. People now send e-mails much more frequently than they do letters. Blogs are popping up daily on the Internet, some sponsored by companies and others maintained by individuals for the sharing of news, viewpoints, and comments. Academics and research scientists regularly exchange theories, views, and research findings with their colleagues around the globe. Patients go on the Internet to research their diseases and acquire information in order to review their options with physicians on a more equal footing. The Internet has profoundly and irreversibly changed the pattern of individual human communication. Although the literature on globalization presents a multitude of definitions, what these seem to have in common is that globalization refers to a process of integration that leads to increased linkages among different countries and individuals around the world.

However, as individuals globalized, so did international corporations. With the modern state system changing as a result, another implication of globalization is the notion that the nation-state was becoming weaker and global corporations were becoming more powerful economically and politically. Susan Strange (2002) makes the argument that this is indeed the case. Strange (2002: 128) says that post-World War II market forces, which are guided primarily by private enterprises, "are now more powerful than states to whom ultimate political authority over society and economy is supposed to belong." Giddens (1990) agrees in that he finds some large business corporations – especially giant transnational firms – may wield immense economic power and have the capacity to influence political policies.

And yet a third facet of globalization is homogenization. That is, as countries experience globalization and become more interconnected, they also become more alike or homogenous. Despite cultural differences, businesspersons will find great similarity in dress, methods, contracts, forms of commerce, and the language of global business (English) around the world, and travelers to major countries will likewise see similar goods and services. Where globalization has been most pronounced, the same retailers will have stores, the same hotel chains will be available, the same airlines will serve the airports, and so forth. Consequently, behind globalization is a process of homogeneity producing a global culture sustaining the exchange and flow of goods and services, people, information, and knowledge worldwide.

The most prevalent global culture today is North American–Western European capitalism (Clark 2007; Frieden 2006; Zakaria 2009). Western-style capitalism dominates the world economy and has resulted in a mode of conducting trade centered on a particular language (English) and norms regarding dress (Western business suits), financing, procedures for record keeping, the use of contracts, methods of manufacture, shipment, sales, and means of communication (e-mail, websites, telephones, cell phones, text-messaging, fax machines, overnight delivery of packages, etc.), which shape social relationships and cultural understandings between people and businesses in different countries. Thus, an Egyptian and a German, a Chinese and an Italian, or a South Korean and an Argentine are as likely to follow the same norms for business methods and communication as an American and a Canadian. As Anthony Smith pointed out several years ago:

> On the one hand, capitalist competition has given birth to immensely powerful transnational corporations with huge budgets, reserves of skilled labor, advanced technologies and sophisticated information networks. Essential to their success is

the ability to deliver suitably packaged imagery and symbolism which will convey their definitions of the services they provide. While they have to rely on a transnational lingua franca (a common language often English), it is the new system of tele-communications and computerized information networks which enable them to by-pass differences in language and culture to secure the labor and markets they require. In other words, the resources, range and specialized flexibility of transnational cor-porations' activities enable them to present imagery and infor-mation almost on a global scale, threatening to swamp the cultural networks of more local units, including nations and ethnic communities. (Smith 1990: 174–5)

However, these methods of doing business, involving common global systems of communication and behavior, go beyond matters of trade and extend to global norms for scien-tific research, higher education, travel, leisure, lifestyles, and health care. They extend to clothing as well. Fareed Zakaria (2009) points out that women's clothing is a powerful indicator of a nation's link to modernity. Traditional saris in India and kimonos in Japan, for instance, are now usually worn only on special occasions. Zakaria (2009: 75) says, "ask a young Indian professional to explain whether wrapping herself in six to nine yards of fabric, often starched, then carefully pleating and folding it, is something of a bother." It is not surprising, in his view, that the sari industry is in decline. He notes that Muslim countries have the biggest problem with their women wearing Western-style clothing and observes that they also represent a region where outside influences are most rejected and women lag furthest behind in literacy, education, and participation in the workforce. As for men, Zakaria finds:

Western clothing is ubiquitous. Ever since armies began dressing in Western-style uniforms, men around the world have adopted Western-style work clothes. The business suit, a descendant of a European army officer's outfit, is now standard for men from Japan to South Africa to Peru – with the laggard (or rebel) once again being the Arab world. The Japanese, for all of their cul-tural distinctiveness, go one step further and on special occasions (such as the swearing in of their governments) wear morning coats and striped pants, the style for Edwardian diplomats in England a hundred years ago. In India, wearing traditional clothes was long associated with patriotism: Gandhi insisted on it, as a revolt against British tariffs and British textiles.

Now the Western business suit has become the standard attire for Indian businessmen....In the United States, of course, many businessmen in new industries dispense with formal dress altogether, adopting a casual jeans and T-shirt style. This, too, has caught on in other countries, especially with younger people in technology-based industries. The pattern remains the same. Western styles have become the standard mode of work dress for men. (Zakaria 2009: 76)

The homogenizing effects of globalization are therefore widespread. For example, as Mike Featherstone (1990: 12) once noted: "It is all too clear that the Indian scientist or intellectual in New Delhi who wishes to develop contacts to exchange information with his Japanese opposite number, must do so in English." Anthony King (1990) adds that people belong to many cultures, but cultural differences are as likely to be within countries (that is, between regions, social classes, ethnic groups, and urban and rural areas) as *between* countries. Consequently, architects and fashion designers, in King's view, move more easily between New York, London, and Mumbai than between Mumbai and the villages of Maharashtra. This ease of movement is possible because of global norms that extend to persons who share a similar global culture. Ulf Hannerz (1990) describes people who fit into this global culture as cosmopolitans. These are individuals who live their lives in an international context rather than purely within the culture of a particular locality. They are open to a variety of cultures and possess a general competence in maneuvering through them. Hence, the cosmopolitan is able to bring a sense of coherence to the diversity of cultures that he or she confronts and can find a similar frame of reference with people of a similar globalized outlook.

A definition of globalization

In order to capture the depth and the breadth of the globalization concept for our examination of its effects on health, we have chosen to adopt the view proposed by Robert Keohane and Joseph Nye. They (Keohane and Nye 2000: 2) define globalization as an increase in globalism, which is "a state of the world involving networks of interdependence at multicontinental distances. These networks of interdependence are linked through flows and influences of capital and goods,

information and ideas, people and forces, as well as environmentally and biologically relevant substances." According to
this view, globalization refers to networks of connections that
span the world and not just links between particular countries.
It also emphasizes the changing role of distance, in that long
distances are no longer a significant barrier to connectivity. The
North American Free Trade Agreement (NAFTA), for example,
establishes connections among the United States, Canada, and
Mexico. NAFTA may be considered to be an aspect of globalization as part of the international trade system, but it is not
globalization per se, since it creates links among only three
states in a regional geographic area. The World Trade
Organization (WTO) would provide a better example, as it
establishes trade rules and helps promote trade links among its
152 member states worldwide.

Before discussing the effects of globalization on health, two
comments need to be made regarding globalization in today's
world. First, even though globalization is regarded primarily as
a post-Cold War phenomenon, it is not new. It is a process that
has been developing since different human civilizations have
come into contact with one another over the course of history,
and its historical context is important in order to understand
how it developed and how it relates to contemporary globalization. Second, although globalization implies interconnections
between countries and people of the world, it is by no means
a universal process. It is important to note that there is a great
deal of variation in the degree to which different countries
participate in globalization. Some states are far more involved
in this process than others. There are barriers, such as a lack of
natural resources, low per capita incomes, ineffective or com-
promised legal systems, and unstable governments, that pose
limitations on the impact of globalization on different countries
and populations. Since these barriers vary quite substantially,
some states and their populations are more influenced by
globalization than others.

Historical context of globalization

The first form of globalization to affect human civilization was
climate change. This change, in turn, affected migration, as
human beings began to move and populate different parts of

the world. For example, the Ice Age caused early groups of humans in Europe to move southward. But, as the glaciers began retreating when the climate became warmer, movement was northward for those humans who depended on the reindeer herds for their subsistence. The spread of disease, however, often accompanies human movement. The first smallpox epidemic was believed to have occurred in Egypt in 1350 BC, only to spread to China in AD 49, to Europe in the 700s, to the Americas in the early sixteenth century, and to Australia in 1789. Territorial expansion was another form of early globalization. The most prominent example would be Alexander the Great's military conquests, which created an empire that spread from Athens to India and introduced Greek thought to the Middle East and Asia. The Roman Empire was another globalizing force, as at its high point it stretched from Great Britain across much of Europe to North Africa and the Middle East. Both the Greek and the Roman Empire were cultural and political global systems (Turner 2004). The spread of religion also presents an example of early globalization, as Christianity, Buddhism, Judaism, and Islam have all spread great distances and reached people in different areas of the world.

The preceding examples demonstrate that globalization is not only an old phenomenon, but it substantially predates the creation of the modern state. Yet the modern state system introduced a major change to the globalization process. This system was created in 1648, at the conclusion of the Thirty Years' War in Europe, as a result of the Treaty of Westphalia, the key principle of which was sovereignty. The idea of sovereignty was that states have absolute authority over their territory and that other states were prohibited from interfering with their authority. State sovereignty continues to be the greatest constraint on the spread of globalization. It provides states with a way to shield themselves from the forces of globalization as well as the influence of other states. As the Europeans began to expand across the globe and develop colonies, they spread a number of ideas, including the principle of sovereignty. Although the modern state system came out of Westphalia, it was not until the late eighteenth and early nineteenth century when sovereignty – the concept of the equality of states and non-interference in affairs of other states – became a core principle of international relations (Held and McGrew 2002). Of course, this international order was confined principally to Europe, as most of the rest of the world consisted of colonies or were countries not recognized as sovereign states by Europeans.

The modern age of globalization begins around the mid-nineteenth century. At this time, much of the American continent had become independent from Europe and the world began to develop truly global linkages as a result of enhancements in technology. By the early 1870s, submarine cables had created a telegraphic link across the Atlantic as well as a link between Britain and India. In fact, in the 1870s a telegram could be sent from London to Bombay (Mumbai) in five hours. By 1900, approximately 190,000 miles of submarine cable had been laid around the world (Thompson 2002). The advent of steamships and railways made travel across great distances much easier and quicker. It was a tremendous improvement over sailing vessels and horse-drawn coaches.

A World Bank Policy Research Report (Collier and Dollar 2001) identifies *modern* globalization as occurring in three separate waves that can be distinguished by their different characteristics. The first wave lasted from 1870 to 1914 and saw the technological advances that enhanced communication and transportation. In addition, national governments reduced barriers to trade and foreign investment, so that during this time exports as a share of world income nearly doubled, to about 8 percent (Maddison 2001). In comparing the ratio of trade to gross domestic product (GDP), Japan, the Netherlands, and the United Kingdom had a higher ratio in 1913 than in 1995, while the ratios for France and Germany in 1913 were only slightly lower (Hirst and Thompson 2002). Foreign capital also increased quite substantially during this time period, from about 9 percent of the income of developing countries in Africa, Asia, and Latin America to 32 percent by 1914 (Collier and Dollar 2001). Another significant indicator of globalization during the first wave had to do with migration patterns. Sixty million people migrated from Europe to the Americas, Australia, and Africa during this period. Millions of people also left China, Japan, and India for East, South, and Southeast Asia. Overall, 10 percent of the world's population moved during the first wave (Collier and Dollar 2001).

Although technology continued to improve, globalization began to decline after 1914. Political rivalries among European powers led to World War I, which decimated an already weak international monetary system. After the war, a global economic depression began, and states responded by engaging in protectionist trade practices to promote domestic economic growth. The United States instituted the Smoot–Hawley tariff on foreign goods, which was reciprocated by other states and led to a significant decline in US trade in the 1930s. Globally, by 1950, trade to GDP ratios were down to about the same level as in 1870, and foreign investment in developing countries dropped below 1870 levels. Migration declined significantly as well. For example, immigration to the United States between 1914 and 1950 was less than half of what it had been during the first wave of globalization (Collier and Dollar 2001).

The second wave emerged out of the reconstruction of the international system following World War II that created the United Nations (UN) and the Bretton Woods system. The UN was an international institution designed to deal with issues of peace and security as well as political rivalries more effectively than the League of Nations had in the 1930s. American and British economists realized that international institutions were needed to cope with the economic problems that had developed in the global economy after World War I, such as protectionism and unstable exchange rates. The Bretton Woods Conference in 1944 led to the establishment of the International Monetary Fund (IMF) and the International Bank for Reconstruction and Development (the World Bank). The IMF would help states maintain financial stability to stimulate trade, while the World Bank would both help national economies recover from the war and provide economic development assistance. An International Trade Organization (ITO) was also proposed, but it failed to get sufficient support for its approval. As a result, states relied on the General Agreement on Tariffs and Trade (GATT) to facilitate international trade until the WTO was established in 1995.

The second wave of globalization lasted from 1945 to 1980. This period saw the enhancement of trade liberalization as well as the absence of war between great powers. However, this wave consisted largely of the economic and political integration of Western Europe, the United States, Canada, Australia, New Zealand, and Japan. The Soviet Union and its Eastern European satellite states and China did not participate fully in the global economic system and became relatively isolated from the globalization process. While developing countries were more involved – with the exception of some of the Far Eastern countries such as South Korea and Singapore – they tended to be less integrated on account of restrictive economic policies.

The third wave of globalization began around 1980 and continues today. It is distinguished from the second wave primarily through a change in economic policy. When Margaret Thatcher and Ronald Reagan came to power in the United Kingdom and the United States, respectively, they promoted an expansion of free market ideology known as neoliberalism, both domestically and through the IMF and World Bank. Neoliberalism favors a greater role for free markets and a minimum role for state control and intervention in a nation's economy. Developing countries thus had an incentive to move toward trade and capital market liberalization, as well as privatization, in order to obtain funds from global economic institutions (Stiglitz 2003). This neoliberal economic orientation was a change from the IMF's Keynesian orientation during the second wave, which emphasized a greater role for government intervention and the public sector in economic development.

In addition, the third wave has seen substantial technological advances accelerating global transportation and communication, especially with the appearance of the Internet in the 1990s. The end of the Cold War reduced political rivalries and led to the integration of more states into the global economy than ever before. The vast majority of countries in the world are members of the IMF, World Bank, and WTO, and twenty-four developing countries, China, India, Brazil, and Mexico among them, have doubled their trade to GDP ratio. Capital flows have increased as well. The flows to developing countries almost doubled from the mid-1970s to the late 1990s (Collier and Dollar 2001). Immigration controls were also not quite as restricted. While international migration is not as extensive as it was during the first wave, it is estimated that about 2 percent of the world's population lives in foreign countries (Collier and Dollar 2001).

Even though globalization is not a new process, and while trade flows and migration during the first wave are somewhat comparable to those in the third wave, today's globalization is still different. More independent states exist in the world than before. A greater number of international organizations are now present. Transportation and communication are now easier, faster, and less costly. Different cultures now have much more of a global reach. More and more states have become influenced by democratization and capitalism. The question, however, is whether the third wave is becoming truly global, and whether, as Friedman (2005) argues about today's globalization, "the world is flat," since it is more interconnected across national boundaries than at any previous time in human history.

How global is contemporary globalization?

While technology has improved and the number of international interactions has increased, the world still has divisions. Most people do not have telephones, let alone Internet access. Millions of people live in remote villages with very little influence on the globalization process (Keohane and Nye 2000). The 2007 United Nations Development Program on Human Development describes some of the divisions that have been developing among people in the third wave of globalization. For example, the richest 2 percent of the world's population owns about half of the global household wealth, while the bottom 50 percent of the population owns about 1 percent of the wealth (UNDP 2007). This inequality is part of a trend that has been characteristic of contemporary globalization. By the end of the 1990s, the fifth of the world's population living in the richest countries accounted for 86 percent of the world's GDP, 82 percent of the world's export markets, and 74 percent of the world's telephone lines, while the people living in the poorest countries had about 1 percent in each of these areas (UNDP 2002). While the Internet is the fastest and least expensive means of global communication and information, 91 percent of users live in the richest states, which have only 19 percent of the world's population. Additionally, about 80 percent of websites are in English, a language spoken by less than 10 percent of the world's population (UNDP 2002). As a result, it is apparent that the world is divided among people that are connected to the globalization process and others who are isolated from it.

States differ in their involvement in globalization as well. The journal *Foreign Policy* and A. T. Kearney publish an annual index of globalization that measures each country's level of globalization based upon four different areas. The first area is political engagement, such as treaties and foreign aid; the second is technological connectivity, such as number of Internet users and servers; the third is personal contact, which includes international telephone calls and travel; and the fourth is economic integration, which measures international trade and foreign direct investment. The 2007 report, which analyzes data from 2005 from 72 states, provides an interesting portrait of contemporary globalization. Singapore was rated as the world's most globalized country for the fourth time since 1998. Hong Kong, the Netherlands, Switzerland, and Ireland rounded out the top five.

Most of the globalized countries were small states, the United States and Canada being the only large countries among the top ten. Why do the more globalized states tend to be small? The 2005 data reveal that economic integration plays a major role. On account of either a lack of natural resources, like Singapore, or a small domestic market, like Ireland, these states globalized in order to be more economically competitive with other states. Those that ranked lowest in the globalization rankings for 2005 included Venezuela, Indonesia, Algeria, India, and Iran.

States seem to vary in terms of their involvement in globalization through a combination of conscious policy choices as well as their level of economic and technological development. Democracies such as the United States, Canada, the United Kingdom, and other Western European countries are more extensively globalized than authoritarian states such as Iran and North Korea. Garrett and Lange (1996) argue that states need to make adjustments in their policies to benefit from globalization and, as long as society wants to globalize, democracies are much more capable of making political changes to suit globalization than authoritarian states. North Korea, which was not included in the *Foreign Policy*/A. T. Kearney index, is a prime example of a state that seeks to resist globalization as much as possible. China is a less extreme example but, with the exception of economic integration, it has also shown some resistance to globalizing influences.

In addition to divisions among people and states in regard to globalization, there appears to be a lack of identification with globalization and a global community. Pippa Norris (2000), using data from the World Values Survey in the 1990s, indicated that local and national identity remain much stronger in the world than a cosmopolitan orientation. In fact, almost half of the public felt the strongest attachment to their specific locality or region. The results did not indicate much difference among developed, developing and post-communist societies. The findings of this study appear to support John Tomlinson's (2003) argument that globalization actually enhances cultural identity rather than suppresses it. For example, the end of the Cold War contributed to the break-up of the Yugoslavian state, as a resurgence of ethnic identities led to a series of violent conflicts in the 1990s, largely through a revived Serbia attempting to dominate its neighbors Croatia, Bosnia and Herzegovina, Kosovo, Macedonia, Montenegro, and Slovenia. Ethnic warfare, repression, and genocide lasted well into the third wave of globalization and ended only with the military intervention of the United States and its NATO allies. Kosovo was the last former Yugoslav province to declare its independence, in 2008.

One aspect in the assessment of whether contemporary globalization is truly global in scope is American power. The United States plays a major role in all elements of globalization. It has the world's largest market, is the only state with a global military reach, and is the leading producer of music, television programs, and film. American power is so pervasive that contemporary globalization has often been considered to be Americanization, especially by non-Americans (Keohane and Nye 2000). Although the United States has more influence over globalization than other states, it is by no means the only influence and its influence is limited. As Nye (2002) suggests, the inevitable spread of technology and increasing economic development globally may lead to a decline in American dominance at some point. But, currently, the US is the world's only superpower, although China is rising and Russia is seeking to regain its former status.

While globalization has been steadily increasing since the end of World War II and technology is more advanced than ever before, the world still has numerous divisions and retains an international rather than a purely global character. Economic and technological inequalities limit access and benefits from globalization to many around the world. State sovereignty persists, and all states pose some sort of limits on the globalization process. As Jeffrey Frankel (2000) points out, even in economic transactions, national borders and geography continue to place significant restrictions on international trade and investment. Identities still retain an ethnic, local, or nationalist flavor. So the world may be becoming flatter through globalization, but there are still some hills and valleys (or bumps and dips) in the process.

Globalization and Governance

Since globalization is a process that transcends national borders, it can create international policy problems, including those that pertain to health, that require some kind of governance. That is, we live in a world society without a world government. Of course, since the modern international system is state-centric, and there is no world government, the question is: How can globalization be regulated if the process is not restricted by borders? The Commission on Global Governance considered this question and developed a definition of governance as "the sum of the many ways individuals and institutions, public and private, manage their common affairs. It is a continuing process through which conflicting or diverse interests may be accommodated and cooperative action may be taken. It includes formal...as well as informal arrangements that people and institutions have agreed to or perceive to be in their interest" (Commission on Global Governance 1995: 2).

While governance is similar to government, in that both promote cooperation through providing structure and regulation, overall the two are quite different. Government is much more formal, legalistic, and hierarchical than governance, suggesting formal authority with enforcement powers. Governance is much more informal and diffuse and includes actors other than national governments, such as intergovernmental organizations (IGOs) and non-governmental organizations (NGOs). It does provide regulation to some degree, mostly by promoting rules and establishing cooperative arrangements. But this means of regulation lacks the authority and enforcement of government. Because of the lack of a world government, however, global governance provides the only constraining influence on globalization issues, such as the spread of infectious diseases, which are beyond control of the state.

The diffuse nature of global governance means that it is a complicated system that involves a number of different actors without a clear, formal relationship. The primary actors are states, which have sovereignty and create and develop IGOs and international law and norms. They are the actors that have the ultimate influence as to whether rules will be established, as well as compliance with those rules. Of course, state power is an important factor in global governance. The United States, for instance, wields predominant power in global governance relative to other states. In addition to its economic, military, and cultural power, the United States has a permanent seat on the United Nations Security Council and has the most voting power in the IMF and the World Bank. The other permanent members of the United Nations Security Council – China, France, Russia, and the United Kingdom – are some of the more influential actors in global governance. Both Germany and Japan, while not holding permanent seats on the council, provide a significant amount of funding to both international institutions and foreign aid, which allow them also to be influential. However, global governance is not all about state power. As Jessica Matthews (1997) pointed out, national governments are sharing more and more powers with IGOs, NGOs, and corporations. As globalization has intensified since the Cold War, power in global governance has become less concentrated in the states.

Although IGOs are created and maintained by states, they are delegated some independence to facilitate cooperation. These organizations, such as the UN, the WTO, the World Bank, the IMF, and the World Health Organization (WHO), all have bureaucracies that help negotiate agreements and seek to promote the organization's agenda effectively. In addition to being actors in global governance, IGOs are part of governance. They provide rules and mechanisms that states are obligated to follow in resolving international policy disputes.

NGOs are another set of actors in global governance. Unlike IGOs, these organizations do not have national governments as members, and so they cannot promote a formal set of binding rules. They are voluntary organizations composed largely of individuals and organized around a specific issue area. Their function in global governance is analogous to that of interest groups in policy-making by national governments. They can influence policies by governments and IGOs by lobbying and providing information to promote policy change. There are thousands of NGOs that operate internationally; however, they vary substantially in terms of size and resources. The Red Cross, Greenpeace, Amnesty International, and Oxfam are some well-known and influential examples.

Multinational corporations (MNCs) form a type of NGO that promotes cross-border business transactions to make profits. The MNCs have their headquarters in one state and branches or subsidiaries in other states. They are influential actors in global governance through their ability to invest capital outside of their home country, and they can lobby for changes in national laws as well as threaten to move capital and jobs elsewhere if they do not care for the policies of a particular state. Since foreign capital can provide a great addition to national income, some countries may be compelled to tailor their economic policies to favor the interest of MNCs.

Another type of actor in global governance that has gained increased significance has been groups of experts known as epistemic communities. These communities emerge from national governments, research institutions, private industry, and academia to deal with certain international problems and are especially relevant in complex issue areas involving science or technology. Because epistemic communities may be perceived as less politically biased than many NGOs, their expertise is potentially very influential on government policy-making.

A feature of global governance that makes it a complicated concept is that all of the actors are linked together through a series of networks. States have the most effect on policy, but policy can certainly be shaped by the actions of IGOs, NGOs, MNCs, and epistemic communities. However, international law is also an important aspect of global governance. This form of law comes principally out of international treaties and customs among states. The resulting agreements and practices are binding on states but, since there is no world government, enforcement is problematic. Another part of governance has to do with international norms, which refer to standards of behavior that, usually because of moral reasons or habit, states should, but are not necessarily bound, to follow. Despite the lack of formal obligation, states usually tend to comply. Overall, international law and norms are directed much more at states than NGOs, MNCs, and individuals.

When it comes to health and global governance, the leading international institution is the World Health Organization (WHO), which was created in 1948. The organization's constitution specifies that its goal is to provide the best possible health for all. It also states that the World Health Assembly (WHA) can adopt regulations that become binding on a WHO member state unless such state expressly refuses to be bound. The WHO includes a role for NGOs such as the Red Cross and Médecins Sans Frontières (MSF) (Doctors Without Borders), while the World Bank plays a role in global health governance with its lending programs. For example, in the mid-1990s, the World Bank funded a smoking reduction campaign in Hungary, which had the highest mortality rates from lung cancer in Europe.

The Organization for Economic Cooperation and Development and the World Trade Organization deal with health issues related to economics and trade, and pharmaceutical companies and public health research organizations such as the US Centers for Disease Control and Prevention (CDC) are key actors in global health governance as well. The global governance of health will be discussed in greater detail in chapter 6.

Health and Globalization

The study of globalization in medical sociology has been slow to develop, but the topic is growing in importance with the increased realization that health and disease have global connections. However, as with globalization, there is no single, all-purpose definition of health. The WHO defines health as a state of complete physical, mental, and social well-being, and not merely the absence of disease or injury. Therefore, being healthy means more than not being sick or injured; it also means having a positive sense of well-being. Most studies suggest that laypersons tend to view health as the capacity to carry out their daily activities. That is, health is seen as a state of functional fitness (Blaxter 2004). Healthy people may not be free of all health problems, but they generally feel good, are able to do what they want to do, are not burdened with illness, and are not handicapped by a serious disability.

Based on our view of globalization as increased connections between interdependent networks of people, goods, information, etc., across continents (Keohane and Nye 2000), we would expect such networks to be conduits for disease. History shows us that this is indeed the case, as bubonic plague reached Europe from China in the fourteenth century, cholera entered Britain by way of India in the seventeenth century, and Europeans brought smallpox to the Western hemisphere during the exploration and settlement of the New World. Bryan Turner (2004) finds the emergence of new plagues, such as HIV/AIDS, SARS, and the West Nile virus, to be a consequence of the present wave of globalization. Other diseases that have jumped continents include the Marburg virus, Lassa fever, and swine and bird flu – and even the deadly Ebola, as noted in the introduction to this chapter.

Consequently, Turner (2004: 230) points out that we can no longer view disease in an exclusively national framework because its character and its treatment are global. This is seen, for example, in the pharmaceutical industry. The ownership, manufacture, marketing, sales, and use of drugs to treat disease span the globe, as does the Internet, with its electronic stores of medical knowledge. Organizations such as the WHO, CDC, and MSF have teams of medical scientists that respond to health threats throughout the world. So it is not just the risks that are global, it is also efforts at containment and resolution. As Turner (2004: 233) finds: "Many sociologists have argued that the conventional theoretical paradigms of the social sciences have to be abandoned in order to grasp a new social reality based on global flows and networks rather than national societies." While studies of national societies still have their place, it is indeed time for a more global perspective in medical sociology, and the remainder of this book will follow this path.

Globalization affects health through multiple pathways by influencing the social and political contexts within which people live. These, in turn, impact on their differential exposure and vulnerability to health risks, disparities, outcomes, and characteristics of their health care system (Labonté et al. 2008). The next chapter will examine the role of globalization with respect to benefits and risks, including the problem of human security and the promotion of disparities. Subsequent chapters will cover pandemics, the characteristics of health care systems in various countries, the global governance of health, and the concept of health as a public good, which is the basis for the formulation of national and international health policy.

Summary

This chapter provides an overview of the relationship between health and globalization that will be discussed in the chapters to come. Keohane and Nye (2000: 2) view globalization as an increase in globalism, which is a state of the world involving interdependent networks stretching across multi-continental distances linked through flows and influences of capital and goods, information and ideas, people and force, as well as environmentally and biologically relevant substances. According to this view, globalization refers to networks of connections that span the world.

The process of globalization is not new. The world has been globalizing for centuries, with the Greek Empire of Alexander the Great and the Roman Empire early examples of the spread of political, economic, and social interconnections across the known world. Currently, we are experiencing a third wave of globalization that began in 1980. While not all parts of the world have become interconnected, the links that do exist are the most extensive in history. These links affect health in a number of ways, including the transmission of disease across continents and the global responses to counter this situation. Without a world government with the authority to direct health activities, actions on the part of national governments and other organizations are dependent upon cooperative agreements. The manner in which this global system functions to promote health and combat disease will be explored in subsequent chapters. However, as will be seen, globalization is a two-sided process, one side bringing benefits and the other side promoting health problems.

2

Globalization: Health Benefits and Risks

As noted in the last chapter, globalization is a two-sided process in that it brings both benefits and risks to health. The purpose of this chapter is to examine some of the most important binary (good–bad) health dimensions of globalization in order to illustrate its varied consequences and provide a background for understanding the issues discussed in subsequent chapters. A logical outcome expected from the process of globalization is that health would be improved for everyone through the diffusion of medical knowledge, and this is true to a certain extent, with respect to the expansion of Western medicine and the rise of medical tourism. Conversely, globalization can bring risks to health through a threat to human security by way of enhancing the transmission of disease and its potential for adversely affecting the environment. These parallel outcomes will be discussed below.

The Globalization of Western Medicine

Globalization has brought the benefits of worldwide monitoring of disease by the World Health Organization and global access to drugs, medical information, health care delivery, and disaster relief. These developments are aided by improved communication and transportation systems, but result primarily from the globalization of Western medicine. In analyzing the history of medicine, Roy Porter (1997: 6) points out that "Western medicine has developed in ways which have made it uniquely powerful and led it to become uniquely global." This occurred, says Porter, because it is perceived by societies and the sick to provide the most effective type of treatment for disease. Western medicine has its origins in Europe, its roots traceable back to antiquity and the ancient Greek and Roman worlds. What allowed Western medical science to achieve global dominance, in Porter's view, is that it developed a radically distinctive approach to exploring the human body through scientific investigation. For much of history, most societies and cultures developed concepts of life, health, and death based on notions of the supernatural in the form of spirits, gods, demons, the underworld, and so forth. An exception was traditional Chinese and Indian medicine, which focused on the structure and force of the cosmos (i.e., balancing the "yin" and the "yang") rather than conceptions of the supernatural. Western medicine, however, disregarded these abstract concepts and concentrated instead on scientifically understanding the functions and dysfunctions of the human body. It did this by probing surgically into both dead and living bodies with the goal of *systematically* improving diagnosis and treatment. Porter finds this was not done in China, India, Egypt, and other important early civilizations, where religious and cultural beliefs discouraged such inquiry.

Max Weber, arguably the foremost classical sociological theorist, helps us to understand the type of rationality that dominated Western thinking at this time. This rationality – what Weber called "formal rationality" – produced the Industrial Revolution and the rise of capitalism, and very likely influenced the development of medical science as well. Weber's analysis did not include medicine, but was applicable primarily to economic activities associated with a competitive free market and the spread of capitalism. Weber ([1922] 1978) believed that a particular type of rationality unique to the West at the time brought about the transformation of society from feudalism in the Middle Ages to modern capitalism. In a systematic fashion, he analyzed the process by which the modern world, especially the West, abandoned the idea that magic and mysticism determined the outcomes of events and substituted in its place the requirement for practicality and logic.

Weber observed that the form of rationality prevalent in traditional Asian societies, in contrast, had emphasized the abstract and the ideal, and had advocated a methodical lifestyle oriented toward harmonious social relationships and the avoidance of embarrassment or loss of face. Conformity, deference to superiors, and obedience to traditional rules and customs were the cultural norm. Innovation and change in the name of efficiency were stifled. While many Asian societies such as Japan, Singapore, South Korea, and, recently, China later embraced modernization and global capitalism, Europeans had done so centuries earlier. As part of this process, Western society featured a rationality that focused primarily on practical outcomes and away from abstract notions and a disregard of strict codes of behavior, dogma, and traditions if they suppressed progress, creativity, and the achievement of desired goals.

Weber maintained that it was not rationality per se, but a particular form of it – formal rationality – that was decisive in determining the dominant direction of Western society. This he defined as the purposeful calculation of the most efficient means and procedures to realize goals. He described the type of rationality that Asian culture and most religions promoted as substantive rationality, which was aimed at realizing values and ideals based on custom, tradition, piety, or personal devotion. Weber believed that substantive rationality had its place in the lives of people and that formal rationality did not characterize Western society as a whole; rather, it was that formal rationality dominated its substantive counterpart in many – especially economic – spheres of life. In fact, it was the large-scale rejection of substantive ends and values that made Western society unique. This Western-adopted rationalism provided an intellectual liberty that was lacking elsewhere. It featured the freedom to inquire, experiment, and dispute, while emphasizing a concern for the practical over the abstract and a belief in the continued possibility of improvement unhindered by cultural and ideological rigidity.

As noted, Weber did not incorporate medical practice into his discussion of formal rationality, but his description of the progressive rationalization of the West mirrors the development of Western medicine. Much of the medical knowledge of the ancient world was lost during the Dark Ages in Europe after the fall of Rome. What knowledge remained was preserved and passed on by the Roman Catholic Church. The position of the Church was that it, not medicine, was responsible for the study of the mind, while the proper role of physicians was to focus on the physical ailments of the human body. The French philosopher René Descartes, considered the most outstanding representative of seventeenth-century rationalism, helped shape the direction of philosophical thought for over two centuries, profoundly influencing the direction of medicine (DuBos 1969). Descartes advanced the concept of a mind–body dichotomy in which the mind was depicted as an expression of God and too mysterious to be approached as an object of scientific study. By contrast, he defined the body as a physical machine whose operation was within the scope of human knowledge and therefore could be studied, much like an engineer studies the inner workings of a machine. While this approach undermined efforts to research problems of mental health, it promoted the investigation of anatomy and body physiology that gave Western medicine its scientific basis. According to the noted microbiologist René DuBos:

> Descartes' philosophy led scientists to neglect questions pertaining to the nature of the mind and the soul and encouraged them to focus their efforts on the much simpler, more concrete, problems of body structure and operation. They could apply knowledge of physics and chemistry, derived from the study of inanimate matter, to the problems of the body without fear of debasing the more lofty manifestations of man's nature, those of his soul. (DuBos 1969: 77)

The approach of Descartes and his followers was in keeping with the Christian notion of the human body as a weak and imperfect vessel intended to transfer the soul from this world to the next. As long as there was a tacit understanding that the investigation of the mind was a religious matter, the Church did not object to the scientific study of the body. The result was that both Western religion and science sponsored the idea "of the body as a machine, of disease as a breakdown of the machine, and of the doctor's task as repair of the machine" (Engel 1977: 131).

Although many of Descartes' theories were later discarded, they nonetheless provided a philosophical framework for the emphasis that at least two centuries of scientists placed on understanding the physical and biochemical functioning of the human body. Over time, the study of the mind and its relationship to health also came under the purview of medical science. But, in the meantime, Western medicine replaced transcendental explanations of illness with scientific accounts of disease and healing. Until the nineteenth century, however, medical practice in the West had a history of mixed success in treating human ailments effectively. Yet, as Porter (1997: 10) observes, in the 1860s it made "a spectacular leap forward." One of medicine's true revolutions occurred in France with Louis Pasteur's germ theory of disease, which provided the foundation for the discovery, classification, and treatment of numerous ailments. This research helped medical scientists uncover the causes of typhoid, tetanus, diphtheria, and a host of other infectious diseases, along with the vaccines providing immunity. Significant advances in anaesthesiology, surgery, pathology, immunology, and many other areas of medicine were on their way as well.

By the last quarter of the nineteenth century, Germany assumed the leading role in the scientific development of medicine. Rudolf Virchow unveiled a general concept of disease based on cellular pathology (1858) and Robert Koch's work in bacteriology led to the discovery of the bacillus for anthrax (1876), tuberculosis (1892), and cholera (1883). Their work and those of their colleagues stimulated the growth of clinics and university-affiliated laboratories and high standards of admissions to medical schools in the West, especially in Germany and Austria. First Vienna and then Berlin became the leading center of medical knowledge and research. The quality of Western medicine was unsurpassed and soon spread to other regions of the globe. By the beginning of the twentieth century, leadership in medical research passed from Europe to the United States. The Americans were ready to forge ahead thanks to vast sums of money poured into medical research by private philanthropic foundations funded by wealthy industrialists.

Western medicine, aided by the extent of its effectiveness and its introduction by Europeans into their colonies in Africa, Asia, and Latin America, spread around the world and became *the* global approach to treating illness. Diseases endemic in colonized areas, such as malaria, yellow fever, cholera, and dengue (sleeping sickness), presented their own challenges, and the scientific medicine of the West was the principal weapon to resolve them. Virtually all medical schools in the world trained students in Western techniques. As Porter explains:

> Before the twentieth century, the health problems of the industrial world were largely distinct and independent from those of the colonized; in many respects, the "West" and the "Rest" were still just making contact. During the twentieth century all grew interlocked, through the transformation of empires, gigantic population migrations, the changes wrought by multinational capitalism, communications revolutions, world war and global politics. (Porter 1997: 483)

Trained physicians all over the world share the same or similar education and understanding of Western medical methods and procedures. Although the quality varies, Western medicine has indeed globalized and is now synonymous with the term "scientific medicine" or "professional medicine." The foundation of global interconnections in medicine is the flow of medical knowledge around the world, promoted by the Internet, journals, seminars, conferences, and activities of multinational health care, medical supply, and drug corporations. On the local level, it is increasingly common for physician researchers to have global connections with colleagues in other countries for the exchange of information and cooperation, leading both medical practitioners to have patients from abroad and markets to exist for drugs and health care products of multinational corporations. Some hospital chains and clinics now extend across national borders. At the global level, there is the World Health Organization and other entities that are taking an increasingly prominent role in the global governance of disease control and prevention (discussed in chapter 6). The threat of global pandemics has made cooperation imperative, and underlying international responses is the worldwide adoption of Western or scientific medicine.

Medical Tourism

Globalization has fostered a rise in medical tourism, which refers to patients in one part of the world traveling to another part in order to obtain medical treatment or drugs. These people shop for better prices or forms of care globally and go to the relevant places to purchase the services or medicines. Among the most popular medical tourism services currently are various types of elective procedures, such as cosmetic surgery, cardiac surgery, orthopedic and spine surgery, gastric bypass and gastric binding, in vitro fertilization, organ and tissue transplants, including stem cell therapy, Lasik eye surgery, and various diagnostic services. Hysterectomies and cancer therapy are also common. Before or after having these procedures, the patients may stay in luxury hotels and engage in sightseeing as part of their tourist experience.

In fact, it is possible to book tours that include medical treatment through specialized tourism companies. Prices depend on what services clients select, where they travel, the length of their visit, and the cost of their hotel or resort (Turner 2007). Travel packages embrace not only travel, food, accommodation, and sightseeing, but also visas, local travel agency representatives, transfer of medical records, and the cost of treatment. The patients pay either out of their own pocket or with health insurance, depending on coverage. While serious concerns may exist about the quality of care in some countries and the continuity of care after returning home, medical tourism has nevertheless become a large business. Some $20 billion annually is spent by people seeking health care internationally.

It has been fairly common for decades for underinsured and uninsured Americans to cross over into Mexico for cheaper medical care and prescription drugs and for affluent Mexicans with insurance or cash to travel to the United States for higher quality medical treatment not readily available in their locale. Much of this medical tourism has been confined to the US–Mexican border and so is regional rather than global in nature. Another international pattern is that between the US and Canada, as Americans go to Canada for less expensive medical procedures and drugs, and Canadians cross to the US to avoid long waits for surgery, cancer treatments, and other procedures.

Today, medical tourism has become global. Major patterns involve patients from the Middle East traveling to the US and Western Europe, and North Americans and Europeans going to India, Singapore, Thailand, and Brazil for less expensive care or for treatments banned in their own countries, such as stem cell therapy. Hip replacement surgery, for example, costs from

$18,000 to $43,000 in the United States, but can be obtained in India for $9,000 or less (Wapner 2008; York 2008). Table 2.1, compiled by the American Medical Association in 2007, shows the comparative costs of selected medical procedures in the United States, India, Thailand, and Singapore. The most expensive procedure is heart valve replacement, which costs $160,000 in the US, compared with $9,000 in India, $10,000 in Thailand, and $12,500 in Singapore. The cheapest procedure in the US is $20,000 for a hysterectomy, which costs $3,000 in India. Clearly, medical procedures in the US are much more expensive than those in the other countries shown in table 2.1.

Some medical facilities in countries such as India have been significantly modernized to attract foreign patients and are able to charge less because the cost of providing quality care is much lower than in North America or Western Europe. India now issues an M-visa (medical visa), valid for one year, for people wanting to visit the country for medical treatment; it is issued for their companions as well. Medical tourism constitutes 5.2 percent of India's current GDP and is expected to expand to 8.5 percent of the GDP in a few years. The time is coming when Western businesses, health insurance companies, and governments will outsource medical services to low-cost providers in other parts of the globe in a similar way to that in which

Table 2.1 *Comparative prices for medical procedures in India, Thailand, Singapore, and the United States*

Procedure	India	Thailand	Singapore	US
Heart valve replacement	$9,000	$10,000	$12,500	$160,000
Heart bypass	$10,000	$11,000	$18,500	$130,000
Spinal fusion	$5,500	$7,000	$9,000	$62,000
Angioplasty	$11,000	$13,000	$13,000	$57,000
Hip replacement	$9,000	$12,000	$12,000	$43,000
Knee replacement	$8,500	$10,000	$13,000	$40,000
Hysterectomy	$3,000	$4,500	$6,000	$20,000

Source: Adapted from American Medical Association data, 2007.

corporations in other sectors of the economy have already done. Already, a few US health insurance companies, such as Aetna, United, and Blue Shield of South Carolina and California, reimburse patients for some foreign care, and state governments in Colorado and West Virginia are considering overseas surgical care for their employees (York 2008). Some US hospitals now send X-rays electronically overnight to India, where they are reviewed by Indian doctors, and the findings are returned early the next morning.

Medical tourism is but one example of how health care functions as a commodity to be sold and purchased in the global medical marketplace. Purchasers include individuals paying for medical treatment, insurance companies covering the bills of their clients, corporations providing coverage for their employees, and governments paying for health care for their populations. In each case, health care is a product of delivery systems that generate incomes for providers and expenses for consumers. Although this commodity has been subject in the past largely to transactions in internal local and sometimes regional and national markets, health care is a growing presence on the global market.

Risk and Globalization

Globalization, however, also brings risks, including risks to health. In economics, business, and gambling we can calculate risks with respect to costs, benefits, and probabilities for success. In these domains, risks can be attractive if the potential for loss is slight while the potential for gain is high as measured by increasing profits. But there is a high probability of disaster if something goes wrong. Sometimes the greater the risk, the greater the benefits as well as the greater the possible loss. The individual must decide if taking the risk is worth the harm that could occur should the action be unsuccessful or worth the benefit if it turns out well.

Although outcomes can be either positive or negative, risks themselves are generally regarded as negative. This is particularly true of disease, as there is nothing to be gained from being sick (with the possible exception of a few days off from school or work) and much to lose (ranging from feeling bad to death).

As Deborah Lupton (1999) points out, over the course of the last century, distinctions in everyday language between good and bad risks tended to fade. For most people, the term "risk" came to mean more or less exclusively danger, threat, or harm. There was no such thing as a good risk, because risks in themselves signified something bad. As Mary Douglas (1992) says, "the word *risk* now means danger; *high risk* means a lot of danger."

According to Ulrich Beck (1992, 1999), we are now living in a global risk society. He argues that, just as modernization dissolved feudal society and produced the industrial society, it is now dissolving industrial society, leading to a new form of society that he calls the risk society. What we need to realize, Beck insists, is that modernization ages, and an important facet of this ongoing aging process today is the emergence of the risk society whose hazards can be global. The risk society is described as an era in which the individual, social, economic, and political risks created by the momentum of modern innovation increasingly elude the control and protective institutions of society. Whereas technological advances are not intended to cause harm, harm may nonetheless be the outcome for some people.

For example, automobile accidents are responsible for a large number of deaths, yet death-dealing automobiles continue to be produced, and people are encouraged through advertising to acquire them. Of course, in this case, autos by themselves do not kill or injure; rather, it is the people who drive them. Nevertheless, even though it is unintended, the operation of an object designed to enhance human transportation can be hazardous to life and limb, and an industry intrinsic to modernization – the automobile industry – produces risks and does so with few limitations. Similar examples may be found in the nuclear, oil, coal, and chemical industries, whose products are essential to modern societies, but whose wastes contaminate the environment.

In sum, the world we live in is a risky place. Moreover, many of its risks are beyond the control of any one individual. People are therefore left to seek out and construct their own certainties. That is, they are required to develop their own protective measures against risk because they cannot always depend on the government – and certainly not on business corporations – to look out for their welfare. Beck does not confront the entire range of risks that individuals may face, including those that threaten their health. But he alerts us to the role of modernization in making life a more risky proposition on a global scale.

Anthony Giddens (2000) depicts modernity as a juggernaut producing a "runaway world," overwhelming tradition with its changes. He argues that, while the idea of risk has always been an aspect of modernity, the current historical period is witness to a new form. We are now exposed to what he calls manufactured risks, which he defines as risks created by the impact of knowledge on the world. Global warming is an example of a manufactured risk, in that it is caused by the adverse effects of chemical gases and fumes released into the air by motor vehicles and industrial plants. This effect is not brought about by nature, but results from products developed through the use of scientific knowledge. "At a certain point," says Giddens (2000: 44), "however – very recently in historical terms – we started worrying less about what nature can do to us, and more about what we have done to nature."

Giddens's position is that the current phase of modernity is not necessarily more dangerous, because there have often been high-risk periods in the past. What is different is that new risks have emerged, caused by the unintended consequences of modernization, such as global ecological damage and nuclear proliferation. To contend with these kinds of risks, people have to rely on scientists and governments. But scientists often disagree, and governments can be slow to respond or be stymied by politics. Sometimes governments may cover up the true extent of a risk so as not to alarm the general population or disrupt the economy. This was the case in 2002, when the Chinese government initially denied that a serious and previously unknown disease – SARS – had broken out and that it had the capability of causing a global epidemic. The speed with which SARS moved around the world was possible because of modern air travel, which allowed infected persons to travel rapidly to distant places.

Human Security

One challenge for the globalization of health is addressing its link to security. Since the end of the Cold War, the concept of security has been changing from one of national security, which focuses on the military defense of sovereign territory, to one of human security, which focuses on a greater variety of threats to ordinary people. The UN has adopted the broader concept of human security and in 2001 established an international commission to monitor and promote relevant activities. The Commission on Human Security has defined the objective of human security as one of protecting the core of human lives in ways that enhance human freedoms and fulfillment (Commission on Human Security 2003).

After five official meetings, in May 2003 the Commission on Human Security issued its final report, and at that point ceased operations. It was replaced by the Human Security Unit (HSU), established a year later in the United Nations Office for the Coordination of Humanitarian Affairs. The goal of the HSU is to help incorporate human security into UN actions. The primary evaluation on human security, however, was in the commission's final report, in which it acknowledged that the responsibility for health is shifting from states to both communities and international institutions. The report recommended building a design for global health that would include cooperation at the local, national, and global level. This would be accomplished through international health rules and public and private sector partnerships. Among its policy conclusions, the commission suggested that greater action should be taken against infectious disease, particularly in regard to surveillance at both the national and global level. It also advocated greater intellectual property incentives for advancing human security and the development of a public primary health care system for each country.

The emergence of the human security concept has led to a greater emphasis on health as a security issue. Almost a third of annual deaths in the world are preventable with existing knowledge and resources (Chen and Narasimhan 2003). Infectious disease, along with poverty, is a health-related area that poses significant threats to human security. The HIV/AIDS epidemic is regarded as the greatest threat, since it is responsible for approximately 3 million deaths annually. According to the report of the Commission on Human Security, HIV/AIDS is emerging as the greatest health disaster in human history. The UN Security Council's declaration in 2000 of the disease's threat to national security emphasized its significance. Although HIV/AIDS has a global effect, its impact is most pronounced in sub-Saharan Africa, which accounts for most of the world's total number of cases. The contributions of the disease to high rates of worker absenteeism, the loss of skilled workers and educators, and increased insurance costs have led to declining economic performances in the region (Heymann 2003). It is estimated among various sources that the incidence of HIV in Africa is in the range of 10 to 50 percent. The risk of HIV-infected soldiers spreading the disease is enhanced by the fact that sub-Saharan Africa is a region that has been experiencing military conflict. Combat increases the chances that non-infected soldiers could come into contact with infected blood on the battlefield. Additionally, soldiers spread the disease through sexual contact, whether it be transmitted through consensual sex, prostitution, or rape (Shisana et al. 2003).

The UN *Human Development Report* in 1994 promoted the link between poverty and health and human security by making the case that freedom of choice in human development would not be possible without security (UNDP 1994). Four of the UN's Millennium Development Goals focus on health objectives. The health-related problems of poverty and inequality are particularly severe in the developing world, where malnutrition accounts for 15 percent of the disease burden and unsafe water and sanitation account for about 6 percent. These factors combined account for less than 1 percent of the disease burden in developed countries, where tobacco use and high blood pressure are the leading cause of disease (Shibuya 2003).

During the most recent wave of globalization, extreme poverty (defined as living on less than US$1 per day) has decreased in developing states. Much of this reduction, however, can be attributed to the rising income of China alone. The number of people living in sub-Saharan Africa in extreme poverty has increased substantially since the early 1980s as a result of a growing population coupled with a stagnation or downturn in incomes. Former communist states in Europe and Central Asia, as well as many Latin American countries, have also seen increases in extreme poverty, although to much less of an extent than in sub-Saharan Africa. Overall, over 1 billion people in the world live in extreme poverty, with almost half of those in the developing world living on less than US$2 per day (Kawachi and Wamala 2007). This situation clearly affects health, in that to be poor by definition means having fewer of the good things in life, including health. It is therefore logical to assume that a reduction in poverty would have a corresponding effect on improving health. Consequently, the lack of progress in poverty reduction is a major problem in securing global health.

However, because of the complexity of the situation and the difficulty of establishing a causal connection, making the case that globalization causes poor health is not an easy task (Bhagwati 2004). Much of the criticism of the globalizing efforts of the World Bank and the IMF in their loan programs for improving health, for example, is directed toward neoliberal policies of cost recovery through users' fees or co-payments (Labonté et al. 2008). User contributions for medical services and drugs in poor countries were initiated to help maintain the health care delivery systems in those countries. The World Bank and the IMF are not charities, but sources for loans to promote economic development, which includes health programs. Co-payments, nevertheless, can be insurmountable barriers to health care for people in extreme poverty.

Giovanni Cornia and his colleagues (Cornia et al. 2008) analyzed the relationship between globalization policies, socioeconomic determinants of health, and mortality using data from WHO's Commission on Social Determinants of Health. Their results can only be considered as tentative because of the methodological problems inherent in establishing causal connections between policies and health status, on account of the possibility of other variables intervening to affect the relationship. Though inconclusive, the study suggests that globalization policies had weakened the role of the state in developing countries in providing basic services, promoted an increase in cigarette and alcohol consumption, and hindered the growth of local economies. Consequently, there may be situations in which globalization and the imposition of external markets and outside creditors on poor countries can adversely affect local economies, levels of employment, and the availability of affordable health services.

Globalization and the Environment

Another challenge posed by globalization is the environment. Although the causal relationship between the two has been debated by scientists and policy-makers, in the most recent wave of globalization the global environment has deteriorated in an unprecedented manner, as reflected in ozone depletion, global warming, and increases in severe weather (Vitousek et al. 1997). All of these negative effects on the global environment have an impact on human health.

Scientific evidence indicates that the production of chlorofluorocarbons (CFCs) has destroyed ozone in the stratosphere. Although the scientific data regarding the effect of CFCs was contested in the 1970s, it became more accepted in the 1980s. The loss of ozone has been responsible for increased exposure to ultraviolet radiation, which has led to a greater risk of skin cancer as well as cataracts and several other eye disorders. It is estimated that skin cancer rates will increase in Europe and the United States by 5 to 10 percent in the mid-twenty-first century (Slaper et al. 1996).

Climate change also appears to be taking place. The UN's Intergovernmental Panel on Climate Change (IPCC) has concluded that the 1990s was the warmest decade in the twentieth century, with 1998 as the warmest year (IPCC 2001). Additionally, the global sea level rose by 0.15 meters during the twentieth century as a result of the higher temperatures. The evidence linking greenhouse gases, such as carbon dioxide and nitrous oxide, to global warming is not as strong as in the case of ozone depletion. The IPCC report, however, concludes that most of the temperature increase is caused by human activity. Carbon dioxide in the lower atmosphere has become more concentrated, and this has been accompanied by increases in the burning of fossil fuels and deforestation. Global warming has a number of implications for global health. The number of infectious diseases could rise through an increased concentration and longevity of viruses, and the production of air pollutants; there could also be temperature-related illnesses and shortages of food and water (McMichael and Ranmuthugala 2007).

Extreme weather events, such as floods, hurricanes, and droughts, are associated with global warming, and scientific evidence suggests that the number and intensity of such events will rise in connection with the increases in temperature (WMO 2003). Extreme weather events can lead to a loss of sanitary facilities and clean water and facilitate the transmission of infectious diseases such as malaria by creating conditions for them to flourish. The World Health Organization (WHO 2002) projected that a 2.4 percent increase of diarrheal disease was attributable directly to global warming. And extreme weather events can lead to a loss of food production, which can be particularly harmful to developing countries and exacerbate malnutrition. Increases in heat waves can also pose direct negative consequences for human life. It is estimated that the summer 2003 heat wave in Europe contributed to almost 15,000 additional deaths in France and more than 2,000 extra deaths in the United Kingdom (WHO 2004). The link between climate change and health is starting to receive greater recognition. The World Health Assembly passed a resolution in 2008 that mandated the WHO to respond more vigorously to climate change risks on health.

Efforts at addressing the depletion of the ozone layer began in 1985 with the Vienna Convention for the Protection of the Ozone Layer. This agreement was signed by only twenty states. Its primary objective was to promote research and the exchange of information. Although the convention, by itself, did not impose much of a legal obligation on the signatories, its significance was in that it was the first treaty directed at a global environmental problem. It was followed by a stronger agreement, the Montreal Protocol on Substances that Deplete the Ozone Layer, which came into effect in 1989 and has now been ratified by over 190 states. The Montreal Protocol focused on a reduction in the consumption of gases that could deplete ozone. Evidence indicates that it has been fairly successful, as the amount of ozone-depleting gases in the atmosphere has been decreasing. Effective stratospheric chlorine, which is based on chlorine- and bromine-containing gases, had been increasing steadily from the 1950s to the 1990s, but since its peak has been steadily reducing. It is estimated that, as long as states continue to comply with the agreement, decreases will continue throughout the twenty-first century and amounts will return to the pre-1980 levels (Fahey 2006). Despite the evidence and progress in its regulation, however, CFC production continues to be a problem.

Climate change has been a much more difficult issue to address than ozone depletion. The two major problems in this area have to do with scientific evidence as well as economic interests. What has been established is that temperature change has been taking place, though there is disagreement as to how great the increase will be and the impact that it will have on the global ecosystem. The burning of fossil fuels plays an important part in economic growth in both developed and developing states. The first step in recognizing the problem occurred with the 1992 UN Framework Convention on Climate Change. This agreement was of a voluntary, non-binding nature in which signatories pledged to reduce their emissions of greenhouse gases. The convention was later supplemented by the 1997 Kyoto Protocol, which provided standards for emissions reductions by industrialized states. The European Union was required to reduce to 8 percent below 1990 levels, and the United States was required to reduce emissions by 7 percent. The protocol did allow for some flexibility in terms of the trading of emission shares if particular states did not reach their limit. In neither the 1992 convention nor the Kyoto Protocol were developing states, including the major polluters China and India, required to meet any limits.

Although it ratified the Montreal Protocol, the United States chose not to participate in the Kyoto Protocol. President Bill Clinton agreed to sign, but it was not submitted for ratification by the Senate by the end of his term of office in 2000. President George W. Bush then withdrew both the signature and US support for the agreement. A primary objection was that the US produced far more greenhouse emissions than Europe or Asia, and so the protocol's effect would create undue levels of hardship on the American economy and lifestyle. Additionally, the exclusion of China and India from the emissions limitations was a cause for concern. China and India both ratified the protocol, but as developing countries they are not bound by its limits on greenhouse emissions, which undermined the status of the agreement. Even without US approval, the Kyoto Protocol came into force in 2005 after ratification by Russia. Overall, over 180 states have now ratified, with the United States being the only developed state not to have done so. Although the large number of international commitments to the protocol signify political recognition of the problem of climate change, the lack of commitment from the US and China make its impact on the problem fairly dubious. The Global Carbon Project, a group formed to assist scientists in establishing a common knowledge base regarding greenhouse emissions, has found that, despite the protocol, carbon dioxide emissions have increased much faster in the 2000s than in the 1990s. The biggest increase was among developing states, with China surpassing the US in 2006 (Global Carbon Project 2007).

Most recently, the new Obama administration in the US supported a new treaty signed in Copenhagen in late 2009 that will differ significantly from the Kyoto Protocol. The new agreement is expected to focus on reducing greenhouse gas emissions and on providing financial support and technical assistance to help developing countries cope with climate change. The US also is working with China to gain its support for the treaty. President Barack Obama is pushing for federal legislation to curb carbon dioxide emissions in the US and to place a heavy tax on industries that violate standards. However, to date, global environmental pollution remains a major unresolved health problem for the world.

Summary

This chapter has discussed the two-sided nature of globalization, both its benefits and its risks. Benefits include the globalization of Western scientific medicine and the rise of medical tourism for patients seeking either better or cheaper medical procedures or drugs. Among the risks are threats to human security, in particular extreme poverty and environmental pollution. One of the greatest risks, however, is globalization's role in the spread of pandemics, and this will be discussed in the next chapter.

3

Globalization and Disease

Risks are "the dark side" of globalization, and this is especially true of the risk of pandemics. Global interconnections between people have historically led to the spread of disease, and these occurrences can be deadly for the people involved. Consequently, one of the major links between globalization and health is the accelerated capability of diseases to spread across continents. This situation has resulted in the establishment of international health agencies such as the World Health Organization, whose mission includes the containment of disease on a global basis. This is seen in WHO's priorities for 2008, among which were the goals of addressing:

1 the threat posed by emerging infectious diseases;
2 the easier spread of disease in a global economy by the movement of people and tainted goods;
3 the need for better management of international health disasters, such as tsunamis and earthquakes;
4 biological and chemical terrorist threats;
5 the health effects of global warming; and
6 AIDS.

Pandemics are the greatest threat in a globalizing world. Pandemics are epidemics that affect people in many different countries, not regional or local outbreaks of sickness. There is a long history of pandemics being introduced in communities of unsuspecting people by infected travelers. The bubonic plague that surfaced periodically in Europe in the years between 1347 and 1750 originated in China. It is believed to have reached Europe on a fleet of trading ships from Genoa that stopped in Sicily with dead and dying crewmen who had been exposed to the deadly disease at a port on the Black Sea. Although the crews were quarantined on their ships, black rats apparently went ashore unnoticed, and the fleas from these rats migrated to humans.

It is estimated that one-third of the population of Europe – about 20 million people – died during the greatest prevalence of the plague (Cantor 2001). In one month (September 1665) in one city (London) some 30,000 people are estimated to have died. What was especially frightening was that no one knew what caused it or how to stop it. There were many theories about its origins, such as its being a punishment from God. But it was eventually realized that it was spread via person-to-person and animal (rodent)-to-person contact. Sanitary living conditions, fresh air, and open spaces seemed to help. The disease finally abated in 1750 after significant improvements in housing and public sanitation, along with the appearance of aggressive brown rats which drove black rats out of Europe's cities. Brown rats tended to avoid humans and had fleas that transmitted the disease less effectively.

Another early example of the spread of disease through globalization is found in the Spanish conquest of the New World. Massimo Livi Bacci (2008) says that three voyages or journeys were important in this circumstance. The first trip was allegedly undertaken by a Siberian hunter or hunters who crossed over the frozen Bering Strait (likely by foot) to Alaska some 15,000 to 20,000 years ago. This individual and others like him began a slow migration over a period of one to two thousand years that reached from Alaska to the southern tip of South America – a movement that established a native population of some 30 to 40 million people in the Americas before the arrival of Columbus in 1492. The journey of Columbus was the second most important voyage, as it initiated permanent contact with Europe.

The third most important voyage was that of an unknown European infected with smallpox, who disembarked on the island of Hispaniola (now Haiti and the Dominican Republic) in the early 1500s. This person, probably male and a Spaniard, was the source of the first major epidemic in the New World, which eventually spread throughout Latin America and brought death to millions of people among the native Indian population, who lacked any immunity to smallpox. The disease arsenal of the Europeans also included measles, scarlet fever, and diphtheria – against which the natives likewise had no immunity. The great empires of the Aztecs in Mexico and the Incas in Peru fell relatively easily to the invaders. The native population was decimated, not only by disease but also by war, devastation of their lands, disruption to their economic and social systems, famine, and enslavement by the Spaniards. The sexual segregation of men into mining and women into work in agriculture affected opportunities for reproduction. Moreover, the hard work and unhealthy conditions in the gold and silver mines promoted high male mortality. For the Indians, contact with Europeans was a disaster of major proportions. The primary cause of their depopulation, however, appears to be disease. As Livi Bacci (2008: 5) describes it: "Only disease could adequately explain the decimation of the native population between contact and a century or so later; indeed, the most extreme estimates suggest that the population declined to a mere one-twentieth of its pre-Columbian size by the end of the sixteenth century."

Compared with the distant past, there are similarities and differences in health-related developments in today's globalizing world. A similar problem, noted as the WHO's leading priority, is that of emerging infectious diseases – infections that have either newly appeared in a population or have previously existed, but are rapidly increasing in incidence or geographic range (Morse 1995). This was a surprising development at the end of the twentieth century because, in the 1960s, there was a widespread belief that most such diseases were on the verge of extinction and that the remainder were controllable through immunization or treatment with antibiotics. The Surgeon General of the United States had declared in 1967 that infectious diseases were no longer a major health threat for Americans. We now know this was wrong: some pathogens have a remarkable ability to resist antibiotics, certain disease-transmitting insects have successfully resisted pesticides in some cases, and humans have created ecological disturbances, uncovering new diseases.

Most emerging infections originate in one geographic area and then spread to new locales. Examples include HIV, SARS, the West Nile virus, Ebola, the Marburg virus, and bovine spongiform encephalopathy ("mad cow disease"). The expanding human settlement of previously unpopulated forests and jungles, ecological changes resulting from agricultural and economic development, human behavior (unsafe sex, intravenous drug use, migration, urban decay), international travel and trade, the globalization of food supplies, and the adaptation of bacteria and viruses to antibiotics are major factors in the emergence of infectious diseases.

Another factor is the capability of contagious diseases to spread more rapidly via air travel. Moreover, a passenger infected with a disease is less likely to be detected on a modern aircraft than travelers in past historical periods, whose outward symptoms would become apparent during their long journey by land or sea. They could then be easily identified as ill and segregated, as historically the preferred method of containing diseases from abroad was to quarantine ships with sick people at ports or turn them away at borders. Sometimes ships were required to remain in port for a certain number of days before they could even be unloaded to ensure the crew, passengers, and cargo were not contagious.

But in today's era of jet air travel, those infected are very likely to be asymptomatic upon arrival at their destination only hours later. That is, they will not appear to be sick and possibly may not feel ill, as their infection is in its earliest stage. Thus contagious travelers can more readily pass unnoticed into the general population where they can infect others. Additionally, the diseases they carry may be previously unknown or new to a particular region of the globe. Of course, most travelers are not a threat to health, yet – as will be discussed – some have spread diseases from one continent to another. Next we will discuss specific examples of pandemics with respect to influenza, SARS, West Nile, and HIV/AIDS, as well as the potential for biological bioterrorism.

Pandemic Influenza

Influenza presents an especially deadly threat of a pandemic. This disease is common among humans and claims lives every year in every country. In a typical year, about 36,000 Americans die from the flu and another 200,000 are hospitalized. Should a flu pandemic occur, these figures would be several times higher. Elsewhere, the UK government published a *National Risk Register* in 2008 categorizing the potential risks facing the country. A flu pandemic was fifth on a list of most likely threats and first in its potential impact on the public. The report said that half of the population – some 30 million people – could be infected and that a million might need to be hospitalized. Some 50,000 to 750,000 people might die.

Pandemics usually occur when a novel flu virus evolves that is transmitted effectively between humans and jumps continents. Influenza pandemics can kill millions of people when they have little or no immunity against the disease. The great influenza pandemic of 1918 ("Spanish flu"), for example, took 40 million lives worldwide, while 2 million people died in 1957 ("Asian flu") and 1 million in 1968 ("Hong Kong flu"). What is scary is that influenza pandemics are unpredictable and occur at irregular intervals, and the potential for one to occur today is high.

The most recent pandemic came in the spring of 2009, when a novel version of the influenza A (H1N1) virus (or "swine flu") was first detected in Mexico before spreading to more than 100 countries worldwide. Its exact origin has yet to be determined. But it appeared centered in Mexico, whose population was hit hard by the flu. Many of the initial victims in other countries had recently visited Mexico as tourists and returned home with the disease. The first fatality in the United States was a Mexican child who had accompanied relatives to Texas. Early tests linked the flu to pigs. More extensive tests showed it to be unique, but the original name of swine flu stuck in the public mind. Some 482,300 people were infected globally by late 2009 and 46,071 had died, including 3,900 Americans, with more infections and deaths still a possibility. Schools and businesses were closed in Mexico and tourism suffered. Schools were also closed in parts of the US and activities such as sports events postponed or cancelled, while in Egypt large numbers of pigs were wrongly slaughtered as a preventive measure. People worldwide became more careful about exposure to those with flu symptoms. While ultimately the disease was not as dangerous as it could have been, its potential return could have a more widespread and deadlier outcome.

Another version of the influenza A virus is the H5N1 strain known as avian flu. This flu has killed over 200 million birds in Asia and was passed to humans in 1997; it refuses to go away and has caused at least 154 human deaths since 2006. Should it mutate or combine with a human influenza virus in a way that would allow it to be readily transmitted from person to person, the world would face a major public health challenge. Such a pandemic could spread around the globe in waves, causing millions of people, including health care workers, to become sick. Some 50 to 80 million people in an unprepared world population could die if the pandemic was similar to the one that occurred in 1918–20. If the 1918 pattern is repeated, people of all ages would be affected, with mortality highest among the young, persons in their thirties, and those over the age of seventy. A major problem is the widespread and timely availability of an effective vaccine. One vaccine considered effective for most types of flu is Oseltamivir ("Tamiflu"), which blocks viral replication. But it is only effective if given within forty-eight hours of infection, and global stockpiles were rapidly increased in late 2009 in an effort to meet worldwide demand.

Consequently, public health fears about avian flu and its potential to become a pandemic have placed the disease at the forefront of the global health agenda along with swine flu. A major factor in avian flu is the close contact between humans and poultry. A pandemic outbreak in this sector of the economy would not only kill people and birds, but have a dramatic effect on local and global economies and food supplies, as chickens have been particularly susceptible to the disease. While the virus has not yet been detected in the Western hemisphere, it may be only a matter of time until it arrives. Despite control measures in Asian countries, where it has infected largely birds, it continues to spread, causing heavy losses to farmers and an occasional human death. Because of the serious health risk it represents, it is monitored closely by national and international health agencies.

SARS

In April 2003, the WHO added Toronto to its list of cities that travelers should avoid because of the outbreak of the new, deadly, and infectious severe acute respiratory syndrome (SARS). Worldwide, some 8,422 persons were infected and 916 died in a span of ten months. The epidemic had struck Hong Kong and Beijing the hardest, but Hanoi, Singapore, and Toronto also had major outbreaks. Altogether, SARS reached fifteen countries. It is a pneumonia-like respiratory disease whose symptoms include fatigue, headache, body aches, chills, dry cough, and difficulty breathing, and it is spread through close contact with infected persons. Many physicians and nurses in hospitals with SARS patients were infected and some died.

SARS first appeared in Quangdong province in China in November 2002. It possibly originated in markets where certain wild animals (the marked palm civet and raccoon dog) were slaughtered as delicacies for human food consumption. The prevalent theory is that it is an animal virus that crossed over to humans by a yet unknown recombination sequence of events. The disease was initially reported by a local hospital to health authorities as an atypical pneumonia. A Chinese businessman died from it and infected enough doctors and nurses to fill a hospital ward. More people became sick and some died. Under Chinese law, the outbreak was classified as a state secret and information regarding it was officially suppressed (Fidler 2004). However, word about the epidemic began to spread on the Internet and by mobile phone. By February 2003, the WHO learned that an epidemic was taking place in southern China and contacted the Chinese government. The information that came back indicated that the problem was under control. But it wasn't.

A 64-year-old physician from Quangdong, Dr Liu Jianlun, who had treated SARS patients, traveled to Hong Kong in February 2003 for his nephew's wedding. He checked into the Metropole Hotel and was given a room on the ninth floor. He felt ill, began coughing, went to a hospital, and later died. As David Fidler explains:

> Dr Liu's stay at the Metropole Hotel in Hong Kong seeded a global epidemic of a disease entirely new to human populations. Dr Liu's coughs spread a new virus, never before experienced by humans, into one of the world's most cosmopolitan and globalized cities. From Hong Kong, the new disease traveled to new destinations within and beyond Asia in the respiratory tracts of a growing number of people, who themselves became

vectors for the transmission of a new plague. Dr Liu's coughs…triggered a global public health emergency the likes of which the world had not experienced in the modern age of public health. (Fidler 2004: 1)

Dr Liu infected at least sixteen other persons at the hotel, including an Asian-American businessman who traveled to Hanoi and died after spreading the disease there. Also infected were people who transmitted the disease to Hong Kong, as well as to Singapore and Beijing. Another person infected at the Metropole Hotel was a 78-year-old Canadian grandmother from Toronto, who infected her doctor and four family members after returning home. She died, along with her son and his wife. Altogether, some 346 persons were infected in Canada, mostly in Toronto, and forty-three died.

An Italian physician, Dr Carlo Urbani, doing research in Vietnam was asked to consult on the case in Hanoi. He determined that the patient there (the Asian-American businessman who had arrived from Hong Kong) had a previously unknown and highly infectious disease. Dr Urbani initiated anti-infection procedures in the hospital that helped contain the disease, convinced Vietnamese authorities they had an epidemic in their midst, and notified the WHO, which, in turn, issued an alert. Countries around the world, the US among them, started screening travelers. WHO insisted on sending inspection teams to China, and the government relented – only to be further embarrassed by reports from Chinese doctors that some SARS patients in Beijing had been kept hidden to avoid disclosure about how serious the disease actually was in the city. The Chinese government finally admitted it had a problem and began to take public measures to halt the infection that included quarantining hospitals, along with their staff and patients.

The real hero in this crisis was Dr Urbani, who sounded the first alarm in Hanoi and later died from SARS himself on a trip to Bangkok. The Chinese government subsequently fired the minister of health and some other officials who had authority in matters of public health. It also changed its policy about classifying epidemics as state secrets (Fidler 2004). SARS was eventually contained, but not before almost a thousand people worldwide had died from it and thousands more had become seriously ill.

The mayor of Toronto was upset about the adverse effect WHO's travel advisory was having on the city's economy. He believed the epidemic to be under control in May 2003 after no new cases had appeared for more than a week, and went on television to tell business travelers and tourists that Toronto was safe. Two fans at a Toronto Blue Jays home baseball game with the Kansas City Royals carried a sign saying "What SARS?" The Canadian prime minister also complained to the WHO, and the advisory was lifted two days later. Some people thought politics had overruled medicine, but fortunately the epidemic had abated. The fact remains that Toronto was the epicenter of SARS in North America. The United States had only twenty-seven cases and no deaths.

The social impact of a global disease such as SARS is immense. In some countries, SARS victims were stigmatized; travelers from abroad were viewed with suspicion; tourism and business were adversely affected; airports screened passengers; flights to and from infected cities were canceled; health care services were strained, some health care workers became sick themselves, and some died; hospitals were quarantined; and schools were closed. These conditions are all linked to globalization.

The West Nile Virus

A new infectious disease in the United States is the West Nile virus, which unexpectedly appeared in New York City in the summer of 1999 and went on to infect people in five north-eastern states. The virus was discovered in Uganda in 1937 and was relatively common in the Nile delta of Egypt, where it made birds sick but did not kill them. Something happened to the virus in the Middle East – most likely a genetic mutation which did kill birds and eventually humans and horses – in the early 1990s. Mosquitoes become infected when they bite birds that have the disease and, in turn, transmit it when they bite humans. In most people the disease feels like a mild headache, but in the very young, the elderly, and those with weak immune systems it can turn into encephalitis, causing muscle weakness, seizures, comas, and a cessation of breathing. The mutated strain of the West Nile virus was found in Israel in 1998 when birds began dying. It found its way to the Queens area of New

York City the following year, which was the first time the disease had ever been seen in the Western hemisphere.

How the new strain of West Nile reached New York is unknown, but it probably migrated in the blood of a traveler who went to Queens and was subsequently bitten by mosquitoes there. Those mosquitoes, in turn, began spreading the disease. Dozens of people became sick and six elderly persons died. The first sign of it was sick and dying birds at the Bronx Zoo, then two elderly persons were admitted to a hospital in Queens with fever and muscle weakness. Lab samples were sent to the New York State Health Department and the Centers for Disease Control and Prevention (CDC) in Atlanta. As the number of sick persons increased, CDC indicated that their tests showed that the virus was St Louis encephalitis (a close relative of the West Nile virus). The West Nile virus was not considered because it had never been known to occur in the United States. The authorities initiated an immediate city-wide campaign to kill mosquitoes, as New Yorkers were growing fearful about a potentially dangerous and unknown virus in their midst. All one had to do was to walk outside and be bitten by a mosquito to become sick.

Yet a pathologist at the Bronx Zoo knew St Louis encephalitis does not normally kill birds. Furthermore, another form of encephalitis, which is deadly to emus, was obviously not the culprit, because the zoo's emus were healthy. CDC was again alerted, and new samples were sent to Atlanta and to an army laboratory in Maryland. In the meantime, Central Intelligence Agency officials were becoming concerned about a possible act of bioterrorism, since an unidentified viral agent was obviously active in New York City (Preston 1999). The army lab and CDC both concluded it was the West Nile virus. Confirmation came a few days later from a lab at the University of California at Irvine that had received brain tissue from some of the people who had died from the disease, sent by the New York State Department of Health. The virus abruptly disappeared and it remained unclear how it would maintain itself in the North American ecosystem. "In discovering the New World," comments Richard Preston (1999: 108), "West Nile has killed a few humans and managed to roil the C.I.A., but now it has more important business – to find a way, somehow, to keep making copies of itself." This was entirely possible if the virus migrated south with the birds and found a place to hide for the winter. Preston (1999: 108) observed that "the only way we will know is if it comes back next year."

It did come back. By 2002, the West Nile virus had spread to forty-three states, and that year over 3,600 Americans became sick and 212 died. About 91,000 birds also died, while 13,000 horses became infected and about a third of them died. Earlier strains of the virus had not affected horses. Nothing like this has ever been seen before in biological history. Not only did a virus in one hemisphere mutate and jump to another, but in its new environment it found a host (birds) that had no immunity and spread via mosquito bites to other species. The epidemic ends with the arrival of cold weather, and each year it has returned. West Nile reached the West Coast of the United States in 2003, when some 9,862 people became sick nationally and 264 died. However, in 2004 the number of both people who contracted the disease (8,219) and deaths (182) declined. While the decline continued in 2005 (3,000 cases, 119 deaths), numbers rose again in 2006 (4,269 cases, 177 deaths) before falling in 2007 (3,623 cases, 124 deaths) and 2008 (1,356 cases, 44 deaths). Why the numbers have fluctuated also remains a mystery.

HIV/AIDS

HIV/AIDS first emerged in Africa, spread around the world in the late twentieth century, and continues to be a problem today. It is transmitted primarily by particular forms of sexual behavior and drug use. The disease presented a formidable puzzle for epidemiologists to solve when it first appeared in strength in the mid-1980s, and a cure has yet to be found. The acquired immune deficiency syndrome, known as AIDS, is a particularly deadly disease that destroys an individual's immunity against infection, leaving them defenseless against a variety of afflictions such as cancer, pneumonia, and a host of viruses. AIDS is a virus itself – the human immunodeficiency virus (HIV) – transmitted through sexual intercourse, intravenous drug use, and blood transfusions, or passed to newborn infants by infected mothers. AIDS is no "ordinary" epidemic: it is a lethal illness with far-reaching implications for individuals, families, communities, health care providers and delivery systems, and societies around the globe. It has become the leading infectious cause of mortality worldwide.

Research has confirmed that AIDS is a virus, but attempts to find a cure have not been successful to date, although anti-retroviral drug therapy has been able to postpone the onset of the disease in many HIV-infected people. It is now known that infection occurs when the virus enters the bloodstream, with anal intercourse and intravenous (IV) drug use the most common means of transmission in Western societies. In Africa and Asia, however, the major route of transmission is hetero-sexual activity.

Routine, non-intimate contact in the home or workplace with persons with AIDS does not appear to spread the infection. Much of the fear about the virus arises from the fact that many people who carry it are unaware of their condition. The virus can remain in the body without causing the disease, but, among those who do develop AIDS, the average time between infection and diagnosis can be five years or longer. Thus, AIDS carriers can unknowingly infect other people for a number of years, since in the absence of symptoms the only method to determine if a person is HIV-infected is through a blood test. People most at risk for developing AIDS are those who have had multiple sex partners and know little about their partners' past sexual behavior.

Worldwide

On a worldwide basis, the Joint United Nations and World Health Organization Programme on HIV/AIDS estimates that 33.2 million people were infected in 2007, with 22.5 million in Africa south of the Sahara Desert. At least 25 million people have died from AIDS since 1981. AIDS is believed to have originated in west central Africa, in Gabon, in one subspecies of chimpanzee (*Pan troglodytes troglodytes*) that somehow trans-mitted the virus to humans, possibly through blood in hunting, the preparation of chimpanzee meat to eat or sell, or bites. As long as infections were confined to a few people in remote areas, the virus in humans remained unknown. The earliest infections may have occurred in the 1940s and 1950s, with the earliest confirmed HIV blood sample dating back to 1959, from a Bantu tribesman living in the Congo. It is not known if the man developed AIDS. Migration from rural areas into cities and the increased commercialization of sex in the region caused the disease to spread among Africans, particularly in the eastern and southern parts of the continent, and to reach Europe and North America in the 1980s or earlier. According to medical historian Roy Porter (1997: 491–92), "It is unlikely that AIDS is a new disease; it probably long possessed its niche in the African rain-forests. The opening up of hitherto isolated areas to economic exploitation, travel and tourism, and the ceaseless migration of peoples have probably flushed it out and unleashed it onto a defenceless world."

African nations such as Botswana, Swaziland, Zimbabwe, and Lesotho have the highest rates per capita of AIDS. Anywhere from 18 to 33 percent of the population in these four countries is HIV-infected. Life expectancy has been reduced to levels not seen since the 1800s and is among the lowest in the world. Elsewhere in the region, South Africa has nearly 5 million HIV-infected people, which is more than any other country (Rensburg et al. 2002). Not surprisingly, both population growth and life expectancy are falling in sub-Saharan Africa. In Swaziland, for example, the average life expectancy declined from 55 years in 1991 to 34.4 years in 2004. The effects of AIDS on Africa south of the Sahara are devastating to individuals, families, communities, and society at large (Hosegood et al. 2007; Rensburg et al. 2002; Rensburg 2004).

However, in striking contrast to the pattern in Western society, AIDS in Africa is transmitted primarily by sexual inter-course among heterosexuals. About 80 percent of all cases on the continent are believed to result from heterosexual relations. AIDS is especially prevalent among prostitutes, migrant workers, and long-distance truck drivers, but reaches up to include significant numbers of people in higher socioeconomic groups. The migrant labor system in sub-Saharan Africa plays a particularly important role in its transmission (Mtika 2007). Whereas African women living in rural areas typically remain in their villages to work and care for their family, African men form a large migrant labor pool seeking greater economic opportunity in mining areas, large commercial farming areas, and major cities. This system of labor promotes long absences from home, family breakdown, and sexual infidelity. Overall, this situation has created a large population that suffers from epidemics of sexually transmitted diseases, thereby making it especially vulnerable to the AIDS virus.

AIDS now affects women in Africa more than men, with adult women comprising 57 percent of all persons living with HIV south of the Sahara. A particular problem faced by many African women is a lack of power to negotiate safe sex, either in marriage or outside of it, because of their dependent status in relation to men. Although this passive victim image may not fit all circumstances, and some African women may be active agents of sexuality (Tawfik and Watkins 2007), many are at a disadvantage in sexual relationships because of their adverse economic situation (Dodoo, Zulu, and Ezeh 2007). Poverty and the widespread lack of employment opportunities in the business sector make many women highly dependent on their spouses or sexual partners and push others into prostitution, while men can often have multiple wives or partners and divorce easily (Dodoo et al. 2007; Hunter 2007; Jewkes et al. 2003).

Why the pattern of AIDS transmission seems to differ so drastically in Africa from that of North America and Europe, where the disease is more prevalent among homosexual males and intravenous drug users, remains a mystery. It may be that the sores and genital ulcers caused by the high prevalence of other sexually transmitted diseases, such as syphilis, enhance the potential for AIDS transmission between men and women. The pattern of gender stratification in which women are severely disadvantaged is also a major factor, along with the political violence in many African states that disrupts efforts to maintain stable and healthy relationships (Jewkes et al. 2003; McIntosh and Thomas 2004).

In Europe, the AIDS epidemic has been most frequent in major cities among homosexual and bisexual men and IV drug users. The UN and the WHO estimated in 2007 that 760,000 people in Western and Central Europe were HIV-infected. The highest rates in Western Europe are found in Spain, Italy, France, and the United Kingdom. In Eastern Europe and Central Asia, at least 1.6 million were HIV-infected in 2007, with Russia and Ukraine having the highest rates of new infections.

AIDS victims in Asia were few until the late 1980s, when the disease began spreading rapidly. The UN and WHO reckoned that 4 million people in South and Southeast Asia were HIV-infected in 2007. As in Africa, the major source of AIDS in Asia is through heterosexual rather than homosexual contact. Thailand, which has many prostitutes and drug users, is a major center of AIDS, with some 860,000 people infected, but the number of new infections has begun to slow. Thailand is the one Asian country that has mounted a major response to the epidemic, with a nationwide program of education, condom promotion, and improved treatment for sexually transmitted diseases generally. Other Asian countries, such as Myanmar, Indonesia, Cambodia, and Malaysia, are now finding that AIDS is entering a new, more visible phase and becoming a major crisis.

In East Asia, the number of infected people in 2004 was estimated to be 800,000, mostly in China. The HIV outbreak in China occurred initially in 1989 among IV drug users in Yunnan province in the southwestern region of the country, bordering on the so-called Golden Triangle area of Myanmar, Laos, and Vietnam, where much of the world's heroin is produced (Deng et al. 2007; Xiao et al. 2007). By 1995, HIV/ AIDS had spread to other parts of China as migrant workers transmitted the disease through drug use and the illicit sex trade. People who become infected with HIV in China are typically subjected to stigma and discrimination which isolates them socially (Deng et al. 2007; Zhou 2007). However, after a slow start, the Chinese government responded to the AIDS menace by launching needle exchange and safe sex initiatives in provinces where the disease is most prevalent.

Sexual intercourse with female prostitutes in Thailand, the Philippines, and other Asian countries by Japanese men is believed to be a major factor in spreading the disease in Japan, but the prevalence of HIV/AIDS remains small. In the past, the Japanese public has not viewed it as a serious problem, believing it to be associated with other countries and confined in Japan largely to small groups of homosexuals and haemophiliacs (Munakata and Tajima 1996). There is no recent evidence this view has changed. Australia and New Zealand were estimated to have about 35,000 HIV-infected persons in 2007.

AIDS was predicted to spread throughout the population in India to a point that the disease would eventually claim more lives there than in any other country. While the epidemic is serious, the extent of the problem is currently not as large as had been expected. India has between 2 and 3 million people infected with HIV, not 4 to 5 million, as was once estimated. Prostitution in large cities such as Mumbai and Chennai, and in places along India's vast system of roadways frequented by some 5 million truck drivers, appears to form the major chain of transmission (Cornman et al. 2007). Homosexual activity is also a factor, along with drug use in northeast India. So far, the AIDS epidemic appears to remain contained largely within these high-risk groups of prostitutes, truckers, male homosexuals, and drug users. If it is not kept in check, because of its large population, India could become the world center of the AIDS epidemic in the twenty-first century.

Another part of the world in which AIDS is on the increase is Latin America and the Caribbean. AIDS first appeared among homosexuals and drug users in Haiti, Argentina, and Brazil and is now spreading throughout the region. Bisexual activity by Latin American men is believed to be important in the infection of a large proportion of females. The UN and WHO estimated that 1.6 million Latin Americans are HIV-infected, with an additional 230,000 cases in the Caribbean. Brazil has the largest concentration of AIDS cases among Latin American countries, while Haiti and the Dominican Republic have the highest rates in the Caribbean. HIV is also spreading in rural Mexico, as Mexican male migrants infected in the US return and spread the disease in their home communities and Mexican border towns provide conditions for transmission by becoming magnets for prostitutes and drug dealers attracted to the flow of workers northward.

United States

Signs of the disease first appeared in the US in the autumn of 1979. Young homosexual men with a history of promiscuity began showing up at clinics in New York, Los Angeles, and San Francisco with an unusual array of ailments. Some had strange fungal infections and others had rare cancers, such as Kaposi's sarcoma, which is found only among elderly men of

Mediterranean extraction or young men from equatorial Africa. Some had a deadly pneumonia, *Pneumocystis carinii*, seldom seen except in cancer and organ transplant patients weakened from prolonged treatment with drugs. Information from physicians in Los Angeles and New York City alerted the CDC in Atlanta to the problems in early 1981. Some fifty cases were initially identified around the country, and each of these individuals was interviewed. But, as the number of victims began to increase at an alarming rate, what caused the disease and how it could be treated remained unknown.

By mid-1984, 4,918 persons in the United States had developed AIDS; many of them died. While homosexual organizations complained that the federal government had little interest in solving the outbreak because most of the victims were gay, a task force was formed at the CDC. At first, it was thought that the cause might be an inhalant, known as "rush" or "poppers," containing either amyl nitrate or butyl nitrate, sometimes used by homosexuals to produce a "high" during sex. But this possibility was ruled out after interviews with gay men who used the inhalants but did not come down with AIDS. This development directed the attention of the investigators toward a virus or some other infectious agent transmitted by sexual contact or dirty needles, since some of the victims used drugs. Support for this theory began to emerge after a few heterosexual drug abusers and a baby in San Francisco, who had received blood from a donor with AIDS, contracted the disease. The strongest evidence on the means of transmission came from sexual histories obtained in Los Angeles. AIDS was consistently linked with the sexual encounters of the victims, with the virus possibly entering the bloodstream through the anus. Three different men, for instance, none of whom were acquainted with each other, identified a man in New York City as a sexual partner; he was found to have AIDS.

The next clues were somewhat puzzling because AIDS turned up in immigrants from Haiti, where homosexuality is considered exceptionally taboo. Many of these victims denied they were homosexual or drug users, but additional investigation showed they might have acquired the disease in this way. AIDS is believed to have originated in central Africa, and it was theorized that it was carried to Haiti, whence it reached the United States through homosexual contacts. In 2007, evidence from 25-year-old Haitian immigrant blood samples stored in Miami showed that it was likely that AIDS entered the US through Haiti.

CDC data for adult and adolescent males living in the US with HIV/AIDS at the end of 2005 show that 59 percent of all cases reported were homosexual and bisexual men, 22 percent were IV drug users, and 9 percent were homosexuals and IV drug users. Of the remaining male cases, 8 percent resulted from heterosexual contacts and 2 percent from other causes, such as blood transfusions. For adult and adolescent females, the majority – some 56 percent – are from heterosexual contact with infected males. Another 40 percent of females are infected from IV drug use and 4 percent from other sources.

Between 1984 and 2006, the total number of AIDS cases in the United States rose from nearly 5,000 to 982,498. Some 60 percent died. However, 1995 was the peak year for mortality, as the number of deaths fell from 49,895 that year to 37,221 in 1996, and dropped even further, to 14,215 in 1999, though it increased to 17,011 in 2005. The incidence of AIDS also fell, from 60,620 new cases in 1995 to 40,230 in 2000 and 36,828 in 2006.

CDC data for 2007 show that, among males, non-Hispanic blacks had the highest rate of infection per 100,000 population, with 81.3 cases, followed by native Hawaiians/Pacific Islanders with 37.5, Hispanics 31.0, American Indians/Alaskan natives 12.5, non-Hispanic whites 10.6, and Asians 7.3. Among females, non-Hispanic blacks also had the highest rate, at 39.8 cases per 100,000 population, Hispanics were next at 8.9, followed by native Hawaiians/Pacific Islanders 7.1, American Indians/Alaskan natives 5.0, non-Hispanic whites 1.8, and Asians 1.6. At the beginning of the AIDS epidemic, in the mid-1980s, those infected in the United States were principally non-Hispanic white homosexual males. That pattern, however, has altered, and the burden has shifted in particular to African Americans and Hispanics.

Table 3.1 shows the mortality rates for HIV for three selected years, 1987, 1995, and 2005. Rates for non-Hispanic white males increased from 8.7 deaths per 100,000 in the general population in 1987 to 20.4 in 1995 before falling to 3.0 in 2005. The highest death rates are associated with black males, with a rate of 89.0 per 100,000 in 1995, followed by a decline to 28.2 in 2005. While there has been an obvious

Table 3.1 *Mortality rates for human immunodeficiency virus (HIV) disease, United States*

	Deaths per 100,000 resident population		
	1987	*1995*	*2005*
Males			
Non-Hispanic white	8.7	20.4	3.0
Black	26.2	89.0	28.2
American Indian/native Alaskan	*	10.5	4.0
Asian/Pacific Islander	2.5	6.0	1.0
Hispanic	18.8	40.8	7.5
Females			
Non-Hispanic white	0.5	2.5	0.6
Black	4.6	24.4	12.0
American Indian/native Alaskan	*	*	1.5
Asian/Pacific Islander	*	0.6	*
Hispanic	2.1	8.8	1.9

*Fewer than twenty deaths.
Source: *Health, United States 2008* (Washington, DC: US Government Printing Office, 2008).

improvement, black male mortality remains the highest of any gender and racial group. Hispanic males had a mortality rate of 40.8 in 1995, but 2005 figures show a decline to 7.5. The lowest mortality rates for males are 1.0 per 100,000 in 2005 for Asians/Pacific Islanders.

For females, table 3.1 shows that blacks have far higher rates than all other groups, even though there was a decline from 24.4 deaths per 100,000 in 1995 to 12.0 in 2005. Female mortality among Hispanics in 2005 was 1.9 per 100,000, and there were even lower rates for American Indians/native Alaskans (1.5) and non-Hispanic whites (0.6) and negligible rates for Asian/Pacific Islanders. While the number of new AIDS cases and mortality rates in the United States started to decline in the mid-1990s, the reversal came later and has been much slower among black women, especially those that live in the South. In states such as Mississippi and North Carolina, more black women than white men have contracted HIV. The center of the epidemic among women was initially intravenous drug users in the urban Northeast, who caught AIDS via contaminated needles, but it is now heterosexual black women in the South. Since 2000, the total number of AIDS cases for both males and females has increased by nearly 30 percent in six Southern states with large black populations: Alabama, Georgia, Louisiana, Mississippi, North Carolina, and South Carolina.

In 2007, the UN and the WHO estimated that 1.3 million North Americans were infected with HIV/AIDS, but no one really knows for sure how many persons carry the virus but are not yet ill. Also, no one knows either what proportion of those persons who are HIV-positive will ultimately develop AIDS or the extent to which it can be contained without a vaccine, the development of which still eludes the best efforts of researchers.

AIDS is an example of how certain types of behavior (namely sexual promiscuity and/or IV drug use) provide a particular virus with the opportunity to cause a deadly disease that spreads globally. HIV/AIDS is the deadliest form of sexually transmitted disease (STD) that has flourished in the last few decades. STDs, such as syphilis and gonorrhea, had declined significantly in the United States and Western Europe during the twentieth century because of the widespread availability of antibiotics. However, beginning in the 1970s, their prevalence increased dramatically and the, as yet incurable, AIDS virus was introduced into human populations in epidemic proportions. In the United States, as recently as 2007, the STDs of chlamydia, gonorrhea, AIDS, syphilis, and hepatitis B accounted for nearly 90 percent of cases reported for the country's ten leading infectious diseases.

What happened? What caused the incidence of STDs to soar around the globe? According to Laurie Garrett (1994), four factors were primarily responsible:

1 the birth control pill, marketed globally, which greatly reduced fears of unwanted pregnancy;
2 an ideology of sexual liberation and permissiveness among young urban adults throughout the world;
3 a new pattern of employment in developing nations, in which young males migrate to cities for jobs and return to

their villages at weekends to spend time with their spouses and girlfriends, thereby spreading STDs acquired in urban areas to the countryside; and, perhaps most importantly,

4   the availability of multiple sexual partners on an unprecedented scale.

As Garrett concludes, the world's leading infectious disease amplifier today is multiple-partner sex:

> At the top of the list has to be sex: specifically, multiple-partner sex. The terrifying pace of emergences and re-emergences of sexually-transmitted diseases all over the world since World War II is testimony to the role that highly sexually active individuals, or places of sexual activity, play in amplifying microbial emergences such as HIV-1, HIV-2, and penicillin-resistant gonorrhea. (Garrett 1994: 610)

Garrett finds that homosexual men in Europe and North America and young heterosexuals in developing countries, especially in Africa, took greatest advantage of the new sexual climate. Globalization promoted ever increasing numbers of urban residents seeking the advantages of city living, while the availability of air travel and mass transit systems allowed people from all over the world to go to cities of their choice. This situation, along with attitudes of sexual permissiveness promoting multiple-partner sex, combined to promote the global spread of HIV/AIDS and other STDs.

Summary

This chapter has examined a particularly dark side of globalization which – in relation to health – is its role in fostering pandemics. The globalization of trade and travel and the more rapid exchanges of people and products around the world enable infectious diseases to be disseminated more quickly and infection to be spread to more places than ever before. Other factors, such as environmental changes, the globalization of food production, the capability of microbes to adapt, and human behavior, are also important in this process. Pandemics are a by-product of globalization, illustrated in this chapter by outbreaks of SARS, West Nile virus, AIDS, and pandemic influenza.

4

Globalization and Health Care: the United States

The purpose of this chapter is to examine the impact of globalization on health care in the United States. As seen in world politics, finance, trade, entertainment, and other forms of global connections, including medical science, the US ranks today among the most influential of all nations. We know, for example, that American medical scientists made numerous significant contributions to Western medicine in the twentieth century. Medical science in the US was influenced initially by Britain during its colonial period, followed by France in the 1860s, and Austria and Germany in the 1870s. Thousands of American doctors received at least part of their medical education in German-speaking universities between 1870 and 1914 (Stevens 1971). However, by the early twentieth century, American medical research began to surpass that of Europe, and the US forged ahead to become the world's leader in Western (scientific) medicine.

Western medicine, in turn, spread around the world and is now the global standard. As new medical knowledge and procedures emerge, the flow of information about them is literally worldwide, and much of it originates in the US. In this respect, globalization has been a benefit for all humankind. We also know that globalization tends to reduce the prerogatives of the nation-state, which suggests a more influential role for international health organizations and multinational corporations in the health field. In this chapter we will review the extent of these global trends in the US.

Determining the Extent of Globalization

Three criteria determine the extent to which globalization affects any country: (1) its level of global interconnections, (2) the degree of global homogenization, and (3) declines in authority relative to non-state actors. First is the extent of a nation's interconnections within the world system. With respect to international trade, finance, politics, media, communications, entertainment, higher education, and a host of other related areas, the United States is the most interconnected country in the world. Facebook and Twitter originated in the US and dominate Internet social "friend" relationships globally with their platforms, and YouTube likewise is the world's leading source of information videos. The United States is currently the only global superpower, a leader in world politics, and possesses trade and financial links spanning the globe. Events happening in the American economy and stock markets invariably have repercussions in the economies and stock markets of other countries, as seen in the 2008–9 recession. Governments around the world were required to stimulate their economies after the collapse of the American real-estate mortgage market. This brought about the demise of several large financial institutions, and federal bailouts of money were needed to save some of the country's largest banks and other lenders. The US presidential elections are also of great interest elsewhere in the world because of their relevance to relationships with other nations, while American political decisions have the potential to affect significantly the political course of other countries around the world.

Second is the degree to which a country has experienced global homogenization – that is, how much it has become similar to other countries with respect to its goods, services, conduct of business, culture, and various other aspects of day-to-day life. The US has produced many (perhaps most) of the norms promoting global homogenization through its extensive worldwide interconnections. This is seen especially in global trade and entertainment. The terms "Americanization" and "Westernization" in many instances are often synonymous. This is because American culture constitutes a significant portion of the Western culture that underlies the global homogenization process.

The dominant role of Western culture in globalization is illustrated by Peter Drucker, who explained in the 1990s that it is impossible for any global culture to be non-Western. This is because science, technological development, economics, banking, and finance *all* rest on Western foundations. "None of these can work," states Drucker (1993: 214), "unless grounded in an understanding and acceptance of Western ideas and of the entire Western tradition." The emergence of a Westernized global culture has not replaced local or national cultures, but instead provides a common frame of reference for the transaction of modern life on an international scale. In essence, it reflects the presence of a cultural unity at the global level existing above and beyond smaller spheres of cultural diversity.

Third is the amount of declining government influence relative to non-state actors. As noted in chapter 1, non-state actors include intergovernment organizations (IGOs) such as the United Nations and the World Bank and non-government organizations (NGOs) such the Red Cross. They can also embrace multinational corporations, such as global pharmaceutical companies. The authority of IGOs and NGOs has not increased relative to that of the federal government in the United States; in fact the US exercises more influence on global entities such as the United Nations, the World Bank, and the International Red Cross than vice versa. Multinational business corporations, however, have extensively penetrated American domestic markets. The policies of state governments have been strongly influenced by such corporations because of the jobs and economic opportunities they provide. Multinational corporations are not partners with the federal government in the US as they are in Japan, nor do they have direct authority or power relative to the government. But they form a highly influential lobbying group in Congress and affect decisions at the federal level through this means.

The United States therefore fulfills the first two criteria for determining the extent of globalization in a country and to a somewhat lesser degree realizes the third. The US has a central role in global homogenization, but still maintains a strong position with respect to the authority of the central government and can unilaterally reject decisions of NGOs and IGOs – although it is subject to the lobbying influence of multinational corporations. Although the US has been subjected to extensive globalization, with its high level of influence throughout the world it is more of a globalizer.

The US: global interconnections

The US is the most interconnected country in the world. American economic, scientific, political, and cultural influence extends around the globe. The terms "Westernization" and "Americanization" are similar in context, thereby illustrating the pervasive influence of and connections to the US on matters large and small. The American media literally covers the world news and financial reports, while major events in America and the activities of prominent people in politics, the economy, film, and television are widely reported in the foreign press. When the American economy enters a recession, the rest of the world is not far behind in experiencing a downturn. As Fareed Zakaria (2009) explains, for three centuries, first Britain and later the US established and maintained an open global economy by encouraging capitalism, protecting trade, providing investments, and keeping markets open:

> For sixty years, American politicians and diplomats have traveled around the world pushing countries to open their markets, free up their politics, and embrace trade and technology. We have urged peoples in distant lands to take up the challenge of competing in the global economy, freeing up their currencies, and developing new industries. We counseled them to be unafraid of change and learn the secrets of our success. And it worked: the natives have gotten good at capitalism. (Zakaria 2009: 48)

American medicine has contributed significantly to solving health problems throughout the world through its technology, high level of medical science, and storehouse of health knowledge. American universities educate thousands of foreign students annually in health-related subjects. American medical research laboratories typically have links to similar labs in other countries, and many of its pharmaceutical corporations and health-based industries are multinational with respect to employment, production, distribution, and marketing. Moreover, the US is well connected to the WHO and other organizations focused globally on health.

The US: global homogeneity

The United States, as noted in chapter 1, is a leader in global homogenization and has had a major role in the emergence of a Westernized global culture. Westernization is not exclusively an American phenomenon, as many Western nations, especially Britain, have also been important in the spread of Western culture around the world. But the US has been exceptionally dominant in this regard since the mid-twentieth century through its business norms, language, computer software, high-speed technology, fashions, and entertainment industry. The result has been a powerful impact on both originating and promoting a standardized global culture.

A similar situation exists with respect to medical training, diagnosis, treatment procedures, technology, laboratory analysis, and many other facets of health care. Western medicine is both the American and global standard. Differences between the US and other advanced societies are largely in organization, financing, and insurance systems. These differences also exist between the US and developing societies, though in addition there are disparities in availability and quality. On the whole, as discussed in chapter 2, Western medicine is the global norm and the US fits comfortably into the Western model.

The US: authority of non-state actors

Non-state actors such as NGOs (e.g., the International Red Cross) and IGOs (e.g., the United Nations) do not have direct authority over policies in the US, including in matters of health. Nor have non-state actors seen their authority increase in the US relative to that of the federal government under the current system of global health governance. While the US cooperates with NGOs and IGOs in health disasters that occur in other countries, such as tsunamis and earthquakes, the relationship is cooperative and advisory, not authoritative, and responsive to critical international events such as pandemics. International agencies have no role domestically.

An exception to outside influence is provided by the large multinational business corporations that have penetrated US domestic markets and evolved into an important lobby in relation to state and federal policy. Many, if not most, of these corporations have American components and interests, since the US is the largest open market in the world. Lobbying Congress and state legislatures for market advantages is common. It is therefore in this manner that globalization is most likely to affect governance in the US with respect to health and other areas of national life.

American Health Care

While the United States has played a dominant role in the development of contemporary scientific medicine, its health care delivery system is not the envy of the world. This is because it is costly and part of the American population lacks health insurance, meaning that they are denied equal access to the system. Practically all advanced societies have universal health coverage, but the US does not. Instead, it has a fee-for-service health care system that restricts access for those unable to pay the fees directly or who lack the health insurance that will pay for them. These persons – some 16.4 percent of the population in 2005 – typically go without needed services or receive care in welfare facilities.

Is globalization responsible for the US having a fee-for-service system and a large, uninsured population? The answer is no. The American health care delivery system evolved out of the unique historical experience of the United States and its dominant social philosophy emphasizing individual self-responsibility. That attitude was seen most recently in the public fears and concerns about a government takeover of health care in the debates about President Obama's health reform agenda. The experience of Europe was different. The provision of health services in European countries was an important feature of paternalistic government policy beginning in the late nineteenth century. Ruling political elites were in favor of government-sponsored health insurance because they desired a healthy population of workers and soldiers in order to project state power. They also wanted to reduce political discontent and contain threats of a revolution by the working class (Cockerham 2010). Germany, for example, wanted to show its working class that the government was interested in their health and welfare and deserved their political support.

Since the government wanted to prevent the Socialist Party from getting the credit for health insurance legislation, in 1883 Germany became the first country to enact a national health insurance program, and other European countries undertook similar measures in the following years. Initially, only wage earners below a certain income level were provided with health protection, but gradually benefits were extended to all or most of the population.

A national health insurance system did not spread to the US as a globalizing event. When, through the early twentieth century, European governments were introducing health insurance as part of a larger package of social benefits for the general population, such as unemployment compensation, family (child support) allowances, and old age pensions, the US government did not become deeply involved in social welfare. The present-day Social Security program to help senior citizens was not established until 1935, when the country was in the late stages of the Great Depression. Earning your own money and paying your own bills was the American norm, not taking government handouts. Americans historically have been less committed to supporting government welfare programs and more in favor of private enterprise in dealing with economic and social problems by providing jobs. The 2008–9 downturn in the economy that was initiated by the collapse of the subprime mortgage market required massive amounts of federal government bailout money. This measure represented a major change in the government's economic role. But this step was not universally popular. Except for elderly retirees, participation in government welfare programs is not considered normative. This situation implies a fundamental difference between Americans and Europeans, with Americans stressing individualism and Europeans viewing government in a more paternalistic fashion. Therefore the lack of national health insurance in the United States is a prime example of what is called "American exceptionalism" (Quadagno 2004).

The existing health care delivery system in the United States is a conglomerate of health practitioners, agencies, and organizations, all of which operate more or less independently. The greatest portion of all patient services, approximately 80 percent, is provided in offices and clinics by physicians who sell their services to patients in return for fees. About two-thirds of all active physicians are involved in treating patients in an office- or clinic-based practice, while the remainder are mostly researchers, residents in training, or full-time staff members of hospitals. The next major form of health care delivery consists of services provided by hospitals. With the exception of tax-supported government institutions, hospitals, like physicians, also charge patients on a fee-for-service basis. Non-profit hospitals charge patients for hospital services from the standpoint of recovering the full cost of services provided and meeting the hospital's expenses. Proprietary or profit-making hospitals not only calculate the cost of services rendered but also operate to realize a profit from those services. Physicians, as well as non-profit and profit-making hospitals, rely heavily on third-party sources, either private health insurance or government agencies, to pay most or all of a patient's bill.

The other types of organizations involved in the delivery of health care to the American public are official agencies, voluntary agencies, health maintenance organizations, preferred provider organizations, and allied health enterprises in the business community.

Official agencies are public organizations supported by tax funds, such as the US Department of Health and Human Services, the Centers for Disease Control and Prevention, the US Public Health Service, and the Food and Drug Administration, which are intended to support and conduct research, develop educational materials, protect the nation's health, and provide services designed to minimize public health problems. Official agencies also have the responsibility for the direct medical care and health services required by special populations, such as reservation Indians, lepers, and tuberculosis patients.

Health maintenance organizations (HMOs) are managed care prepaid group practices, in which a person pays a monthly premium for comprehensive services. HMOs are oriented toward preventive and ambulatory (walk-in) services intended to reduce the need for hospitalization. Under this arrangement, HMOs derive greater income from keeping their patients healthy, and not having to pay for their hospital expenses, than they would if large numbers of their members were hospitalized. Physicians participating in HMOs may be paid according to a fee-for-service schedule, but many receive a salary or are paid on a capitation (set amount per patient) basis. Membership entitles patients to receive physicians' services, hospitalization, laboratory tests, X-rays, and perhaps prescription drugs and other health needs at little additional cost. There are also *individual practice associations*, which are solo practitioners or small groups of physicians who contract independently with HMOs to provide care to patients enrolled in their plans.

There are some disadvantages to HMOs, namely that patients (especially at night or on weekends) may be treated by whoever is on duty rather than the doctor they regularly see, and a patient may need a referral from his or her primary care practitioner to consult a specialist. HMOs have attracted considerable attention because of their cost control potential and emphasis on preventive care. The number of HMOs and their enrollment has been rapidly increasing in the last few years, and by 2006 there was a total of 539 enrolling nearly 78 million people, constituting about 26 percent of the U.S. Only 3 million people were served by HMOs in 1970.

Preferred provider organizations (PPOs) are managed care health organizations in which employers who purchase group health insurance agree to send their employees to particular hospitals or doctors in return for discounts. PPOs have the advantage of being added to existing networks of hospitals and physicians, without having to build clinics or convert doctors into employees. Doctors and hospitals associated with a PPO are expected to provide their usual services to PPO members, but lower charges are assessed against the members' group health insurance. Thus, the health care providers obtain more patients and in return charge less to the buyer of group insurance. PPOs served over 81 million people, or 27 percent of the population, in 2006.

Voluntary agencies are charitable organizations, such as the Multiple Sclerosis Society, the American Cancer Society, and the March of Dimes, which solicit funds from the general public and use them to support medical research and provide services for disease victims. *Allied health enterprises* are the manufacturers of pharmaceuticals and medical supplies and equipment, which play a major role in the research, development, and distribution of medical goods.

The majority of Americans have health insurance benefits provided through their place of employment and paid for by contributions from both the employee and the employer. In 1984, some 96 percent of all insured workers were enrolled in traditional health plans that allowed them to choose their own doctors and have most of their costs for physician and hospital services covered in an unmanaged fee-for-service arrangement. However, this situation changed dramatically because of the soaring costs of health care and through limitations being placed on the insurance benefits provided. By 1998, only 15 percent of all insured workers had unmanaged fee-for-service health plans, while the remainder had managed fee-for-service plans, in which utilization was monitored and prior approval for some benefits, such as hospitalization, was required. This means that physicians are shifting away from their historical roots in self-employment toward group and salaried practices that are more closely aligned with the shift to managed care. Their incomes are increasing less rapidly than in the past, and professional autonomy is declining as well. The day in which doctors and their patients decided just between themselves what care was needed, without considering cost, appears to be over, as financial concerns are increasingly influencing how patients are cared for.

Some features of the health care delivery system in the United States remain unchanged. As Marsha Gold (1999) points out, the system is still pluralist. That is, it has more than one major client. These clients are (1) a substantial private sector, (2) the elderly and the poor with government-sponsored health insurance, and (3) a large uninsured population. But the major pattern for medicine has been widespread change. Both government and private corporations (employers) now dominate health policy as the major purchasers of health services and support managed care as the primary form of medical practice. This development means that more people with private health insurance are now limited in their use of health services to a particular managed care network, such as an HMO or a PPO. The changes began with Medicare and Medicaid in the 1960s, and are continuing today with the dominance of managed care systems.

Medicare

By the early 1960s, it was clear to most Americans that private health insurance had not met the needs of the aged and the poor (Light 2004). Much of the research in medical sociology during the 1950s and 1960s documented the disadvantaged position of these groups in obtaining adequate health care. Although the medical profession strongly resisted, in 1965 Congress passed the Medicare and Medicaid amendments of the Social Security Act. These amendments were a compromise between what was ideal and what was politically feasible, but their passage was a turning point in the history of medical politics in the United States. Congress for the first time emerged as a dominant voice in health care delivery and demonstrated that the control of health care was no longer the sole prerogative of organized medicine. In addition, the resistance of the medical establishment to Medicare made it clear to the general public and lawmakers that the medical profession could not always be relied upon to place the public's interest ahead of that of the profession.

Medicare is a federally administered program providing hospital insurance (part A) and medical insurance (part B) for people aged sixty-five or older, regardless of financial resources; disabled people under the age of sixty-five who receive benefits from Social Security or railroad retirement programs; and certain victims of chronic kidney disease. It also provides prescription drug coverage. Medicare offers two types of plan: (1) the Original Medicare Plan and Medicare Advantage and (2) other Medicare Health Plans. There are deductible and co-insurance amounts, for which the beneficiary is responsible, and limitations on benefits. The hospital insurance is financed primarily through social security payroll deductions, while the medical insurance plan, whose participation is voluntary, is financed by premiums paid by the enrollees and from federal funds.

Medicare Advantage and other Medicare Health Plans link original Medicare benefits with either managed care plans such as HMOs and PPOs or private fee-for-service plans. Enrollees receive all of their Medicare benefits under the original plan, but may get extra benefits such as prescription drugs or additional days in the hospital. However, there may be additional expenses of monthly premiums, higher and more frequent co-payments, and supplementary charges for the type of care needed.

The Medicare program is under the overall direction of the Secretary of Health and Human Services and is supervised by the Bureau of Health Insurance of the Social Security Administration. Most of the day-to-day operations of Medicare are performed by commercial insurance companies and Blue Cross/Blue Shield plans that review claims and make payments. Reimbursement is made on the basis of reasonable charges, as determined by the private insurance companies which issue the payments. Medicare covered 14.3 percent of the American population in 2006.

Medicaid

Medicaid is technically a welfare program. It provides for the federal government's sharing the payments made by state welfare agencies to health care providers for services rendered to the poor. Medicaid provides federal matching funds to the states, ranging from 50 to 80 percent of the costs, depending on the per capita income of the states involved. Each state is required to cover all needy persons receiving cash assistance. Eligible health care services are inpatient and outpatient hospital services, laboratory and X-ray services, skilled nursing home services, and physicians' services. Other forms of health care are covered at the option of the individual states – for instance, states can include not only the financially needy but also the medically needy, the aged, the blind, and the disabled poor, as well as their dependent children and families. In 1986 Congress passed legislation extending Medicaid coverage to children under five years of age and pregnant women with incomes below the poverty level, which in 2009 was $22,050 for a family of four.

In 2006, 45.4 million people, or 15.1 percent of the population, received Medicaid benefits. While Medicaid was originally intended to cover people on welfare, the extension of benefits to children and pregnant women from low-income families, who may or may not be on welfare, indicates that the insurance is also being used to cover people with medical expenses who have no other source of health insurance. However, since Medicaid is administered by the individual states rather than the federal government, it is subject to variation in levels of benefit.

The effects of Medicare and Medicaid on health care

Medicare and Medicaid were not designed to change the structure of health care in the United States. These programs did not place physicians under the supervision of the federal government or attempt to control the distribution or quality of medical practice. Instead they were based on pre-existing patterns of insurance coverage, involving the participation of private health insurance companies, and they allowed physicians to continue to set their own fees and conduct business as usual.

Medicare and Medicaid turned out to be a financial boon to the medical profession and to hospitals, as they channeled billions of federal and state government dollars into health care. Yet the general public does not really escape from paying higher prices, as the costs of the programs have to be met through payroll deductions and tax revenues. Nevertheless, Medicare and Medicaid accomplished two highly important goals on a national scale. First, while they may have been expensive and may not have met all the needs of the aged and the poor for which they were intended, they have provided much needed health services for the old and those in poverty that were not previously available. In this regard, both programs have been a major success.

Second, Medicare and Medicaid established the precedent for the federal government's involvement in the administration of health care, and this situation is key to future health care planning and reorganization. The time has long passed when the question of whether the federal government should be involved in health matters is a subject of debate. Its participation in health care is now an important and substantial reality, and whatever happens in the future organization, financing, and scope of health care services in the United States is dependent on its decisions.

One far-reaching measure is the 1983 federal legislation to curb Medicare spending by setting fixed amounts – diagnostic related groups (DRGs) – to be paid for services provided under its coverage. DRGs are schedules of fees placing a ceiling on how much the government will pay for specific services rendered to Medicare patients by hospitals and doctors. The Medicare payment system was passed by Congress with relatively little debate, as part of a plan to guarantee the financial status of the social security program. Hospitals make money if they keep costs below what Medicare pays, and they can lose money if their costs exceed the rate. Under the law, hospitals cannot collect additional money from Medicare patients if they find federal money does not pay the entire bill. This situation requires hospitals to be both cost conscious and more efficient when it comes to treating patients covered by Medicare.

A major overhaul of Medicare fees (the Physician Payment Reform Act, passed in 1989) set fixed fees for physicians as well. This federal legislation lowered the amounts (by 20 percent) usually paid to doctors providing specialized services, such as those performed by surgeons and radiologists, while increasing amounts (by 40 percent) for general and family practitioners and internal medicine physicians for preventive care. Physicians' fees dropped another 5 percent in 2006. A major goal was to focus Medicare more toward prevention and health maintenance than toward treatment per se, especially treatment involving very expensive medical procedures. The amount physicians can charge patients in excess of payments they receive from the government was also limited. Most physicians accept the amount paid by Medicare as payment in full.

The extent to which globalization played a role in Medicare and Medicaid is not clear. The examples of Canada and Western Europe may have been important influences, but these countries all featured universal coverage for their citizens, while the US sought to provide only for the health insurance needs of special populations – namely, the poor and the aged. However, given the historic distrust of extensive government control ("American exceptionalism"), partial coverage may have been the best outcome available at that time. As it was, it took the opportune combination of several factors to establish Medicare and Medicaid: the lack of past effective health care legislation, the changed composition of Congress in the early 1960s, the personal commitment of President Lyndon Johnson, the decreasing credibility of professional medicine's claim of support for the public's welfare, and the consistent rise of health care costs serving as ever more powerful barriers for the poor and the aged in obtaining medical treatment.

Managed care

The other major change to health care delivery is managed care. In the early to mid-1990s, private health care in the United States experienced a dramatic reorganization into managed care plans. Changing from a largely office-based, fee-for-service system increasingly to a group or an organization-based managed care system, American medical practice took on a dramatically different new structure (Pescosolido and Boyer 2005; Pescosolido, Tuch, and Martin 2001). Some of this restructuring was in response to the anticipated health reforms of the Clinton administration and some was because of a "buyer's revolt" by business corporations and insurance companies seeking to manage health care costs by controlling medical work (Budrys 2001, 2003; Stevens 2005). The medical market was under considerable pressure to contain costs, and managed care was considered the most effective means of doing so. In 2006, about 53 percent of all Americans (some 159 million people) with health insurance were enrolled in managed care programs, while in 1988 only some 29 percent of the insured were members of such plans. Managed care, as noted, refers to health organizations such as HMOs and PPOs. These organizations "manage" or control the cost of health care by monitoring the work of doctors and hospitals, limiting visits to specialists within a particular managed care network and to all physicians outside it, and requiring prior authorization for hospitalization.

Managed care alters the patient–physician relationship by introducing a third party – the case manager – to the decision-making process. The case manager represents the bill payer, usually an insurance company, who certifies that the care to be rendered is the most effective and the least costly alternative and also authorizes hospitalization. Another feature of managed care is its reliance upon capitation financing. Capitation (per capita) financing is a fixed monthly sum paid by the subscriber and his or her employer that guarantees care to that person and the person's immediate family, with little or no additional out-of-pocket cost. Health care providers, in turn, supply the necessary care and are not paid for any additional services. This measure discourages inefficient and unnecessary treatment.

Patients are allowed to see a specialist only after being screened by the primary care physician who routinely cares for them. Since specialist care is usually more costly, the primary care physician serves as a gatekeeper to the use of specialists and is usually rewarded by keeping referrals to a minimum. Finally, patients are required to use the physicians within the managed care network – unless the subscriber or a family member has a medical emergency outside the plan's geographical area.

Managed care organizations emerged because corporate and government purchasers of health care faced a crisis of excess spending by the physician-dominated system and a new concept was needed to control costs. According to Donald Light (2004: 19), "they sought to rein in the excesses, replace professional autonomy with accountable performance measures, and reorganize the center of health care from hospital-based acute intervention to community-based prevention and primary care." Light finds that a large new secondary industry arose in support of managed care organizations. These new businesses designed benefits, selected providers, managed services, defined outcomes, and established systems measuring quality and performance. Control was stripped away from physicians as the managed care model became a product of big business (Mechanic 2004). The attraction for business corporations was to keep costs down through greater efficiency that would nonetheless provide a pipeline into the huge profit potential of the health care market. Managed care is no longer the alternative delivery model that it once was; rather, it has become the dominant model (Pescosolido and Boyer 2005).

Has managed care controlled costs? The answer appears to be that the system initially kept rising costs in check. Between 1993 and 1997, health care's portion of GDP fluctuated around 13.5 percent. In 1995, the US Department of Commerce estimated that expenditures would exceed 15 percent of GDP. Yet only 13.4 percent of GDP was spent on health that year – the smallest increase in several years. By 1997, this had fallen to 13.1 percent. However, by 2005, the percentage of GDP spent on health care rose to 16.0 percent and the total amount of spending had soared to $1.97 trillion. In 2006 health spending in the US reached $2.1 trillion. While the extent of the increase between 2005 and 2006 was not large (6.7 percent), it is clear that health expenditures are still rising. If health spending continues to grow, then the percentage of GDP spent on health care is certain to rise. Moreover, pressure from patients, physicians, and employers to give patients more choice in obtaining services has ended the requirement in many managed care programs for a patient to obtain approval from a primary care physician before seeing a specialist. And rising costs within managed care plans have resulted in higher insurance premiums and co-payments.

David Mechanic (2004) forecasts that the managed care model will continue to dispense with gatekeepers and limited choices, but will institute other ways of forcing patients to be more frugal in their choices and likely will reintroduce rationing. Given the magnitude of these changes – the reorganization of a considerable portion of medical practice into managed care, along with constraints on income and autonomy – it is not surprising, as Gold (1999: 14) points out, that the satisfaction of physicians with their work situation has decreased. However, as Mary Warren and her associates (Warren, Weitz, and Kulis 1998: 364) explain, "Whereas physicians 20 years ago may have been horrified at the prospect of managed care, physicians now accept it as the rules of the game – at least in areas in which high percentages of patients belong to such plans – and recognize that the price of refusing to play by those rules is bankruptcy." Thus, many physicians have had to make the adjustment to managed care, and the revenue, especially capitation fees, from this type of practice now constitutes a growing percentage of physicians' incomes.

Mechanic (2004) observes that some sources suggest that, as its controls on costs have weakened, the managed care model is either "dead" or has been transformed into "managed care lite." He suggests the primary reason for this decline is the repudiation by the middle class of its rationing services. Mechanic points out that Americans are accustomed to having choice and autonomy in their utilization of health services, and the middle class in particular reacted negatively to restrictions. Pressure on managed care plans by physicians, the media, and politicians responding to patients also helped dilute cost controls. Employers and health care plans offering managed care health insurance relaxed cost constraints. Managed care plans, in turn, adapted to the changing environment by devising new provisions and practice arrangements. As Mechanic (2004: 81) explains: "By the new century, health providers were increasingly successful at consolidating and strengthening their bargaining position as well, making it more difficult for health plans to demand low reimbursement rates." The result was a return of upwardly spiraling costs for health care which are ultimately passed on to patients in the form of higher out-of-pocket expenses and health insurance premiums.

With the domestic market presenting less opportunity for profit, national managed care organizations expanded into multinational companies exporting managed care plans to other countries (Jasso-Aguilar, Waitzkin, and Landwehr 2004). European welfare states such as the United Kingdom, the Netherlands, and Sweden have sought to contain the rising costs of health care for the government, and in doing so they have introduced principles of managed care, market competition, and privatization of some public services. While the US is moving away from unrestricted free enterprise in health care, other countries are experimenting with American initiatives such as DRGs and managed care measures such as capitation payments (Lassey, Lassey, and Jinks 1997). Even though welfare states guarantee a basic level of health benefits to all citizens, additional benefits – private or semi-private hospital rooms, co-payments, and other services – can be covered by private insurance. This development creates new markets for managed care strategies exported by multinational corporations to Latin American nations such as Argentina, Brazil, Chile, and Mexico for patients who can afford private health insurance (Stocker, Waitzkin, and Iriart 2008). Consequently, the managed care model not only survives in the US, but is experiencing globalization.

Health Reform

The election of Barack Obama as president of the United States in 2008 brought an individual to office whose campaign rhetoric showed him to be aware of the nation's health problems, especially the plight of the uninsured. The final changes he and

Congress may bring to the health care sector had not been fully decided as this book went to press. However, with the president's Democratic Party having the majority of votes in both the House of Representatives and the Senate, passage of health reform legislation seemed likely. There was strong opposition to the plan on the part of Republicans, who were emboldened by widespread public criticism in many of their home states, and few of them supported the measure. Concern was centered on how to raise revenues to pay for it, the public health insurance option, access for illegal immigrants, and abortion coverage. Some elderly were fearful of a reduction in Medicare benefits, and persons with private health insurance did not want to see a decrease in their coverage or an increase in their costs.

The plan passed by the House – the Affordable Health Care for America Act – and sent to the Senate for approval in the late fall of 2009 preserved private health insurance but added a public insurance plan sponsored by the federal government to cover the uninsured. It could also compete with private plans and be available for purchase by employers and individuals, including illegal immigrants. Employers were required to provide health insurance for their employees or pay the government a tax equal to 8 percent of their payroll, with small businesses being exempt. Payments to doctors and hospitals under the public plan were to be negotiated. Coverage for abortions was limited to pregnancies that endangered the life of the mother or resulted from rape or incest. All Americans would be required to have health insurance, either public or private, or pay a fee equal to 2.5 percent of their adjusted income. Subsidies, government-mandated changes in private health insurance, and changes in Medicare and Medicaid were also included. To help pay for the plan, a surtax of 5.4 percent was to be levied against married couples earning $1 million or more a year and individuals making over $500,000. The final version of the plan is not known at this time, as the Senate will debate the House version and advance its changes and additions, or deny passage of the bill.

Previous presidential efforts to secure universal health insurance coverage have failed. President Harry Truman proposed a national health insurance program for all Americans in 1945, when health care costs consumed only 4 percent of GNP. But

Truman's plan died in Congress after strong opposition from the American Medical Association and public concerns that such a program was a form of socialism. In 1974, Richard Nixon began pushing for a national health insurance scheme that was closely tied to the concept of HMOs, only to become politically crippled by the Watergate scandal that ultimately forced him to resign. Jimmy Carter suggested national health insurance was needed during his first term in office but lost re-election in 1980. Only Lyndon Johnson had success with his limited reforms, which established Medicare and Medicaid in 1965, and George Bush secured coverage for prescripton drugs for Medicare patients in 2006.

The most recent attempt to provide health insurance for the entire country was President Bill Clinton's failed effort in 1994. The problems of rising costs and increasing numbers of uninsured persons – which continues today – pushed public demand for universal coverage to one of the top positions on the nation's political agenda. At the time, this plan, or a modified version of it, seemed likely to become reality because of its popularity. However, when it was delivered to Congress in 1993, numerous interest groups lobbied legislators to adopt provisions favorable to them or to oppose it altogether (Quadagno 2004, 2005). Delays in bringing the health reform bill forward through various congressional committees gave vested interests more time to mobilize. The small business lobby was especially influential in opposing the plan, since it required even businesses with few employees to pay most of the costs (80 percent) of health insurance for their workers. The AMA opposed government control over health care delivery and losses in income for doctors; hospitals, drug companies, and insurance companies were opposed to price controls; labor unions and the elderly were against losses or caps on health benefits that they already had; and some consumer groups were dissatisfied with various aspects of the plan. These anti-insurance lobbying efforts, lack of consensus between the Democrats and the Republicans in Congress charged with drafting the legislation, and growing public uncertainty resulted in congressional inaction.

In 1994 the White House conceded there was no chance of passing national health insurance that year, but vowed to make it a priority in 1995, which it did not do as the Republican Party gained control of both the House and the Senate. Weakened by a sex scandal, leading to an unsuccessful impeachment trial, President Clinton did not advance national health care legislation again. The Clinton plan nevertheless had two major effects. First, it stimulated movement toward the massive reorganization of American health care into a delivery system in which managed care is now the dominant approach in the private sector. Second, it moved health care to the forefront of domestic politics, with both the Democrats and the Republicans in Congress recognizing that changes needed to be made. One legacy of this situation is the passage by Congress in 1996 of the Health Insurance Reform Act, whose major provisions guarantee that workers in employer-sponsored health plans will be able to maintain their insurance after changing or losing their jobs and that insurance companies are barred from denying coverage to people who have pre-existing medical conditions.

Whether Obama will be able to establish a national health insurance program where other presidents have failed remains to be determined. However, some type of national health reform eventually seems likely, since the problem of health care for the uninsured in a liberal democracy requires a humane resolution. As large numbers of people continue to go without coverage, and those with insurance have benefits cut or canceled by employers and health insurance companies because of cost-saving measures, pressures to act will continue to resurface. The impending decision in Congress on the House's 2009 health reform plan is supported by the AMA and has the highest likelihood of any previous measure of bringing equity to health care. While internal pressures stemming from the unmet needs of the uninsured push the US toward national health insurance, globalization enters into reform by pulling the country in the direction of Canada and the European Union, with their examples of universal health care coverage. The internal push is by far the strongest pressure, but convergence with health care delivery systems in other countries in the capitalist world system is a feature of global homogenization that is also at work to promote change (Lassey et al. 1997).

Summary

The extent to which globalization affects any country can be determined by three criteria: (1) its level of global interconnections, (2) the degree of global homogenization, and (3) declines in authority relative to non-state actors. The US is the most interconnected country in the world and the leader in global homogenization, as seen in its role in the emergence of a Westernized global culture. However, while non-state actors such as NGOs and IGOs have not seen their authority increase in the US relative to that of the federal government, multinational business corporations have penetrated American domestic markets extensively. They are now an important lobby with respect to both state and federal policy. The US therefore fulfills the first two criteria for determining the extent of globalization in the country, but meets the third only in relation to the lobbying influence of multinational corporations.

When it comes to health care, American medicine has contributed significantly to solving health problems on a worldwide basis through its technology, high level of medical science, and storehouse of medical knowledge. Its system of health care delivery, however, is not the envy of the world on account of its high cost and the large proportion of uninsured persons. But changes in this system brought about through Medicare and Medicaid providing state-sponsored health insurance to the elderly and the poor, along with the emergence of the managed care model to contain costs, are evidence of decisive alterations in the traditional free enterprise American health care delivery system. Yet the persistent problem of a large proportion of people being uninsured – some 16.4 percent of the population in 2005 – remains unresolved. Pressure to deal with this problem continues, and it is likely to be addressed in some manner by the federal government in coming years. Whatever approach is eventually taken will probably be influenced by the global homogenization of health care delivery in Canada and the European Union.

5

Globalization and Health Care in Selected Countries

Globalization is an uneven process. It affects different countries in different ways and to varying degrees. This is true not only in trade and politics but also health matters. An anticipated outcome of globalization is better health for all – namely, a worldwide convergence or similarity of health trends in a positive direction. However, Anthony McMichael and his colleagues (2004) found that, while trends in life expectancy since the 1960s have generally been upward, this outcome has not been consistent. Some national populations have experienced stagnation in longevity and others a reversal of previously positive trends.

For example, unhealthy lifestyles, primarily heavy drinking and smoking, have caused life expectancy to reach a plateau in Denmark and to decline in Russia. Elsewhere, McMichael et al. noted the role of famine and political mismanagement in downturns in longevity in North Korea, infectious diseases in Haiti, and the deadly impact of AIDS and civil wars in Africa. Conversely, Japan began this period with relatively low life expectancy, but rapidly surged to the highest longevity in the world. France and Sweden saw life expectancy increase, as was typical in wealthy developed countries, while longevity in developing nations such as Mexico, Chile, and Tunisia followed the expected pattern of convergence toward that of developed nations. Consequently, McMichael et al. made the important observation that:

Globally, life expectancy has been on a long uptrend. However, the emerging picture of variable mortality trends and regional setbacks indicates that future health gains are not guaranteed by any general deterministic process of convergence. Rather, there is an increased heterogeneity between countries, here summarized as those achieving rapid gains, those achieving slower or plateauing gains, and those having frank reversals. (2004: 1158)

With heterogeneity rather than worldwide convergence the current health outcome, the purpose of this chapter is to examine how globalization has impacted on health care delivery systems in selected countries at various stage of development. The United Kingdom, Japan, China, Russia, Trinidad, and Kenya were chosen for discussion because each has had a different experience of globalization. The UK, Japan, and China are globalizing forces, Russia has resisted globalizing influences, while Trinidad and Kenya have experienced one-sided globalization.

The United Kingdom

The UK is one of the most globalized countries in existence. This is seen in its worldwide trading and banking connections, its high level of global homogeneity, and its respect for the authority of non-state actors such as the World Bank and World Health Organization. It has a lengthy history of globalization going back to the period when it governed and "civilized" an empire that once spanned the globe. British influence – ranging from Anglo-Saxon legal principles to norms concerning dress and manners – is worldwide. Today, London joins New York City as a leading financial center, while British corporations control much of the world's publishing and media outlets and are leaders in a number of global corporate enterprises. Along with the Americans, the British continue to be a major influence on the globalization process – a role they have occupied since the Industrial Revolution spread outward from Britain. Great Britain became the world's leading naval power back in the days of eighteenth-century sailing ships and established a network of trade and military outposts in the New World, Asia, and Africa. The United States, Canada, the Bahamas, Hong Kong, Malaysia, Singapore, Burma, Australia, New Zealand,

India, Sri Lanka, Kenya, Uganda, South Africa, and a host of other countries are all former British colonies. Britain is no longer a colonial power, but nonetheless it remains globally connected. The language that binds the world together is English.

Although Germany was the first country to enact national health insurance, Britain established the first system in any Western society to offer free medical care to the entire population. Before 1948, the quality of care a person received in the United Kingdom clearly depended on that individual's financial resources. The poor suffered from a decidedly adverse situation, since the country's original national health insurance program was primarily for the working class. The Labour Party, which came to power after World War II, enacted measures to ensure that the entire British population would receive medical treatment free of charge. To accomplish this, the government took over privately owned hospitals and made doctors state employees. The National Health Service Act of 1948 reorganized health care delivery by creating a national health service with responsibility for providing health care on behalf of the state. In such circumstances, the government becomes the employer for health workers, maintains facilities, and purchases supplies and equipment through the use of funds collected largely through taxation. Health services are thus provided at little or no cost, apart from paying taxes, to those who use them. Private health insurance is available for those persons and families who want health benefits supplementing those provided by the state, such as paying for semi-private rooms instead of being housed in a hospital ward with several other patients.

How has globalization affected health care delivery in the UK? It can be argued that the National Health Service (NHS) was an innovative means to meet internal health needs without reference to other countries. However, in the 1990s, when the NHS was having serious financial problems, greater privatization featuring a fee-for-service scheme similar to that of the United States was instituted to allow hospitals and doctors to make a profit out of patients with private health insurance. One result of the privatization process encouraged by government policies is the growth of private hospitals providing upgraded facilities and more amenities to patients with private health insurance than those found in state-owned hospitals. Another is that, when state hospitals are overcrowded, NHS patients can be referred to private hospitals. The UK is also a major site for medical tourism, especially on the part of patients from the Middle East, who travel to British doctors and facilities for their care. A further measure of globalization supported by government policy is the infusion of foreign doctors and nurses into the domestic health care market to alleviate local shortages of personnel.

British health care is not only subject to trends in globalization, it also influences other countries. Sweden, for instance, has a national health service similar to that of the UK, a key difference being the level of government responsibility. In Sweden, the county (or municipal government in the case of large cities such as Stockholm) rather than the central government is responsible for health care delivery. Furthermore, some of Britain's former colonies have been influenced by the UK model of health care. This is seen in Kenya, for example, which modeled its system after that of the British.

In the UK, the first line of medical care remains the general practitioner (GP), who works from an office or clinic either solo or as part of a group practice. GPs are paid an annual capitation (per capita) fee for each patient on their list, as part of a contractual arrangement with the NHS, regardless of how much or how little of the doctor's time and services are required by a patient. The size of a solo practitioner's list usually falls somewhere between 2,000 and 3,500 patients. A higher capitation fee is paid for patients who are sixty-five or older, and additional sums are paid by the government to meet certain basic office expenses, if a doctor wishes to join a group practice, for additional training, to recognize seniority, and for those who are practicing medicine in underserved areas. Group practices can have larger patient lists, depending on the number of doctors involved. The GP is required to provide medical services at no direct cost to the patient.

Except in the case of emergencies, if treatment by a specialist (called "consultant" in the British system) or hospitalization is warranted, the patient must be referred by their GP. Generally, consultants are the only physicians who treat patients in hospitals and are paid a salary by the government. About 11 percent of the funds to support the NHS are derived from payroll deductions and employer's contributions; thus most of the revenue for health care comes from general taxation. The average worker pays about 9 percent of his or her earnings for national health insurance, which is matched by employers.

Because of strong opposition from physicians when the NHS was first organized, doctors are also allowed to treat private patients, and a certain number of hospital beds ("pay" beds) are reserved for this type of patient. Private patients are responsible for paying their own bills, and most of them have health insurance from private insurance companies. The advantage of being a private patient is less time spent in waiting rooms and obtaining appointments and, of course, more privacy. In addition to the medical care provided by the NHS, the British have a sickness benefit fund to supplement a person's income while he or she is sick or injured, death benefits paid to survivors, and maternity benefits.

The British Medical Association (BMA) initially opposed the formation of the NHS after World War II. However, the government was determined to establish the program, and enough inducements were offered to physicians to reduce the strength of their opposition. In the face of strong government determination and skillful politics by Health Minister Aneurin Bevan at that time (1946), the BMA was rendered ineffective. Bevan refused to be drawn into lengthy negotiations with the BMA but did provide concessions to teaching hospitals and consultants and permitted the treatment of private patients in state hospitals to gain the support of many in the medical establishment. It also became increasingly clear to the medical profession that the government was going to turn the measure into law, either with or without the support of the BMA. In the end, the BMA became a partner with the government in instituting changes.

Initially, the NHS was marked by controversy and subject to criticism, but the problems concerning health care delivery in the UK are largely between health care providers and the government, and the general public has little direct involvement. It is the state's role to act as the protector of patients' rights and interests, yet only in the last few years have there been channels for members of the public to voice their concerns directly. The primary problem faced historically by the NHS is its lack of financial resources. Although the UK has a relatively high standard of living, there are large pockets of poverty.

Moreover, the NHS has worked hard to hold down medical costs, and only about 8.1 percent of Britain's GDP was spent on health care in 2004. This is less than that of many Western European countries. Though relatively successful in combating rising expenses, this policy has had its drawbacks. British doctors and nurses are paid considerably less, on average, than their American counterparts. Occasionally British doctors, nurses, or other health workers will threaten to go out on strike in order to increase their salaries. Many doctors, especially consultants, do a considerable amount of private work in order to increase their income.

However, criticism in the 1990s about long waiting periods, both for appointments and in doctors' offices, delays in obtaining elective surgery, and low staffing levels in hospitals convinced the British government, led by Prime Minister Margaret Thatcher, to initiate reforms. These reforms, a globalizing influence from the US, resulted in the creation of a competitive "internal market" within the nation's socialized health care delivery system (Annandale and Field 2005; Light 1997). The most important measure was enactment of the NHS and Community Care Act of 1990. The provisions of this act made the NHS more responsive to the needs of patients by delegating greater power and responsibility to local health districts and hospitals. Hospitals could be self-governing as NHS hospital trusts and finance themselves by contracting directly for their services with district health authorities (DHAs). DHAs are responsible for paying for health care in their area, managing the provision of that care, and planning in accordance with regional and national guidelines. They are managed and receive their resources from NHS executive regional offices, which are funded, in turn, by the central government. Additionally, GPs in group practices with at least 5,000 patients can have a budget, as GP fundholders, to purchase services from hospitals for their patients. GPs are also given higher incomes from capitation fees and encouraged to compete for patients. Patients, in turn, are allowed to choose and change GPs more readily. And, finally, the work of consultants is audited and reviewed regularly to determine satisfactory performance.

Furthermore, hospitals providing services to private patients are allowed to make a profit from those services. Hospitals are also allowed to market their services to make them more attractive to private patients, and NHS patients can be admitted by their doctors to the best hospitals available – not just those in their district. These measures were intended by the government to improve efficiency, reduce delays in providing treatment, and assist doctors and hospitals to increase their incomes by attracting more patients. Although they signified the application of free-market methods to a state-financed system, the principle of state-sponsored health care remained in place. In addition to reforming the health care marketplace, a *Patient's Charter* was provided that assured patients of ten basic rights, including the right to receive care; be referred to a consultant, if necessary; be given a clear explanation of treatment; have access to health records and have the confidentiality of those records maintained; receive detailed information on local health services; be guaranteed admission to treatment by a specific date; and have any complaints about the NHS investigated.

Despite these reforms, however, serious problems remained. Conditions in hospitals, many of them old and in need of renovation, worsened; waiting lists for surgery lengthened beyond a year; different regions of the country had different standards of care; and there was deepening dissatisfaction among doctors, nurses, and other health care workers over government budget cuts. Market reforms did not eliminate shortages caused by government underfunding. In 1997 the Labour Party came to power (after an eighteen-year absence) under its prime minister, Tony Blair, who proposed to reorganize the health care system and abolish the internal market of the NHS established by the Conservatives. Yet the internal market has remained largely intact, with its emphasis on primary care, contracts, and NHS trusts. But there were changes under Blair, as new primary care groups, consisting of local networks of general practitioners and community health nurses, replaced the fundholding and non-fundholding general practices in purchasing care from hospitals and consultants.

Primary care groups were planned to evolve administratively from providing direct care to purchasing care for their patients from both public and private sources, depending on costs. New medical schools were established to reduce doctor shortages, and one-stop drop-in medical centers were authorized. A 24-four hour medical hot line (NHS Direct), staffed by doctors and nurses, was established, and medical information was posted on the Internet for both doctors and patients. In 2004 the NHS also allowed patients who had been on waiting lists for more than six months to choose care at a variety of hospitals, including private or foreign ones. The trend in the NHS is toward greater choice and decision-making for informed patients in a partnership arrangement.

Although reforms have been found necessary, the NHS has accomplished what it set out to do – provide free comprehensive medical care to the residents of the UK. It has shown significant results. On balance, health care in the UK is of a high quality, despite problems, and particular success has been achieved against heart disease. While significant inequalities in health remain between social classes (Chandola 2000; Lahelma et al. 2002; Nettleton 2006; Reid 1998), these differences are not as substantial as those in Third World countries. Poor health among the lower classes in the UK is a result more of the unhealthy lifestyles and living environment associated with poverty than a lack of access to quality health care (Jarvis and Wardle 1999; Marmot 2004; Reid 1998; Shaw et al. 1999).

Japan

Japan spends about 8 percent of its GDP on health care (more than half that of the United States), but the Japanese have achieved striking results over the last five decades or so. For example, in 1955 the average life expectancy of the Japanese was more than four years lower than that of an American. By 1967, Japan's life expectancy had passed that of the United States and, as shown in figures for 2003, is the highest in the world for both males (78.4 years) and females (85.3 years). Japanese rates for infant mortality are the second lowest in the world (2.8 per 1,000 live births in 2004), after Singapore.

Japan, like the UK, is highly globalized. It has extensive global interconnections, subscribes to the Westernized cultural homogeneity while strongly maintaining its own distinct national culture, and typically cooperates fully with non-state actors such as the United Nations and WHO. Its globalization is linked to its drive to modernization, which began with the Meiji Restoration in 1868. After the United States forced Japan to open its ports to international trade in 1858, ending 217 years (1641–1858) of isolation from the outside world, the Japanese government embarked on a policy of modernization to avoid becoming a colony of the Western powers, as had happened in the Philippines, Indonesia, Southeast Asia, and certain coastal regions of China.

Before modernization, Japan had been exposed to Western medicine through Christian missionaries in the middle of the sixteenth century, Dutch medical officers at a lone trading station in Nagasaki, and various Japanese interpreters of Western medical works (Anesaki and Munakata 2005). With the end of isolation, the country adopted German medicine as its model for modernization, as well as the German constitution and military system. As Japanese medical sociologists Masahira Anesaki and Tsunetsugu Munakata (2005: 447) explain: "The Japanese government invited two instructors from a German army medical school to be part of the institution that was the forerunner of the University of Tokyo Medical School. The two instructors were empowered with full authority to establish a new medical education system at Tokyo University that would disseminate western medicine all over Japan."

Before this time, the sick in Japan typically were treated by traditional Chinese medicine. Beginning in 1876, Chinese medical practitioners were excluded from the health care system and licenses to practice medicine were granted only to doctors trained in Western medicine, as Japan was intent on being a modern country. Since there were no hospitals before modernization, Japanese doctors began establishing their own private hospitals using the German model, and some public hospitals were organized as well. Consequently, from its very inception, Japanese medicine has been associated with globalization and modernization.

Japan has a national health insurance plan, introduced in 1961, but its benefits are relatively low by Western standards. Japanese patients pay 30 percent of the cost of health services, with the national plan paying the remainder. However, patients are reimbursed for expenses over 60,000 yen ($570) for medical care during any given month; low-income patients are reimbursed for amounts spent over 33,600 yen ($320) a month. People over seventy years of age have all of their costs covered. Patients are allowed to choose their own doctors and are encouraged to visit them regularly, and these policies more than likely promote the longevity of the Japanese, since health problems can be diagnosed during early stages. About one-third of Japanese doctors are in private practice and are paid on a fee-for-service basis. All the rest are full-time, salaried employees of hospitals. Physicians not on a hospital staff cannot treat their patients once they are hospitalized.

Physicians' fees for office visits and examinations are low because they are set by the government. Regardless of seniority or geographical area, all Japanese doctors in private practice are paid the same amount for the same procedures. Fee revisions are negotiated by the Central Social Medical Care Council in the Ministry of Health and Welfare, comprised of eight providers (doctors, dentists, and a pharmacist); eight payers (four insurers, two from the government, and two from management and labor); and four who represent public interests (three economists and a lawyer). However, because government subsidies must be kept within general budgetary limits, any changes in fees are ultimately decided by the Ministry of Finance. In effect, the government virtually determines fees for doctors and hospitals. Hospital costs tend to be low because the government refuses to pay high fees in that area as well.

The government fee schedule is the primary mechanism for cost containment. Providers are prohibited by law from charging more than the schedule allows. Japanese doctors do receive a substantial supplementary income from the drugs they prescribe (25 percent or more of the price of the drug). Also, the Japanese use more prescription drugs than patients anywhere (Ikegami and Campbell 1995; Powell and Anesaki 1990). Private practitioners in Japan earn significantly more (about four times as much) than hospital-based doctors.

The Japanese national health insurance plan does not cover all the population. Instead, private organizations were encouraged to keep government involvement at a minimum by setting up their own welfare programs. Part of the normative structure of the Japanese business world is that companies are responsible for taking care of their own employees. In Japan this responsibility includes offering retirement plans, helping retired employees find post-retirement work, arranging vacations, offering low-cost loans for housing, and providing medical care. Consequently, there are separate programs of health services for employees of large companies, small and medium-sized companies, and public and quasi-public institutions. Some large companies even employ doctors and own hospitals. There is also a program for citizens who are not covered under other plans. The entire population is therefore covered by some type of health insurance plan, and the average Japanese has a much greater measure of security concerning health care than the average American (Anesaki and Munakata 2005; Ikegami and Campbell 1995).

The concept of having a decentralized system of health care based largely on occupation is supported by Japanese businessmen, who generally provide more benefits than are required by law. Business leaders oppose a heavy welfare burden for government, as they want to pay lower taxes and avoid the governmental administrative overhead required for a large public welfare system. The tax burdens in welfare states such as Sweden and Great Britain are undesirable, as is the type of welfare system in the United States. Also important is the desire of Japanese businesses to provide security to their employees in exchange for loyalty and productivity. This policy gives large Japanese corporations an advantage in attracting workers because of the greater benefit packages they can offer. As a result, some Japanese have better health care benefits than others, although the overall provision of benefits in Japan is highly equitable.

Some 80 percent of all Japanese hospitals are privately owned by physicians, but many facilities are old and lack space. Because the government limits how much they can charge, Japanese hospitals are often required to admit more and more patients in order to meet their expenses. Overcrowding has therefore become common in most hospitals. The average length of hospitalization in Japan is also longer than that in the West. Hospital administrators complain that it is difficult to finance updated facilities or hire additional personnel without increases in the amounts charged to patients.

There are changes in disease patterns. Heart disease is on the rise and is now the second leading cause of death after cancer. Historically, Japan has had low mortality rates from heart disease in comparison to Western countries. This trend undoubtedly influences higher levels of life expectancy among the Japanese, especially among males. The traditional low-fat, low-protein and high carbohydrate Japanese diet of fish, rice, and green vegetables is a major factor in this situation (Cockerham, Hattori, and Yamori 2000; Powell and Anesaki 1990). Also important may be the stress-reducing aspects of Japanese culture, such as strong group solidarity and cooperation in dealing with problems, as well as after-work socializing on a regular basis by males with close friends in bars or noodle shops. These drinking places are often designed to encourage relaxation and allow a temporary escape from the tensions of modern living. After-work socializing with co-workers seems to have become a routine activity in the lifestyle of many men in industrial Japan.

Nevertheless, a more Westernized diet and an increase in the consumption of animal fats and proteins, along with the stresses of living in a dynamic, hard-working, and densely populated society, have promoted more heart disease (Anesaki and Munakata 2005). Research examining socioeconomic differences in risk behavior for coronary heart disease in urban Japanese civil servants shows that persons with less education and lower status jobs smoke significantly more than those with a university education and higher status positions (Nishi et al. 2004). Alcohol consumption, however, was widespread at both the top and bottom of the social scale. The shift toward higher fat in Japanese diets has contributed to a rise in colon and pancreatic cancers, and heavy smoking among Japanese males has led to an increase in mortality rates from lung cancer. The Japanese also have the highest rates of stomach cancer in the world. Increases in death rates from cancer and heart disease, as well as the highest mortality rates from stroke of any advanced country, suggest that improvements in life expectancy for the Japanese may be slowing down and perhaps reaching a limit.

These changes, combined with the rapid growth of its elderly population, are likely to place tremendous pressure on Japan's health care delivery system in the future. The proportion of people living to old age is increasing faster than in any other society in the world, and this situation is going to require a significant response from Japan's system of health care delivery. Despite these problems, the country has an exceedingly healthy population overall, and the twin processes of globalization and modernization contributed significantly to this situation.

China

The People's Republic of China remains a socialist country politically, but its economic transition from socialism to market-driven participation in the global economy has been accompanied by a dramatic transformation of its health care delivery system. China's former socialist system, in which the state controlled, organized, financed, and allocated medical treatment directly to all citizens free of charge, literally collapsed in the 1980s, when the central government ended its financial support and transferred responsibility to local authorities. This had the effect of privatizing most of China's health facilities and doctors (Blumenthal and Hsiao 2005). China now has a fee-for-service health care system financed largely by payments from patients, employers, and health insurance companies (Chen 2005). As will be discussed, much of the population, especially those living in rural areas, lacks health insurance and has difficulty paying the fees charged by doctors and hospitals.

The Chinese are major participants in the globalization process, as they flood the world with less expensive Western-style consumer goods and other products. However, it cannot yet be demonstrated that China is fully globalized. The three criteria determining the extent to which globalization affects a country help us understand this situation. First, China has indeed established a high level of global interconnections through its worldwide trade activities and its financial and political influence. It has become a wealthy country through its manufacture of goods for Western and other consumers. While China meets this first criterion of far-reaching global interconnections, and despite massive economic and social change, it is still a developing country. Globalization and modernization go hand in hand, and large swaths of rural China are not modernized. Metropolitian centers such as Beijing, Shanghai, and Hong Kong are generally (but not exclusively) modern and globally connected, in contrast to far-flung areas in northwest China lacking extensive international links. Second, the degree of global homogenization is well developed with respect to the influence of Western global culture in corporate business matters and the conduct of life for affluent and well-educated urban residents. Some large areas of China, such as Shanghai and its surrounding cities, are also highly exposed to global culture. However, the influence of indigenous Chinese culture remains all-powerful in the country as a whole and in overseas Chinese communities. Cultural globalization therefore remains limited, despite its large-scale and continuing penetration into the daily lives of many Chinese people.

Third, declines in authority relative to non-state actors are not apparent; indeed, such authority is typically rejected or ignored by the state. The Chinese government allows only limited freedom of expression for its own population, while dissent, criticism, and political protest are suppressed. Information is often classified as a state secret, and people do not always trust the government to be truthful about problems (Becker 2000). However, such control is becoming increasingly difficult with the spread of mobile phones and the Internet. An example is the 2003 SARS outbreak, which was, as noted in chapter 2, officially suppressed until it became impossible to conceal (Fidler 2004). Word about the epidemic had spread unofficially on the Internet and by way of mobile phones. Alerted by an Italian doctor in Vietnam who subsequently died from SARS, the WHO learned in February 2003 that an epidemic had migrated there from southern China. The WHO contacted the Chinese government, which responded that the epidemic was under control. It soon became clear that this was not the case, and the WHO therefore insisted on sending its own inspection teams to China. The central government relented, only to be further embarrassed by reports from Chinese doctors that some SARS patients in Beijing had been kept hidden to avoid disclosure about how serious the disease had actually become in the city. The Chinese government finally admitted publicly that it had a problem and began to take public measures to halt the infection, which included quarantining hospitals along with their staffs and patients. The minister of health was fired.

Before the 1949 revolution that brought the communists to power under Mao Zedong, there were few Western-trained physicians in China. These doctors typically lived in major cities, where they commanded high fees for their work. Although there were a few missionary doctors in the countryside, the bulk of the population received medical care from folk practitioners and herbalists schooled in traditional Chinese medicine. Many lacked adequate training in prevention and treating infectious diseases (Chen 2005). There was a heavy death toll from communicable diseases associated with poor sanitation and widespread ignorance about health matters. In 1949, the average life expectancy of a Chinese was less than thirty-five years.

Improvement in health became one of the major goals of the communist government after it came to power following the civil war with nationalist forces. One of the first public health measures was the "Patriotic Health Movement," in which millions of Chinese killed flies, removed trash, and worked to improve sanitation. Two other measures were also important. First, traditional Chinese medicine was revived, featuring the use of herbal medicines and techniques such as acupuncture, in which pain is controlled by the insertion of needles into certain designated points in the body. Even though its therapeutic value is not fully understood, traditional medicine is still used today throughout China, with considerable effectiveness for many health problems. China is the only country that consistently treats traditional and scientific medicine equally, making both legally available and requiring Western-style physicians to learn traditional methods (Hesketh and Zhu 1997).

Another important measure was the so-called barefoot doctors movement, in which 1.8 million paramedical personnel were eventually trained in rudimentary medicine. They were sent to rural areas in order to staff clinics on communal farms, where they provided basic medical treatment and assisted efforts at preventive medicine and public health. Through this movement, the majority of the population was able to have at least some routine access to very basic health care.

China's attempts at improving its health care system suffered a serious setback during the Cultural Revolution between 1966 and 1977. The Cultural Revolution was intended by Mao and other leaders to be a mass movement of the people that would expose corruption and rid the government of unnecessary bureaucracy. Many influential people were subjected to severe public criticism and were persecuted by revolutionary groups such as the Red Guards, whose membership included thousands of zealous young students. Schools and universities were closed as young people abandoned their studies to participate in revolutionary activities. Factions developed within the movement itself, and this period of Chinese history is marked by chaos, as power struggles were waged within the hierarchy of the government and the Communist Party. There was widespread disruption of work and education.

For nearly four years there was virtually no medical research or training of medical students. Thousands of doctors were forced to leave their positions and were sent into the countryside to work with peasants in agricultural communes. When medical education was resumed in 1970, the time for training was cut from eight years after high school to three years, with an emphasis on practical and applied medicine. Almost anyone could gain admission to medical school, and few or no examinations were given during training. The quality of Chinese doctors declined accordingly, and the old system was revived, but many valuable years were lost in regard to both medical education and research.

After the death of Mao in 1976, significant changes transformed the economy, the health care delivery system, and many other aspects of daily life. At the Third Plenary Session of the Communist Party in December 1978, the new head of state, Deng Xiaoping, called for greater trade with the outside world and said he favored market-oriented reforms designed to make China part of the global economy. This policy was later referred to as "socialism with Chinese characteristics." China's one-party rule was maintained, but state control over the economy was relaxed, and people were encouraged to make money and accumulate wealth. As Merle Goldman explains:

> Because the Cultural Revolution had been so destructive and had decimated the Chinese Communist Party, Deng and his colleagues had the support of most of the party's rank and file in their efforts to abandon Maoist policies. Most of them rejected not only Mao's utopian visions of an egalitarian society, which he and they had promoted in the Great Leap Forward, and unending class struggle, which was Mao's goal in the Cultural Revolution, but also the Stalinist model of state control of the economy, collectivization of agriculture, and emphasis on heavy industry that China had copied during a ten-year alliance with the Soviet Union in the 1950s. By the late 1970s, this model had produced a faltering economy in China as well as in the rest of the Communist world. (Goldman 1998: 407)

In 1979, China began its policy of economic reform and greater openness to the outside world. For the remainder of the twentieth century China was transformed from an isolated, largely rural, and poor nation to a modern urbanized society. Its economy grew faster than that of any country in the history of the world and the standard of living improved significantly for many Chinese (Goldman 1998). It allowed private ownership of land, farms, and factories, while promoting entrepreneurship in business similar to that of the capitalist West and the East Asian nations of Japan, Taiwan, Hong Kong, Singapore, and South Korea. Thousands of Chinese students flocked to Western and other foreign universities to study a variety of subjects, including sociology, business, engineering, mathematics, and the physical sciences. In a few years China became the world center for manufacturing export-oriented light consumer goods, such as clothes, shoes, toys, flat-screen TVs, and auto parts. Foreign countries also invested in or contracted with factories inside China to take advantage of the lower cost of labor to make goods for sale in their markets and gain entry to the immense Chinese marketplace. Globalization brought not only exposure to the Westernized global culture but also modernization of China's factories and educational institutions, an expansion in the number of personal computers and the use of the Internet, and a mass migration into cities for factory work. China had changed from a largely rural country into an urbanized nation with a rising middle class and a wealthy elite.

In the process, China became a very wealthy country, largely because it was buying significantly less from the United States and other countries than it was selling in return. Had this trade gap persisted, the US economy would have become bankrupt. However, China loaned money to the United States at low interest rates to keep America's consumer society on a buying binge. Using some $1 trillion in profits from exports to the United States over the most recent decade, China invested in US government bonds and government-backed mortgage debt that lowered American interest rates and helped promote both a massive buying spree and a subprime mortgage bubble. When the housing bubble burst in 2008 as a growing number of Americans were unable to meet their mortgage payments, an economic recession spread into the general economy, triggering high unemployment, bank and business failures, and stock market losses. Government bailouts (loans) were required in countries around the globe to restore banks and key businesses. China, in turn, was adversely affected, as fewer Chinese goods were sold for export and factory orders declined, resulting in layoffs and some factory closures. Regardless of economic recessions, China has become an integral part of the global economy.

Today an extensive network of health care facilities exists in urban China. Clinics providing basic care, preventive medicine, birth-control measures, and first aid are readily available, while people with serious illnesses or injuries are referred to local, district, or regional hospitals. Many factories have their own clinics and hospitals. Medical care for factory workers is paid for by health insurance established by state-owned, collectively owned, and privately owned factories with money obtained from the sale of goods. A few Chinese can afford private health insurance. In 1998, China mandated that all private- and state-owned enterprises should offer workers medical savings accounts combined with insurance coverage for catastrophic illnesses and injuries. Medical savings accounts require people to save up to 10 percent of their annual wages to pay for the costs of their routine health care needs – at which point catastrophic coverage begins. But not all employers and workers participate in the program, dependents may not be covered, and workers lose coverage when companies disband; consequently, about 51 percent of all urban residents lack health insurance (Blumenthal and Hsiao 2005).

In rural areas, China's transition from a communal (collective farm) agricultural system in the 1980s to one centered on households led to the collapse of the collective farm health care system (Chen 2005). Without collective farming income, farm health clinics were dissolved, and many barefoot doctors left the profession altogether or went into private practice (Blumenthal and Hsiao 2005). The financial burden in rural areas was shifted to individual households, which have to pay for health care out of their own income. Those who cannot afford to pay may go without care, as the Chinese government struggles to find an equitable and efficient way to deliver health services to rural areas (Bloom and Tang 1999). A health reform plan has been introduced to provide universal insurance coverage with comprehensive benefits, first in the cities and later in the countryside, with financing by contributions from employees, employers, and local governments. It has yet to be fully implemented.

At present the central government provides less than 1 percent of all health expenditures. The responsibility for health services was delegated to the provincial and local governments (Hesketh and Zhu 1997). But the amount of money available covers only minimum wages for health care workers and capital investment for the construction of new facilities. The remaining expenses are to be covered by patient fees. Basic levels of health care tend to be provided below cost, but profits can be made from the sale of drugs and use of technology. Hospitals and health centers have to generate their own incomes from the services they provide to patients, but they control the allocation of profits. The result is the end of China's system of universal access to free health care and its replacement by a fee-for-service model. Although incomes have risen throughout China in recent decades, the urban and especially the rural poor are the most disadvantaged in obtaining health care (Hesketh and Zhu 1997; Liu, Hsiao, and Eggleston 1999).

In 2005, the average life expectancy in China for males was seventy-one years and for females seventy-four years; the infant mortality rate was twenty-seven infant deaths per 1,000 live births. Acute infectious diseases were largely under control or had been eliminated, but the global SARS epidemic started in China and caused considerable problems in Hong Kong and Beijing. Infectious diseases therefore remain an important threat. Heart disease and cancer are the major problems in most parts of the country, but one that is increasingly important is lung cancer. China has an estimated 350 million smokers, who account for 30 percent of the world's tobacco consumption. Some 70 percent of the adult male population smokes, and the proportion of adult female smokers is about 7 percent. Lung cancer rates are increasing by 4.5 percent a year, and smoking-related deaths are expected to reach around 3 million annually by 2025, or about 30 percent of worldwide deaths from cigarettes. Already some 1.2 million Chinese die annually from smoking-related causes. The government has initiated a nationwide campaign against smoking, but this effort is counter to the interests of the vast state-owned tobacco monopoly, which is the world's largest producer of cigarettes. Tax revenues from tobacco sales are the government's single largest source of income. Consequently, the Chinese government is faced with an important dilemma: if smoking declines, its greatest single source of income will be reduced.

Although it is a major component in the globalization of the world through its wide-ranging trading networks, China itself, as noted, is not fully globalized. However, the process is under way, and the effects are producing ongoing social and economic changes. China's decision to globalize led to the loss of its former socialist system of health care delivery, as that system imploded from within after state subsidies were drastically lowered. The current system has been largely privatized without the financial underpinning of private or public health insurance to support the care of the general population. As less than half of urban residents and most of the rural population are without health insurance, and fee-for-service arrangements are unaffordable for many people, the problem of the uninsured is not going to disappear. Unless resolved, this situation could one day result in massive social discontent. The globalization–health care delivery relationship in China is still evolving.

Russia

In contrast to Britain and Japan, the Russian Federation and its predecessor, the Soviet Union, have not had a major role in globalization. This is because the USSR was a largely a closed society, intent on securing its borders and dominating its close neighbors. Trade and business connections were limited, global homogeneity was not encouraged, and any authority on the part of non-state actors external to the state was unequivocally rejected. The old Soviet economy was based on the command system of centralized planning, which was a means by which the state directed the nation's resources to the production of goods required. As described by Hungarian economist János Kornai (2008: 3), the characteristics of the classic socialist system exemplified by the Soviet Union were the undivided power of the Communist Party, the domination of its ideology of Marxism–Leninism, state ownership of the means of production, bureaucratic coordination of production, paternalism, forced growth, and shortages of consumer goods because the state gave higher priority to the needs of the military and heavy industry.

The most obviously unique characteristic of a socialist economy is the replacement of individual private property (except for personal items) by collective (usually state) ownership. Socialism originated as a moral ideal, that of equality, and culminates in a practical program – the end of private property and the free market (Malia 1994). Any measures short of this do not equate to full socialism. As Kornai points out:

> It is not the property – state ownership – that erects the political structure of classical socialism over itself. Quite the reverse: the given political structure brings about the property form it deems desirable. Although in this case the ideology plays a marked role in forming society, it is not the sole explanation for the direction of influence. The indivisibility of power and concomitant totalitarianism are incompatible with the autonomy that private ownership entails. This kind of rule demands heavy curtailment of individual sovereignty. The further elimination of private ownership is taken, the more consistently can full subjection be imposed. (Kornai 2008: 5)

The unpredictability of the marketplace is theoretically replaced in socialism by long-term central planning setting rational objectives and allocating resources on an equitable scale. The state acts on behalf of its citizens to eliminate the class system and to redistribute goods and services equitably, thus ending the socioeconomic basis for exploitation, alienation, oppression, and injustice. The state provided for the needs of the individual, and the individual, in turn, gave up personal reliance and freedom. According to Polish sociologist Zygmunt Bauman (1992: 167): "Under the rule of the patronage state, freedom of individual choice in all its dimensions was to be permanently and severely curtailed, yet in exchange the less prepossessing aspects of freedom – like individual responsibility for personal survival, success, and failure – were to be spared." The state was thus a haven providing free health care and education, while old-age pensions, low-cost housing, and food, along with guaranteed employment, were state benefits.

In order to maintain the state's extensive system of control, globalization was curtailed, as was the freedom to travel and have unsupervised contact with the West. As Kornai (2008: 10) puts it: "The mature classical [socialist] system cannot tolerate contrary political opinions, self-governing institutions,

and organizations independent of the political institutions organized from above; cultures and world views other than the
official ones; or free-market exchange between autonomous
economic entities." Moreover, Soviet specialists in all fields
lacked the freedom to innovate and make decisions on their
own. They had quotas and directions from above and were
discouraged from going beyond boundaries set by the Communist Party. Consequently, the Soviet Union missed the
revolution in information technologies that occurred in the
mid-1970s (Castells 1998). The flow of free and uncensored
information was incompatible with the communist system. At
a time when there was a critical shift in computer capabilities
in advanced capitalist countries, the Soviets were unable to
integrate the rapid diffusion of the new information technologies into their controlled system. "In short," states Fred Coleman
(1996: 124), "forced to choose between progress and control,
the Communists choose control." Coleman found that few
Soviet scientists ever lived up to their potential because of
limitations on funding, computer time, and access to Western
scholarship. Talent was wasted largely for political reasons.

Unable to modernize at the same pace as the West, and
lacking extensive global trade connections, the Soviet economy
began floundering by the early 1970s. The Soviet Union did
not manufacture goods in demand in the West or Japan – that
is, they did not make anything Westerners wanted to buy in
quantity and lacked access to the world's richest markets for
products other than the raw materials of heating oil, gasoline,
and gold. Industrial performance slowed, money-losing state
enterprises were kept open in order to maintain full employment, and investment remained concentrated in heavy industry
and weapons production. Except for weapons exports to developing countries, most of the Soviet Union's trade was with
other communist countries in Eastern Europe. In addition, the
Soviet Union purchased sugar at inflated prices from Cuba in
order to keep the Cuban economy viable. Profits from oil and
gas revenues helped offset losses from manufacturing for some
time, but this only forestalled economic decline. Agricultural
production was unsatisfactory, as the nation's state-owned collective farm system was unable to produce and deliver enough
food to feed the country. Economic and political reform was
desperately needed but was not possible under the communist

system, which collapsed in Eastern Europe and the Soviet Union during the years 1989–91.

Before the implosion of communism, the health care delivery systems in the former Soviet Union and Eastern Europe were philosophically guided by Marxist–Leninist programs for reshaping capitalism into socialism. However, Marxist–Leninist ideology pertaining to health was never developed in depth. The new Soviet state established in the aftermath of the 1917 revolution nevertheless faced serious health problems, including large-scale epidemics and famine. More out of practical than theoretical necessity, the Soviet government mandated that health care would be (1) the responsibility of the state, (2) provided without direct cost to the user, (3) controlled by a central authority, and (4) allocated priority for care to workers, with (5) an emphasis on preventive care (Cassileth, Vlassov, and Chapman 1995). Because of the critical need for doctors and a shortage of manpower resulting from industrial and military demands, large numbers of women, especially nurses from working-class backgrounds, were sent to medical schools, where they were given cram courses and certified as physicians. As William Knaus explains:

> Many had no ambitions beyond a weekly paycheck. The Soviet government responded in kind with a low wage scale and a social status for medicine that treated the new physician with no more respect given a factory worker. Professionalism was not rewarded nor even encouraged. Medicine became a job and women were the ones chosen to do it. (Knaus 1981: 83)

Russia has more doctors per capita than any major nation (about 4.7 physicians for every 1,000 people) and some three-quarters of these are women. However, men hold the majority of academic positions in medicine and medical posts in the Ministry of Health.

In 1987, four years before the collapse of the Soviet regime, the average salary for health care providers was about 30 percent less than the national average for all salaries (Mezentseva and Rimachevskaya 1992). Prominent physicians, however, had special privileges with respect to housing, vacations, schools for their children, access to restricted stores, and the like. The general public did not have a choice of physicians, but assignment to a medical practitioner was made on the basis of residence. In order to receive personal attention from their doctors and better care, patients typically offered gifts or bribes, which evolved into a second economy within the overall health care system. Mark Field (1993: 167) referred to the bribery system as the "commercialization of Soviet medicine" and noted that it was paradoxical that payments by patients were reintroduced in a system designed to remove financial incentives from the patient–physician relationship. Russian doctors now have a payment structure based on income from insurance and patients for services rendered.

Following the collapse of the Soviet Union, the new Russian Federation passed legislation establishing a system of health insurance consisting of compulsory and voluntary plans (Twigg 2002). The compulsory social health insurance plan is financed by contributions (3.6 percent of payrolls) from employers to cover their workers along with central government subsidies for pensioners and the unemployed. Health insurance is mandatory for all employees, provides the same basic benefits without choice, and is administrated by eighty-nine regional government health insurance funds that make payments to participating private insurance companies. Individuals or employers have a choice of insurance companies, and competition between these companies is expected to control costs and ensure quality services. There is also a voluntary plan of private insurance, available to anyone to purchase out of his or her own pocket, that provides supplementary benefits. The intent is to move away from the former Soviet method of paying for health care directly out of the central government's budget and replace it with a universal system of health insurance providing basic benefits for all citizens in the form of payments to providers.

Nevertheless, serious problems remain, including low financing, and the declining male life expectancy is causing a major health crisis. In the mid-1990s, less than 2 percent of GDP was spent on health, and the figure in 2002 was only 6.2 percent of GDP. This is a low percentage in comparison with other industrialized countries and less than would be expected, given the magnitude of health problems in the Russian Federation. Health care costs have typically been financed by funds left over after providing for the needs of other sectors of the economy.

From the end of World War II until the mid-1960s, health progress in the former Soviet Union was rapid and consistent.

Table 5.1   *Life expectancy at birth in Russia, 1896–2005*

Year	Males	Females
1896	30.9	33.0
1910	—	—
1926	39.3	44.8
1938	40.4	46.7
1958	61.9	69.2
1965	64.0	72.1
1970	63.0	73.4
1980	61.4	73.0
1984	61.7	73.0
1985	62.7	73.3
1986	64.8	74.3
1987	64.9	74.3
1988	64.8	74.4
1989	64.2	74.5
1990	63.8	74.3
1991	63.5	74.3
1992	62.0	73.8
1993	58.9	71.9
1994	57.6	71.2
1995	58.3	71.7
1996	59.8	72.5
1997	60.8	72.9
1998	61.8	72.8
1999	59.9	72.0
2000	59.0	72.3
2001	58.9	72.2
2002	58.7	71.9
2003	58.6	71.8
2004	58.9	72.3
2005	58.9	72.4

Source: Russia State Committee on Statistics, 2007.

This situation is depicted in table 5.1, which shows that, in Russia, life expectancy for males was 40.4 years in 1938 but reached 64.0 years in 1965; for females, life expectancy increased from 46.7 years to 72.1 over the same period.

However, in the mid-1960s, life expectancy began a downward trend, brought on largely by rising mortality from heart disease among middle-aged working-class males. The mid-1960s was also a period when the Soviet Union reached its highest stage of development, which occurred about the time (1964) when Leonid Brezhnev ousted Nikita Khrushchev as premier and Communist Party leader. At that time, the Soviet Union was a military superpower, showed significant economic growth, and was making scientific advances, including a space program.

Russia had apparently reached a point in its modernization when an epidemiological shift in the major cause of mortality from infectious diseases to chronic diseases had taken place; however, by the mid-1960s, the accumulated effects of a generally unhealthy lifestyle in the post-World War II period – involving high levels of alcohol consumption, smoking, poor diet, and little or no exercise – triggered an epidemic of heart disease among susceptible middle-age males (Cockerham 1999, 2006, 2007). The Soviet health care delivery system, oriented toward treating infectious diseases, was ill-prepared and not geared toward coping with chronic illnesses. These disorders, such as heart disease and cancer, are more expensive to treat, require an individual approach to patients, and often involve a modification in lifestyle habits. Yet this method was not compatible with communist values, which emphasized the welfare of the state and the collective over that of the individual. Under Brezhnev, the collective focus on patient care remained unchanged and no more medical resources were provided; rather, it was "business as usual" in both the economy and health care.

But it was also a time when the Soviet state entered a period of economic and political stagnation from which it never recovered. This was marked especially by its over-extended military and industrial development, its poor quality consumer goods, its insufficient agricultural production, and its failure to lift party controls and participate on a broad scale in the emergence of new information technologies – technologies that were common in the West.

Table 5.1 shows that male life expectancy in Russia fell from 64.0 in 1965 to 61.4 in 1980, but improved to 64.9 in 1987. Russian demographers credit this brief rise to Gorbachev's anti-alcohol campaign in the mid-1980s, which significantly curtailed both the production and consumption of alcohol. For example, Vladimir Shkolnikov and Alexander Nemtsov (1997) calculated the difference between observed and expected deaths by sex and age and found that longevity increased by 3.2 years for males and 1.3 years for females during the campaign's duration, with the greatest advances occurring in 1986. Shkolnikov and Nemtsov (1997: 239) concluded that "the rapid mortality decrease in the years 1984 to 1987 can be assumed to reflect a pure effect of reduced alcohol abuse on mortality, because there were no other significant changes in conditions of public health in that short period." But the campaign was discontinued in late 1987 because of its widespread unpopularity, and both alcohol consumption and male mortality correspondingly increased. As shown in table 5.1, the average life expectancy for Soviet men had declined to 64.2 years by 1989.

With the collapse of the former Soviet Union in 1991 and the continued decline in Russia's standard of living in the 1990s, the decrease in life expectancy for both men and women accelerated. Table 5.1 shows the life expectancy of Russian males dropping from 64.9 in 1987 to a low of 57.6 in 1994. For females, there was a relatively slow but consistent upward trend between 1965 and 1989, from 72.1 to 74.5 years. In 1991, in the new Russian Federation, females lived 74.3 years on average, but by 1994 life expectancy for women had fallen to 71.2. Consequently, both men and women had a lower life expectancy in 1994 than their counterparts in 1965. Between 1995 and 1998, however, there was a slight increase for both men and women on account of a reduction in alcohol-related deaths (Shkolnikov, McKee, and Leon 2001). The most vulnerable people had died, and their premature deaths had less effect on life expectancy as a result. This was not a genuine improvement in longevity, as table 5.1 shows that figures resumed their downward movement, from 61.8 for males in 1998 to 58.9 in 2005, meaning that males averaged 5.1 fewer years of life in 2005 than they had in 1965. Longevity for females rose only 0.3 years during the same period. With rising death rates and falling birth rates, it is not surprising that Russia's population declined from 147 million persons in 1989 to 142.2 million in 2007.

The reduction in life expectancy in Russia and elsewhere in the old Soviet bloc countries was one of the most significant developments in world health in the late twentieth century. It continues today in Russia and a few other former Soviet republics (Belarus, Ukraine, and Kazakhstan). This situation is without precedent in modern history. Nowhere else among industrialized nations in peacetime has health worsened so seriously and for so long. Ironically, the former socialist countries espoused an ideology of social equality that theoretically should have promoted health for all. However, the reverse occurred, and life expectancy turned downward in the mid-1960s; in some parts of the former Soviet Union it has never recovered. This is a surprising development, as such a prolonged decline in public health was completely unexpected.

The rise in mortality was greatest in Russia and came very late to East Germany, but virtually all former Soviet bloc countries were affected to varying degrees. The deaths stemmed largely from higher rates of heart disease and to a lesser extent from alcohol abuse and alcohol-related accidents. An unhealthy lifestyle appears to be the primary cause of the increase in heart disease and other health problems leading to the downturn in life expectancy (Cockerham 1997, 1999, 2000, 2006, 2007; Cockerham, Snead, and DeWaal 2002; Medvedev 2000). This lifestyle was characterized by extremely heavy alcohol and cigarette consumption, high-fat diets, and little or no leisure-time exercise, and was noted to be particularly common among middle-aged working-class males, who were the principal victims of the rise in premature deaths. Thus, gender (male), age (middle age), and class (working class) were the key sociological variables in this health crisis. Medical treatment could not compensate for the damage to the circulatory system caused by unhealthy lifestyle practices, and the pathological effects they engendered overshadowed the contributions of infectious diseases, environmental pollution, and medically avoidable deaths to the increase in mortality. A health policy that failed to cope with the rise in heart disease and stress was also an important causal factor. The Soviet system lacked the flexibility, both administratively and structurally, to adjust to chronic health problems that could not be handled by the mass measures successful in controlling infectious ailments (Field 2000). Ultimately the unhealthy lifestyle of a particular segment of the population appears to be the major social determinant of the downturn in life expectancy.

For example, the amount of taxed alcohol consumed in Russia annually is about 7 liters per capita, but the real figure appears to be at least 13 to 15 liters when the consumption of unregistered imports and home-distilled beverages is taken into account (Nemstov 2002). This is the highest per capita consumption in the world. When it is noted that adult males consume 90 percent of the amount, yet comprise only 25 percent of the population, it is apparent that the drinking practices of males far exceed per capita consumption and reflect a tremendous concentration of drinking. Not only is per capita consumption extraordinarily high; the type of alcohol typically consumed (vodka) and the manner of consumption (oriented toward drunkenness and binge drinking) are considerably more harmful than the moderate drinking of wine. Smoking is also higher in Russia than in the West, and male deaths from lung cancer are extremely high by international standards (Lopez 1998; Oglobin and Brock 2003). As for nutrition, the Russian diet has changed considerably since the 1960s, moving away from cereals and potatoes toward much greater consumption of sugar and red meat. By 1990, over 36 percent of Russian food provided energy from fat, making it one of the fattiest diets in the world (Popkin et al. 1997). Furthermore, men consume about 50 percent more fat than women (Shapiro 1995). There are few data on healthy exercise, but what studies exist show the amount of exercise taken to be minimal (Palosuo 2000). As the Russian medical sociologist Elena Dmitrieva (2005) concludes, Russia lacks a self-protective health culture.

As unhealthy lifestyles continue, the Russian Federation appears to be returning somewhat to the old Soviet model, with restrictions on the media and government takeovers of former private corporations whose products are vital to the state, such as oil companies. The extent to which globalization will ultimately affect Russia and the resolution of its health crisis remains an unanswered question. However, one negative aspect of globalization is the marketing of cigarettes by multinational tobacco companies. Between 1992 and 2000, these companies invested over $1.7 billion in marketing their products in Russia, and there has been an increase in smoking among younger persons, women, and urban residents (Gilmore and McKee 2004a, 2005). Between 1992 and 2003, the prevalence of smoking doubled among Russian women, from 6.9 percent to 14.8 percent, and increased for men from 57.4 percent to 62.6 percent (Perlman et al. 2007). Russia has the highest percentage of male smokers in Europe. Low cigarette prices, public ignorance about the effects of smoking, a weak legislative branch of government, the absence of an effective anti-tobacco public health campaign, and the influence of multinational tobacco companies have been important factors in the rise in smoking (Danishevski, Gilmore, and McKee 2008).

Trinidad

Trinidad is one part of a two-island democratic republic (Trinidad and Tobago) in the Caribbean. The country is a former British colony with a population of about 1.2 million people; most live in Trinidad. The two largest racial/ethnic groups are of African (40 percent) or East Indian (40 percent) descent, and the remainder are whites, Asians, and mixed races. Oil and gas, construction, manufacturing, and tourism are major sources of revenue. The health care system was modeled after that of the UK, with some 4.3 percent of GDP being spent on health care in 2003. Life expectancy in 2008 was 66.1 years for men and 67.9 years for women.

Since independence from Britain in 1962, Trinidad has established a public health system with its own hospitals, clinics, and other services providing care. An expanding private health care sector also exists, which largely serves the affluent and has relegated the poor to public services. Globalization affected the health care delivery system in a number of ways: loans from the IMF and the World Bank changed what had previously been a government welfare service into a cost recovery system, Western medical equipment and drugs were imported, and Western medicine was adopted as the standard for care (Reznik, Murphy, and Belgrave 2007). As part of this process, local remedies and healers were increasingly abandoned, and patients turned to doctors for treatment of their afflictions. Globalization was considered by many residents to be both beneficial and inevitable, as it represented progress toward modernization in all areas of life, including medicine.

According to participants in a study of medical globalization by Reznik et al. (2007: 542), people in Trinidad often indicated a sense of helplessness with respect to the inevitability of globalization, and the process was described as an autonomous force immune to the efforts of the public to change or stop it. Globalization included extensive multinational corporate marketing, product advertising, and the promotion of consumption and materialism. An expanded market mentality was observed by Reznik et al. to have influenced professional medicine as well, as seen in a growing emphasis on profits over public health needs:

> A 'Total Market' philosophy and its manifestation in medicine are perhaps most clearly illustrated in the current restructuring of the Trinidadian healthcare system. As one participant explained, 'the private healthcare market is increasing, certainly by the number of private healthcare institutions that are being developed.' Hence medical practice is becoming increasingly a for-profit industry, with the patient transformed into a consumer of the physician's products and services. (Reznik et al. 2007: 543–4)

This change was seen as beneficial by many, as it promoted a higher standard of care, including an adherence to Western medical standards of high technology. Others were concerned that the country was moving toward a two-track system of private care for the affluent and public care for the poor. By globalizing, Trinidad itself was viewed as integrating with the rest of the world by way of a macro-level process that was beyond the control of any individual or local institution to change.

Kenya

Kenya is located in East Africa and covers an area approximately the size of France. As a result of a high birth rate (37.9 births per 1,000 persons in 2008) and declining mortality, the population increased from 5.4 million in 1948 to 37.9 million in 2008. With such a rapidly rising population and a depressed agricultural economy, based largely on the production of coffee and tea, Kenya has serious economic and social problems – although the economy is somewhat stronger than that of other nations in the region.

Kenya's national health service was inherited largely without modification from the former colonial power, Britain. It employs physicians and other health personnel and owns regional and district hospitals and a network of rural health clinics, but private practitioners, mission clinics run by church organizations, and traditional native folk healers are also available. The system was established in the early 1950s under the colonial administration. Modern, Western-style health care in Kenya, as also throughout Africa south of the Sahara, is provided primarily by the state and is concentrated almost exclusively in major urban centers (Rensburg and Ngwena 2005).

Kenya's experience of globalization rests largely on its history as a British colony (the former British East Africa) from 1886 until independence in 1963. It does not have widespread interconnections on a global scale, and exports of its agricultural products and imports of consumer goods provide the bulk of its foreign trade. Kenya sells coffee and tea and buys finished products largely from elsewhere. Tourism is also a major source of income. There is some global homogeneity, as seen in the use of English as one of the country's two official languages, the inclusion of English case law in the legal system, and other vestiges of British influence. Overall, Kenya occupies a marginal position in the world economy and its experience with globalization has been generally one-sided, with influences coming in but not going out. Like Trinidad, it is a passive participant in globalization.

Despite good intentions, Kenyan health policy is typical of that in other African states, in that most of the national health budget is spent in the capital, Nairobi. On average, urban health institutions in Kenya receive 80 to 85 percent of the total annual national health budget. Almost every hospital is located in an urban center. The best-educated and most wealthy members of Kenyan society also live in urban areas, especially in Nairobi and Mombasa, where the highest quality health services are available.

Consequently, there is a considerable disparity between urban and rural health care. Some 85 percent of Kenya's population lives in the countryside, where dispensaries and clinics are poorly equipped and understaffed by trained personnel. Kenya has one doctor for every 20,000 persons, but less than 10 percent of its physicians are located in rural settings. Another major problem that rural residents face is that they must often travel great distances to reach a health clinic. Even though care is free – as it is for all Kenyans who use public facilities – travel expenses, a lack of transportation and roads, and the time involved are major considerations in making the decision to seek medical care. In some areas, professional health care is simply not available.

Many people turn to traditional folk healers, even in large cities, not only for treatment, but also to find out why they contract certain illnesses and who or what is responsible. Traditional healers are widely available to the African public, although their popularity varies, and they remain the most common source of health care in rural Africa. Traditional healers are inexpensive, effective in reducing anxiety and stress, and embedded in the culture of the groups they serve. Consequently, they are likely to persist as health providers in a developing country such as Kenya, where there is an acute shortage of trained health professionals.

Although the Kenyan health care system is financed by revenues from the country's general budget and public services are provided at no cost, there are sometimes small fees for consultations and charges for drugs. However, even small fees, as low as 50¢, have been barriers to health care for rural Kenyans living in poverty (Mbugua, Bloom, and Segall 1995). Private care is also available to those persons who want it and can afford it. A new development in 2004 was legislation to establish a national health care fund providing national health insurance to all Kenyans, which would be paid for largely by deductions from employee wages and salaries. Unemployed persons would pay $5 annually for coverage.

Kenya has a medical school and nursing schools for the training of its own health professionals, and health care delivery remains an important government priority in the nation's development. Infant mortality has decreased from 68 deaths per 1,000 births in 2003 to an estimated 56 per 1,000 in 2008, which is lower than in nearby countries such as Rwanda, where the rate was 83.4 per 1,000, or Uganda, with a rate of 65.4 per 1,000. Life expectancy in Kenya in 2008 was estimated to be 56.4 years for males and 56.9 years for females, which reflects the impact of AIDS on the population. As the twenty-first century progresses, Kenya confronts increasingly serious problems in public health. Many people, perhaps a majority in rural areas, are infected with malaria. But the most life-threatening epidemic at present is AIDS, which, while not as prevalent as in nearby Rwanda and Uganda, is nevertheless extensive and spreading throughout the population. About 2 million people are believed to be HIV-infected.

Summary

This chapter reviews the manner in which globalization has affected health and health care delivery in the UK, Japan, China, Russia, Trinidad, and Kenya. These countries were selected for discussion because each has had a different experience in relation to globalization. Britain and Japan have positive overall levels of health and are both globalizing and globalized countries. China entered into globalization in a major way in the late twentieth century, but continues to resist being globalized. In the process, its former socialist system of health care disappeared with the end of state support and in its place a fee-for-service has evolved that excludes many Chinese. Russia has resisted globalization and is undergoing a long-term health crisis characterized by premature mortality, especially among middle-age males. Trinidad and Kenya, conversely, are not globalizing influences, but have been subjected to globalization, since they were both British colonies. Kenya and Russia have the worst health status of the states discussed in this chapter. In each instance, globalization can be related to the level of health: the more globalized countries have the best health and the least globalized the worst overall health profile.

6
Actors in Global Health Governance

As the world has become more globalized over time, a number of health issues have become prominent because of their global impact. Greater worldwide human mobility as a result of enhancements in technology and transportation have contributed to the spread of disease across continents, as discussed in chapter 3. Additionally, the distribution of medical technology and pharmaceutical products between developed and developing states has been as uneven as it has between rich and poor people. However, health issues have not generally received as much policy emphasis from international institutions as other issues, especially economic ones. Nevertheless, there are more health issues today that transcend national boundaries than in the past. Consequently, some degree of global governance is necessary to promote cooperation among states to help resolve common problems. This chapter explores the role of global governance in health by discussing the key actors involved and how their linkages can affect global health issues.

For most of the twentieth century, international policy-making in health was dominated by nation-states. After the Cold War, the scope of international health issues expanded and the role of non-state actors increased. The state, however, still plays the key role in global governance.

States are the most powerful actors and have historically dominated the process of international cooperation. This was seen in the previous two chapters, where the different experiences of the United States, the United Kingdom, Japan, China, Russia, Trinidad, and Kenya were reviewed in relation to globalization and the health of their respective populations. This chapter will examine other actors in the global governance of health, namely international governmental organizations (IGOs) such as the United Nations (UN), World Health Organization (WHO), World Bank, International Monetary Fund (IMF), and World Trade Organization (WTO). The role of multinational corporations (MNCs), especially pharmaceutical companies, and non-governmental organizations (NGOs) will also be discussed.

Early forms of international cooperation on health matters involved direct relationships between two or more states. This cooperation was usually intended to stop the spread of infectious diseases. Such efforts included quarantine measures and the requirement that ships have bills of health certifying they were disease free. Institutions did not become part of international cooperation in health until the mid-nineteenth century. One impetus for the formal institutionalization of cooperation in this area was the growing level of international trade. Quarantine procedures incurred delays and increased business expenses, so other measures to stop infectious diseases from spreading were sought (Howard-Jones 1975). The first step to improve matters was the International Sanitary Conference held in Paris in 1851. This was followed by a series of conferences over the next several years and led to four international treaties which came into force before 1900. The International Sanitary Conventions of 1892, 1893, 1894, and 1897 dealt with quarantine and hygiene practices for the participating European countries, primarily in regard to cholera and the plague. These conventions were consolidated into a single document at the Paris conference in 1903.

The second impetus for institutionalizing cooperation was the fear of diseases being imported from outside Europe. In fact, Norman Howard-Jones (1975) suggested that the main purpose of the 1903 conference was to keep diseases from being imported from the East.

The next step in cooperation was the establishment of formal institutions. The world's first permanent international health organization, the International Sanitary Bureau of the Americas, was established in 1902, and evolved over time to become part of the Pan American Health Organization in 1958. The Office International d'Hygiène Publique, a forerunner to the WHO headquartered in Paris, followed in 1907. It included a permanent secretariat and a senior committee of public health officials; when it was shut down in the 1940s, part of it was merged into WHO. The Health Organization of the League of Nations was established in 1920 to assist member states with public health problems.

While the first wave of modern globalization represented a surge in international law and cooperation in solving health problems, its impact was strongly mitigated by a concern for state sovereignty. As Fidler (2004) points out, the international health agreements reached before World War II never required states to improve their national sanitation and water systems. He suggests that the reason the agreements took this shape was owing to political considerations by the leading powers. State cooperation was structured around the effects disease had on trade and travel rather than on efforts to eliminate diseases altogether.

The UN and the WHO

The United Nations was established towards the end of World War II. Although its purpose of maintaining peace and security was similar to that of the League of Nations, which failed to prevent the outbreak of the war, the Allied powers were convinced that they could create a new organization that would have a broader scope and be more effective than the League.

Since its founding, the UN has emerged as a central actor in global governance. Among IGOs, it is the only one that has a global scope and almost universal membership. The UN Charter, drafted at Dumbarton Oaks in Washington, DC, in 1944 and finalized in San Francisco in 1945, established some key principles for international relations. One principle has to do with the sovereign equality of all states, while others address peace and security. States are restricted from threatening or using force against other states, although they are permitted to use force for individual or collective self-defense. They are also obligated to settle disputes through peaceful means and to fulfill their obligations in good faith. Despite the responsibilities placed upon states to abide by the agreement, the charter did provide protection for state sovereignty. Article 2 states that "nothing in the present charter shall authorize the United Nations to intervene in matters which are essentially within the domestic jurisdiction of any state or shall require the Members to submit such matters to settlement under the present charter..."

Although the charter provides an exception to this provision for enforcement actions that have been approved by the UN Security Council, it indicates the importance of state sovereignty in the international system. The UN also provides a forum for multilateral diplomacy through its General Assembly, which is composed of representatives of all member states. The Security Council, which is composed of fifteen states, only five of which are permanent members, deals with threats to international peace and security and has the power to issue sanctions for non-compliance with its resolutions.

During negotiations to establish the UN, one of the items for discussion was to continue the role of the Health Organization of the League of Nations by establishing a global health organization for the new entity. These discussions culminated in the establishment of the World Health Organization as a specialized UN agency. Its constitution establishes the objective of the organization as the highest attainment of health for all people and stipulates its functions include that of collaboration with the UN and other specialized agencies, assistance with health services to states upon request, and proposing conventions, agreements, regulations, and recommendations with respect to international health. Membership is open to all states.

The primary decision-making body of the WHO is the World Health Assembly (WHA), composed of three delegates from each member state. These delegates are all experts on health. Each state gets one vote. The WHO also has an executive board with thirty-two representatives chosen by the WHA which operates to give effect to the WHA's decisions and policies. The day-to-day operations of the WHO are administered by a secretariat led by a director-general. The secretariat is the most independent body in the organization, and the director-general and staff are required to refrain from taking instructions from states or other outside actors in performing their duties.

Under Articles 21 and 22 of the WHO constitution, the WHA has authority to adopt regulations that are binding on all member states unless a particular state rejects them within a designated period of time. These regulations are an important aspect of global governance in health. One set of regulations provides international legal rules on the spread of infectious diseases. In order to consolidate the international sanitary conventions put into effect before World War II, the WHO adopted the conventions in the form of the International Sanitary Regulations in 1951, the name of which was changed to the International Health Regulations (IHR) in 1969 (Fidler 1999).

The objective of the IHR was to facilitate cooperation among states to control the spread of infectious diseases. Among other things, the rules required states to notify the WHO of the outbreak of cholera, plague, smallpox, or yellow fever. This requirement assisted the WHO in tracking the spread of disease globally. In addition, the IHR established public health standards at ports and airports.

As also indicated in the UN charter, the IHR demonstrated an international norm of non-intervention. Although the WHO constitution allows states to opt out of the IHR, provided that they do so expressly, the regulations were not particularly burdensome. They did not provide standards for national public health capabilities but were directed mostly at international travel and trade. In fact, Article 23 of the IHR provides that the regulations are the maximum measures that a state may apply to international traffic to protect itself from the diseases specified.

In addition to the IHR, the activities of the WHO were very much constrained by the norm of non-intervention until a change was sought in the 1980s. Cold War politics played a major role in its actions in the early years. The WHO was closely aligned with the interests of the United States and its allies, while the Soviet Union chose to opt out of the UN system between 1949 and 1956 (Brown et al. 2006). One of the key goals for the WHO during this time was the eradication of malaria. The US wanted to eliminate the disease in order to create greater access to foreign markets for American goods as well as to promote support against communism (Packard 1997).

The dynamics of the WHO began to change when the Soviet Union returned to the UN. The malaria eradication program proved to be unsuccessful, and in 1969 the WHA declared that this goal was not viable (Brown et al. 2006). The Soviets wanted to focus in the 1960s more on the elimination of smallpox, and were successful in encouraging the WHO to promote this objective, which by 1965 was strongly backed by the United States. The WHO was able to certify the eradication of smallpox in 1979.

Although the WHO experienced success with its smallpox campaign, a growing concern began to emerge in the late 1960s and the 1970s that it was largely ineffective in promoting its objective of attaining the highest level of health for all people. In developing countries, it became more of a belief that its agenda had been related primarily to economic interests and that it needed to focus more at a grassroots level to be effective in eliminating disease. One critique of the failed malaria campaign was that it relied too much on technology brought in from developed states and did not do much to involve local populations in the campaign (Brown et al. 2006). Another problem for the WHO was the ineffectiveness of the IHR as a result of non-compliance, as several states failed to report outbreaks of the diseases specified in the regulations. This was largely because of concerns over the economic costs associated with any outbreak (Fidler 2004).

Under pressure from the Soviet Union and developing states, the WHO executive board called for a conference in Alma Ata in Kazakhstan. This conference proposed a primary health care strategy, which was endorsed by the WHA in 1981. This strategy was to achieve the objective of "Health for All in the Year 2000." The idea was that the WHO should strive for a comprehensive health care system that would suit its constitutional objective and translate health as a human right. Thomas and Weber (2004) suggest that the Alma Ata declaration indicated a shift from symbolic global politics to more substantive policy development in UN governance.

This change was more representative of a social democratic shift in global governance (Thomas and Weber 2004: 190). Some governments, international agencies, and private groups found the Alma Ata declaration to be too idealistic and a radical departure from WHO practices and the IHR. A conference in Bellagio, Italy, promoted an alternative concept of selective primary care, which was supported by US interests and policies.

The focus of this approach would be on specific diseases in developing countries and on immunization. However, the primary health care policy would prove to be too ideologically costly for developed states, especially since most of the benefits would go to developing states. In the 1980s, the selective primary care strategy gained more acceptance and became the norm for the WHO. The failure of the primary health care strategy was not strictly on account of ideological reasons, however. Some developing states failed to implement the policy, which also contributed to its lack of acceptance (Cueto 2004).

The third wave of globalization that began in the 1980s brought additional challenges to the WHO. The controversy regarding selective versus primary health care contributed to a loss of prestige, which was reflected in the WHO's budget problems during this time. The WHA voted to freeze the budget of the organization in 1982. This problem was exacerbated by the decision of the United States to withhold contributions from the WHO's regular budget. This decision was in part a result of the WHO's essential drug program, which was opposed by some major pharmaceutical companies based in the US (Godlee 1994).

The greatest challenge for the WHO would be the neoliberal economic policies promoted by the Washington Consensus, which held that the "correct" economic policies that were promoted by the IMF, World Bank, and the United States were the best path for economic development. These policies encouraged reduced government intervention in the economy, trade, and investment, as well as privatization. The World Bank, in particular, would begin to have an increased influence on global health beginning in the 1980s. The World Bank, unlike the WHO, was a funding organization that could offer financial assistance to states to influence policy change. The bank encouraged greater reliance on privatization and the reduction of public involvement in health services to improve national health care systems (World Bank 1987). Its financial resources gave it an advantage over the WHO, and by 1990 the bank's loans for health surpassed the WHO's total budget (Brown et al. 2006).

The WHO began to see in the 1990s that major reforms were necessary to increase its political influence. The end of the Cold War led to a transformation in international politics, as the world became less divided and states began to move to adopt democracy and more market-oriented economic systems.

In 1998, Gro Harlem Brundtland became director-general and instituted a series of reforms for the WHO to respond to global political changes. One important step was the creation of the Commission on Macroeconomics and Health, the purpose of which was to advocate the importance of health in economic development. Brundtland also instituted a strategy of public–private partnerships (PPPs) to bring together private groups to work with governments and international organizations. A prime example of a PPP is the Global Fund to Fight AIDS, Tuberculosis, and Malaria, which involves both states and NGOs with voting power in decision-making. To receive monies from the Global Fund, proposed projects must include participation from the government as well as NGOs (Global Fund 2008). The dynamic of the Global Fund differs substantially from the traditional reliance of global health needs on international organizations and international law (Fidler 2004).

Another major innovation supported by WHO was the Framework Convention on Tobacco Control in 2003. The treaty agreed upon contains a comprehensive ban on advertising tobacco products and regulations on the content, packaging, and labeling of tobacco products, as well as a reporting requirement in which states should provide periodic reports on implementing the treaty to the Conference of Parties, an institution created by the treaty to oversee and implement it. The tobacco treaty represented a move on the part of WHO to become a more influential political actor. In fact, it was the first treaty adopted under Article 19 of the WHO's constitution (Fidler 2004).

The WHO also sought to revise the IHR in the 1990s. It approved a new set of rules in 2005 that went into effect in June 2007. The first major change was to expand the scope of diseases covered by the regulations. After smallpox was removed from the 1969 IHR, only cholera, malaria, and yellow fever were covered. The 2005 IHR defines disease as "an illness or medical condition, irrespective of origin or source, that presents or could present significant harm to humans" (IHR 2005). The new regulations also require states to notify the WHO of all events that may constitute a public health emergency of international concern. To facilitate notification, the IHR now requires notification go through specific national and WHO IHR focal points. States are also required to develop and maintain public health capacities for surveillance.

The new IHR does not have an enforcement mechanism for non-compliance, but it does include a provision for the settlement of disputes. While the revised regulations provide an enhancement of surveillance of diseases, as with the 1969 IHR, states were not permitted to provide additional health measures that would significantly affect international traffic, unless these were supported by scientific evidence and submitted to the WHO for evaluation.

Despite the growing role of the World Bank, WTO, pharmaceutical companies, and NGOs in global health governance, the UN and the WHO continue to play a key leadership role in the process. Although global health issues traditionally fall under the purview of the WHO, the UN has become more concerned with health during the post-Cold War period. The UN Security Council held its first session on health in July 2000, when the Security Council passed Resolution 1308, which recognized HIV/AIDS as a potential risk to international peace and security, and encouraged states to increase cooperation in creating and implementing policies for HIV/AIDS prevention.

Even though WHO lacks the capacity to provide funds to states for health development, it continues to have significant power in this area on account of its moral and expert authority. Morally, the WHO is the only IGO that has the objective of obtaining the highest level of health for all as part of its constitutional mandate. The members of the WHA are experts on health matters, and the secretariat also includes medical doctors, health specialists, and epidemiologists. Taken together, this expertise makes the WHO a persuasive actor in shaping health policy.

The World Bank and the IMF

As globalization has accelerated, the World Bank, in particular, and the International Monetary Fund (IMF) have become more important actors in global health governance. Both of these organizations were established around the same time as the UN and WHO. Delegates from several countries met at Bretton Woods, New Hampshire, in 1944 to discuss an international framework for economic cooperation. The chief planners of the conference were Harry Dexter White of the US Treasury and the British economist John Maynard Keynes. The purpose of the conference was to provide greater economic stability at the international level, and to avoid the increased monetary exchange controls and trade protectionism that contributed to the Great Depression in the 1930s and during World War II. The result was the creation of the International Bank for Reconstruction and Development, or World Bank, and the IMF.

The World Bank's initial function was to assist reconstruction efforts in Europe after the war. Its focus, however, changed from reconstruction to development in the 1950s. Unlike WHO, the World Bank can provide funding resources, which it acquires from private capital markets as well as member states. The bank provides interest-bearing loans to states to assist them with development projects that private banks would not support, such as education and health care. However, it attaches economic and, sometimes, political conditions to these loans in the form of policy changes that it would like to see in the recipient state in order to promote economic development. This practice is known as a structural adjustment program (SAP), and began in response to the debt crisis in developing states in the early 1980s.

In the 1950s and 1960s, the bank was interested primarily in funding large infrastructure projects in poor countries, such as the construction of dams and bridges, to promote economic development and improve the quality of life. The idea was that these projects, along with financial stability and a robust private sector, were the path to successful development (Asher and Mason 1973).

This focus began to change in the 1970s, under the leadership of Robert McNamara, to a basic needs approach where the bank would seek to address areas of family planning, education and health. These areas had largely been ignored by the bank up until this time. The first step in this approach was directed at population control. Although the bank granted its first family planning loan in 1970, overall the program was not successful: it had failed to become sufficiently attractive to borrowers and bank shareholders (Kapur et al. 1997). McNamara then began in the mid-1970s to turn the bank's attention to health and nutrition programs. In 1979 it created the Population, Health, and Nutrition Department and allowed loans directed specifically at health (Ruger 2005). During the 1980s, the bank provided a number of health-related loans as well as co-sponsoring (with the WHO) two conferences on safe motherhood.

The bank's increased role in global health governance had become much more evident by the 1990s. *The World Bank Development Report, 1993* was devoted entirely to health. It identified the inefficient use of funds, inequitable access to adequate health, and rising costs as major problems in global health and recommended that economic conditions needed to be improved so that households could better improve their own health, especially by educating girls in health matters. It also recommended that government spending should be redirected from specialized care to primary care, such as immunization and treatment and control of infectious diseases. Additionally, the report suggested greater competition in health services, particularly by non-state actors (World Bank 1993). The bank has followed through on its emphasis on health through research and funding, and its own policy research department spends $1 million annually on health, nutrition and population studies. In terms of funding, the bank made just one health-related loan in 1970; in 1999, there were 199 active health, nutrition, and population projects in eighty-four states (de Beyer et al. 2000).

Additionally, the bank has established a more collaborative relationship with the WHO in global health governance. The WHO has provided technical assistance allowing the bank to evaluate development projects related to health, and the two organizations have worked to promote greater global understanding of health issues.

The IMF does not play as prominent a role in global health governance as the World Bank, but it is a relevant actor. The difference in roles between the two has to do primarily with their different mandates. While the bank's emphasis is on development, the fund's mission is directed at finance, which is not as directly related to health. As with the bank, the purpose of the IMF has changed and expanded over time. Its original purpose was to lend money to states to meet fluctuations in currency exchange rates, thus allowing exchange rates to be stabilized, which would permit easier convertibility of currency. The funds for the IMF came from member state contributions based upon a quota for each state. Although it was not intended to be involved in development, over time its assistance with currency exchange rates became associated with trade and economic development. In a similar way to the bank, the IMF offered SAPs as part of its lending program, and the conditions attached to the loans had potential effects for the national health care systems of the various debtor nations.

The Center for Global Development conducted a study of the IMF's programs and health spending in poor countries and issued a report in June 2007 that included detailed case studies on Mozambique, Rwanda, and Zambia. It emphasized how IMF programs can have important indirect effects on health through public spending. When such programs advocate a reduction in public spending, this can affect health spending disproportionately in states with poor economies and disrupt services. The report found that IMF programs were too restrictive on national fiscal policies and recommended that the fund needed to develop more flexible programs that would allow for greater public spending as circumstances changed. It should also be more proactive in promoting a wider range of policy options for aid recipients (CGD 2007).

Along with the privatization of public health services, SAPs have been one of the major criticisms of the World Bank. These programs have followed the neoliberalist ideology of encouraging both the reduction of public spending and the privatization of state-owned enterprises (Ruger 2005). As indicated in the Center for Global Development report, the concern with SAPs is that they have not been beneficial for health care. For example, Nuria Homedes and Antonio Ugalde (2005) conducted a study of the reforms sponsored by the World Bank and the IMF. The Latin American debt crisis of the 1980s had led to a call by both the bank and the fund for health reforms in the region. These institutions called for cuts in government spending, including that on health, and encouraged the private sector to become more involved in health care. Chile and Colombia were the two states that most closely followed the neoliberal reforms. In the case of Chile, Homedes and Ugalde (2005: 88) found that the reforms had contributed to inequities in the health care system, as 22 percent of the population was enrolled in private health insurance programs, which accounted for 43 percent of all health expenditures. Interestingly, Colombia was regarded by the WHO and the World Bank as having the best health care system in Latin America. This system, however, has developed inequities. A significant part of the population is not covered by insurance, and the poor have had more difficulties accessing health services, despite the fact that more money is being spent. Overall, Homedes and Ugalde argue that Latin American countries have spent more money on health after the reforms without improving coverage or access to care.

Amit Sengupta (2003) argues that India experienced similar problems after adopting policies influenced by the bank and the fund in the 1990s. Health care suffered major cuts in India's budget reforms in the 1990s, especially that in rural areas.

Despite these negative findings, Joy de Beyer et al. (2000) argue that the policies are designed to assist states in improving health care. Countries spend much of their national income on health, and the bank encourages responsible spending, because inefficient spending can hinder economic growth and restrict spending on social programs other than health. In addition, the authors maintain that the diversity across national health care systems makes it challenging to find the most effective form of bank intervention in all cases (de Beyer et al.). Breman and Shelton (2007) conducted a review of the literature examining the relationship between SAPs and health. Out of the seventy-six articles that they identified as exploring this relationship, 47 percent were from Africa while 18 percent were global studies. They found that, although most articles were written by opponents of SAPs, the empirical evidence was both positive and negative on health outcomes. While the studies on sub-Saharan Africa were consistently negative in regard to the effect of SAPs and health, the findings on other regions, and globally, did not exhibit a clear consensus.

Although the World Bank has been only a relatively recent actor in global health governance, it has made a substantial impact in the area. It has an advantage over other IGOs in that it is a funding institution, and it is now the largest external funder of health care (Ruger 2005; de Beyer et al. 2000). Since it is an economic rather than a social institution, it lacks the moral authority of the WHO. It does, however, have financial power, and, with its increased spending on health, nutrition, and population research, it is developing more expertise in the area. Despite the controversy over SAPs, the bank has realized the need to develop more efficient health policies and is seeking to work with other IGOs, such as the WHO, as well as NGOs and the private sector in doing so (de Beyer et al. 2000).

The WTO

In addition to the World Bank and the IMF, an International Trade Organization (ITO) was also proposed at the Bretton Woods conference. It was designed to provide a framework for international trade rules and to restrict protectionist practices by states. Owing to disagreements over the scope of the rules, however, the ITO failed to gain enough support to become established. Instead an alternative arrangement, the General Agreement on Tariffs and Trade (GATT), was developed. The GATT was expected to be a temporary arrangement, but it provided the framework for international trade rules from 1948 to 1994. In 1995, the World Trade Organization (WTO) was created as a formal organization for international trade matters. It also expanded the scope of the GATT by including a General Agreement on Trade in Services (GATS) and the Agreement on Trade-Related Aspects of Intellectual Property Rights (TRIPS).

The highest level of authority in the WTO is the Ministerial Conference, which includes representatives of all 152 member states and is required to meet at least once every two years. Unlike the World Bank or the IMF, which have weighted voting procedures, WTO decision-making is based upon one vote per state. In practice, however, decisions are made by consensus rather than formal voting. The WTO also has a dispute settlement mechanism, which involves both a dispute settlement body and an appellate (appeal) body.

The key principles of both the GATT and the WTO are the most favored nation treatment and national treatment. Under most favored nation guidelines, countries cannot discriminate against other WTO members. If a country lowers a tariff against one state, it must lower tariffs against all other member states.

Exceptions, however, do exist in some instances for regional trade agreements and developing states. National treatment refers to equal treatment between foreign and domestic goods and services, as well as trademarks and patents. Open trade is related to the neoliberal perspective on development, in which free trade theoretically leads to economic growth, which, in turn, benefits health. As Meri Koivusalo (2003) points out, potential sources of conflict exist between the promotion of unrestricted trade and health regulation.

One concern has to do with trading in goods that may have been produced through an unhealthy process. These goods cannot be restricted by the WTO unless their production clearly presents a danger to public health. Another concern is that the trade in the products themselves may be unhealthy, such as trade in tobacco and alcohol. Since these products are not considered under WTO rules to be a public health threat, they cannot be restricted only on account of their potential harmful effects on health. Three agreements that fall under the purview of the WTO have exhibited an impact on or have the potential to affect health policy: the Agreement on Sanitary and Phytosanitary Measures (SPS), the Agreement on Trade-Related aspects of Intellectual Property Rights (TRIPS), and the General Agreement on Trade in Services (GATS).

The SPS agreement is directed at trade issues relating to food safety as well as animal and plant regulations. It relates to Article XX of the GATT, which allows states to take action that would restrict trade if it is based on a threat to public health. The SPS agreement, however, provides that such measures must be based on scientific evidence, should not discriminate between member states, and are to be used only to the extent necessary to protect public health. The interpretation and application of the SPS was an issue brought before the WTO's dispute settlement body in 1996 and 2003. In 1996, the United States requested a panel to resolve a complaint against the European Community (EC). The complaint was that the EC took measures that effectively banned the import of hormone-fed cattle from the United States. The panel found that the EC's ban was inconsistent with the SPS agreement. Although the EC appealed the decision to the appellate body, the ruling of the panel was upheld in 1998. Despite the judgment, Gregg Bloche and Elizabeth Jungman (2007) argue that the decision was a close one, and it did represent a certain amount of deference to national health policy. The appellate body found that the EC failed to conduct a risk assessment to evaluate its claim that the hormone-fed cattle created a health hazard to humans. As a result, it opened the possibility for such a ban to be acceptable if it was supported by sufficient scientific evidence.

A similar situation emerged with the genetically modified (GM) foods case in 2003. The United States filed another complaint against the EC based on the latter's strict interpretation of GM foods as a violation of the SPS agreement. As in the earlier decision, the WTO panel found in its 2006 report that the EC's measures were not supported by a scientifically based risk assessment. In doing so, it rejected the EC's claim that risk assessment was inadequate on account of insufficient scientific data.

The decisions by the WTO dispute resolution panels have revealed a narrow construction of the public health exception to GATT. Critics of these decisions have been concerned that they represent a loss of national control over risks to health. They have also indicated that the WTO favors the market over other values, such as culture (Zurek 2007). Another cause for concern among health advocates is with the dispute settlement process itself. The panels are composed of only senior trade officials, without any consultation with health experts being required, even in health-related matters (Koivusalo 2003). An alternative perspective has been that the decisions indicate an increased awareness by the WTO of public health. According to Bloche and Jungman (2007: 257), in regard to the SPS risk assessment, "once this low empirical barrier is crossed, emerging SPS jurisprudence protects health to a remarkable degree, through a policy of exceptional deference to member states' assessments of and responses to health risk."

The TRIPS agreement also has implications for national health policy. This agreement covers protection for trademarks, copyrights, and patents and provides for minimum standards of intellectual property protection. Patents protect the right of the innovator to benefit commercially from an innovation over a certain period of time. TRIPS provides patent protection for twenty years, with certain exceptions. While patents help to encourage innovators to assume research and development costs, they also contribute to higher prices for pharmaceuticals and block competing products from entering the market (Koivusalo 2003; Abbott 2002). When TRIPS took effect, developed states had one year to modify their national laws to conform with the agreement while developing countries were given five years or more.

The TRIPS Agreement does allow for exceptions to patents in the case of compulsory licenses. Such a license is granted by a WTO member to another producer, giving them the right to produce the patented product without the consent of the patent holder, albeit with some constraints. Some developed states have threatened trade sanctions against WTO members who have proposed granting compulsory licenses. The United States, for example, pressured Thailand to change its patent law to be more restrictive than TRIPS (Thomas 2003: 182). The applicant must first seek a license from the patent holder under reasonable terms and conditions, unless it is for a national emergency or non-commercial public use, and the patent holder must be paid adequate compensation. The majority of pharmaceutical patents are held by pharmaceutical companies in only a few developed states (Abbott 2005: 323). A further problem is that many developing countries do not have the capacity to produce the drugs themselves, so they have to rely on exports from other states – for example from those states that produce such drugs under a compulsory license. Article 31(f) of TRIPS, however, requires licensed products to be used mostly for domestic markets, which limits the amount that can potentially be exported.

In response to the HIV/AIDS epidemic in South Africa, the government passed a law in 1997 to introduce compulsory licenses that would allow local companies to produce cheaper, generic substitutes of patent-protected HIV/AIDS medications. Several pharmaceutical companies filed a lawsuit against the South African government, claiming that the law violated the TRIPS agreement. The United States also responded by denying South Africa benefits under the Generalized System of Preferences, which would allow South Africa to export items to the US at a reduced duty. After three years the lawsuit was dropped by the pharmaceutical companies, in large part as the result of an activist campaign in which hundreds of NGOs took part (Lanoszka 2003). The US also curtailed its trade pressures.

The controversy surrounding the affordability of medicines and the TRIPS agreement was addressed by the WTO in its 2001 ministerial conference at Doha, Qatar, where a policy known as the Doha declaration was adopted. This affirms "that the Agreement can and should be interpreted and implemented in a manner supportive of WTO members' right to protect public health and, in particular, to promote access to medicines for all" (WTO 2001: paragraph 4). The declaration also stipulates: "We recognize that WTO members with insufficient or no manufacturing capacities in the pharmaceutical sector could face difficulties in making effective use of compulsory licensing under the TRIPS Agreement. We instruct the Council for TRIPS to find an expeditious solution to this problem and to report to the General Council before the end of 2002" (WTO 2001: paragraph 6).

A debate developed over the interpretation and application of paragraph 6 of the Doha declaration, centering on the scope of diseases to be covered and how the eligibility of states would be determined. The General Council of the WTO decided in 2003 that individual states should determine which health problems should be allowed to have compulsory licenses for export to WTO members that had insufficient pharmaceutical manufacturing capacities. Both the scope of diseases and eligibility requirements were to be broadly construed (Hein 2007). This decision, however, was subject to certain safeguards, such as a notification requirement and the limiting of exports only to the amount necessary for an eligible member state. In order to enhance the legality of the General Council's decision, another debate began on whether it should become a formal amendment to TRIPS. At the WTO's ministerial conference in Hong Kong, the General Council agreed on an amendment, which will become effective once it has been ratified by two-thirds of WTO members. Once it has been adopted, the amendment will be the first change to any WTO agreement (Hein 2007).

Although the 2003 decision has not led to much of an increase in the use of compulsory licenses by developing states, it has given them a better bargaining position vis-à-vis pharmaceutical companies. These companies have been selling their own products more cheaply and providing more licenses to produce drugs (Hein 2007). The position of the United States has been to continue to promote high standards for intellectual property rights. The US was the first state to accept the TRIPS agreement and has declared respect for the Doha declaration, though its consistently strong commitment to property rights could weaken its support for both. Frederick Abbott (2005) points out that other trade agreements could weaken the amendment. He suggests greater implementation of the declaration will indicate whether it will be effective.

The General Agreement on Trade in Services (GATS), the purpose of which is to promote free trade for services, is another WTO agreement that may have important implications for health policy. This coverage could include health services such as health insurance and hospital treatment. The GATS agreement allows states to choose which sectors fall under its terms as well as what limitations they would like to make to those commitments. Those governments which largely control their health service sector tend not to make commitments to health under the agreement (Belsky et al. 2004), which does not cover services that are provided by the government on a non-commercial and a non-competitive basis. It is not clear whether or how a mix of public and private providers would be affected by commitments under the GATS. When a state makes a commitment, it must allow market access to foreign companies in that sector, and it must treat foreign companies in the same way as domestic companies.

The potential application of the GATS to a national health care system that has some commercial and competitive elements has brought concerns that the treaty could intrude on health care regulation by national governments. The United States has agreed to grant market access to foreign health insurances providers and hospital service providers, although it retains the right to place a quota on the number of hospitals entering the market. If it decides to restrict access to these foreign providers, under the agreement it will either have open equivalent sectors to foreign competition or allow those states to close access to US providers (Belsky et al. 2004).

Some developing states may be tempted to make health service commitments under the GATS both because they could export health services abroad, which could provide additional income, and because importing foreign services could help improve domestic health services. David Woodward (2005), however, argues that a greater concern for developing states is that they would be restricting their health care policy on the basis of trade considerations. He suggests that committing health services to the GATS would not provide much of an economic or health benefit to these states, and would make it more difficult for them to regulate health care policy. States have therefore been more reluctant to include health services under the agreement than other services. As of 2000, fifty-four WTO members had made commitments to medical and dental services, while forty-four had committed to hospital services. States such as Burundi, Zambia, Malawi, Jordan, Estonia, and Latvia have made fairly extensive commitments for their health services (Adlung and Carzaniga 2001). The effect of the GATS on health policy remains uncertain. It has not been addressed by the WTO to the same extent as the SPS and TRIPS. Potentially, however, it could prove to be a significant factor in some states' national health care delivery systems.

While the WTO is a relative newcomer to global health governance, it has made an impact on health policy in its less than two decades of existence. Its purpose is to promote trade and economic liberalization, and as a result it lacks moral authority in the area of health. It also lacks the expertise on health issues of the World Bank. It seems than the WTO is in a learning process on how trade affects national health. The Doha declaration indicates that it is becoming more aware of the impact of its rules on health, and it will be interesting to see if it begins to weigh health considerations more heavily in the future, or if health issues will be consistently subordinate to trade liberalization.

Multinational Corporations

Multinational corporations (MNCs) are also participants in global health governance. MNCs are private actors whose purpose is to make profits and conduct business operations across multiple states. As globalization has increased, they have become more powerful. They offer both financial resources that can influence national governments through lobbying and incentives for investment that may lead to job creation (Karns and Mingst 2004). MNCs are primary movers in the process of globalization. Given their motivation to maximize profits, they support open markets and economic liberalization. In response, they deliver goods, services, and technology across national borders.

In the area of global governance, multinational pharmaceutical companies play a significant role. Developed states spend approximately 15 percent of their health expenditures on pharmaceuticals while developing states spend about 25 percent (Wogart 2007). Worldwide sales of pharmaceuticals were expected to total $735 billion in 2007–8, with North American sales constituting approximately half of that and North American and European sales combined three-quarters of the total (Williams, Gabe, and Davis 2009). Pharmaceuticals tend to be fairly expensive on account of research and development costs. The companies, however, face increased competition from the production of generic drugs that enter the market at a much lower price, many of which are unauthorized copies of patented drugs. It is estimated that these drugs compose about 25 percent of pharmaceuticals sold in developing states (Wogart 2007). In order to protect their interests, the multinational pharmaceutical companies have been strong advocates of promoting intellectual properties internationally, and during the TRIPS negotiations they successfully lobbied the US trade representative to promote stronger patent protection in the agreement. In particular, the firms were able to acquire twenty-year patent protection and make it more difficult for some of the least developed states to purchase drugs from states that produced a large number of generic drugs, such as India and Brazil, through placing export restrictions on compulsory licenses. Pharmaceutical companies have also sought to protect their patents through legal means. Several of them filed a lawsuit against the South African government in 1998 based upon its passage of the Medicines Amendment Act, which would allow domestic production of generic drugs. The companies argued that the Act was both unconstitutional and a violation of South Africa's obligation under TRIPS. Although they chose to drop the suit in 2001, it indicated how important patent protection was to them.

Another area where multinational pharmaceutical companies have exerted an influence has been the price of drugs. Brazil, for example, was the first developing country to adopt an official policy that provided universal access to antiretroviral drugs (ARVs), in 1996. In 2007, approximately 200,000 Brazilians were taking ARVs paid for by the government (Biehl 2007). Brazil tried to limit the costs of ARVs through the promotion of generic drugs. Additionally, Brazil negotiated with several multinational pharmaceutical companies for a substantial price reduction by threatening the issuance of compulsory licenses. This tactic proved to be successful, as Brazil was able to receive a substantial price reduction, including over 60 percent from Merck and 30 percent from Hoffman–La Roche on patented ARVs (Cohen and Lybecker 2005). Brazil's bargaining position relative to the pharmaceutical industry had been strengthened as a result of the protest by the international health community over the lawsuit in South Africa and the fact that the US did not provide full support to the companies in the dispute. The Clinton administration had filed a complaint against Brazil in the WTO against its threat of compulsory licenses, but the Bush administration withdrew the complaint in 2001. The resolution of this dispute has worked out quite well for Brazil. Deaths resulting from AIDS and the need for AIDS-related hospital services have dropped by 70 percent, and by 2000 the United Nations program on AIDS, UNAIDS, recognized the Brazil AIDS program as the best in the developing world (Biehl 2007). Although it remains to be seen if its success is applicable to other developing states, one advantage that Brazil has in such a negotiation is its capacity to produce generic drugs.

The pharmaceutical industry argues that patent protection of drugs is necessary to create financial incentives for expensive research and development. The US Congressional Budget Office has stated that pharmaceutical companies spend as much as five times in research and development, relative to sales, as the average American manufacturing firm (PhRMA 2008). If states purchase more generic drugs, this will lead to a loss of income for the companies, and so they will have neither the funding nor the financial incentive to develop new and effective drugs.

A primary counter-argument to this claim is that the pharmaceutical companies are motivated by maximizing profits rather than promoting public health needs. Jagdish Bhagwati (2004), a leading international trade theorist, argues that intellectual property protection is unnecessary in poor countries because it is not feasible to make a profit selling drugs in these countries. He suggests that the multinational firms want to prevent generic drugs from being sold from states such as India and Brazil because the influx of more drugs on the global market will reduce prices. This is especially apparent in drugs for diseases, such as HIV/AIDS, which cut across both rich and poor countries. Pharmaceutical companies have generally not spent much time or funding on the research and development of drugs that are associated much more with developing states. Patrice Trouiller et al. (2002) found that, of 1,393 new drugs that entered the market between 1975 and 1999, only sixteen were for tropical infectious diseases and tuberculosis. Considerably more funding had been spent on health problems germane to developed states, including baldness and obesity (Thomas 2003).

Despite the shortcomings of pharmaceutical companies in providing drug access to developing states, some innovations have taken place to help address this problem. One important innovation has been that of PPPs in the pharmaceutical sector. These PPPs, such as the Medicines for Malaria Venture, help to address the problem of neglected drugs by allowing funding for research and development by the public and philanthropic sectors. This financial support allows large firms to lower the cost and the financial risk of developing such drugs. As a result, more attention has been paid to neglected diseases, as sixty projects have been initiated between 2000 and 2004 (Moran et al. 2005). Another innovation is the non-profit drug company, such as OneWorldHealth, which was founded in 2000 and became the first non-profit pharmaceutical company to be founded in the United States. The non-profit companies differ from PPPs in that they have larger research and development teams and can address a greater number of neglected diseases (Hale et al. 2005) and can assume the financial risk in the early development stage that most pharmaceuticals would deem too costly.

Both the PPP and the non-profit model have demonstrated some early success, but their impact on global health is hindered by a number of obstacles. First of all, these models are very new in the landscape of global health governance, so it is difficult to assess how successful they will be beyond drug development. Distribution of the drugs will prove to be a problem, as many developing countries lack an adequate health infrastructure to distribute them to all of those in need. Secondly, funding is a continuous challenge to the non-profit enterprises. Members of the Organization of Economic Cooperation and Development, which is composed mostly of high income states, have offered little financial support to PPPs (Moran et al. 2005), and most of the funding comes from phil-anthropic sources, such as the Gates Foundation. Drug development is expensive, and so it will be difficult for these companies to produce drugs at a low cost without more support from the public sector.

Another type of MNC that has become more influential during post-Cold War globalization has been the managed care organization, which provides a wide variety of managed health care services. Jasso-Aguilar et al. (2004) conducted a compre-hensive study on the migration of multinational managed care organizations from the United States to Mexico and Brazil. They suggest that, in the late 1990s, some of these corporations began to withdraw from American markets because of a declin-ing rate of return in the US and policy decisions in Latin America to privatize the health care sector. In the United States, the managed care industry experiences heavier costs on account of the increasing price of both medications and doctor and hospital fees. Medicare and Medicaid markets also proved to be less profitable, as Congress and state legislatures limited premiums and lowered payments to managed care organiza-tions. Latin America, in particular, emerged as an attractive market for these firms during this time. The IMF and the World Bank's promotion of open markets influenced Mexico and Brazil to reduce public spending and open their markets, includ-ing the health care sector, to private investment. Rebecca Jasso-Aguilar et al. (2004) found that the increased role of private care organizations has led to a lack of access to health care for individuals who cannot afford the required co-payments under the managed care plans. Although these individuals can turn to government-supported programs, the latter have limited their services following the government's increasing efforts to priva-tize the health care sector.

In the area of global health governance, MNCs are primary agents of globalization. Open markets and a limited amount of government intervention help facilitate their goal of maximizing profits. Although corporate actors are motivated more by profits than public health needs, their income does promote innovation as well as more effective research and development. The major dilemma in the case of both pharmaceutical companies and managed care organizations is that their practices can lead to inequality and a lack of access to health care benefits.

NGOs

Non-Governmental Organizations (NGOs) are actors in global governance that are independent of national governments. They can, however, be distinguished from MNCs principally because of their non-profit motivation. NGOs are voluntary organizations that have a variety of purposes and a series of different roles, especially in political and operational capacities. They are much more numerous than other actors in global governance: approximately 6,500 of them operate at the international level, and there are thousands more at the national and local levels (Karns and Mingst 2004). NGOs, however, are relatively weak actors. They lack the legal power of states to implement policies, and they do not have authority delegated by states, as do IGOs. On account of their non-profit nature, they lack the financial resources of MNCs, and they cannot provide the same economic benefits, such as job creation, to influence national governments. Despite these weaknesses, globalization has helped to empower NGOs in the governance process. As a result of enhancements in communications technology, NGOs have established links among different organizations to provide greater information sharing and influence across borders. These organizations represent individuals who are left out of the government and business sectors and are considered part of the larger civil society.

The influence of NGOs in governance is associated largely with their political and operational functions. Politically, they can perform a number of different tasks. They represent civil society as advocates of policy change, and through the use of providing information and lobbying, NGOs seek to influence both national governments and IGOs in developing and implementing particular policies. Additionally, they play a watchdog role by monitoring and reporting on the activities of governments, IGOs, and MNCs. NGOs have also been developing closer relationships with other actors in global governance. The PPPs, such as the Global Fund, provide one example of this cooperation. Others are increased participation in international conferences and a consultative status with WHO and the Economic and Social Council of the United Nations. For instance, only 250 NGOs participated in the 1972 UN conference on the environment, while over 1,400 participated in the UN environmental conference in Rio de Janeiro twenty years later (Karns and Mingst 2004). Operationally, NGOs may provide humanitarian relief and developmental assistance.

NGOs tend to play a greater role in global health governance than in other areas of global concern. One reason for this role has to do with tradition. The International Committee of the Red Cross was established in 1863 in Geneva, Switzerland, as an organization that would care for wounded soldiers. It was also associated with the only NGO provision in the League of Nations covenant, which encouraged the promotion of national Red Cross organizations. The Red Cross is one of the oldest and largest international NGOs. It consists of the International Red Cross and Red Crescent Movement, the International Committee of the Red Cross, and the International Federation of Red Cross and Red Crescent Societies, as well as national societies. Together, these groups are involved in disaster relief, health care, fundraising, and improving international humanitarian law.

Another reason has to do with the lack of IGOs in the health area. Until the Bretton Woods institutions began to deal with health-related issues in the 1980s, the WHO was the only IGO coping with global health issues. In the meantime, in addition to the Red Cross, NGOs such as Médecins Sans Frontières (MSF) and Oxfam filled some of the need to assist with these transnational problems. MSF, also known as Doctors without Borders, was established in 1971 by a group of French doctors. It collaborates with health authorities in more than seventy states that have inadequate health care infrastructures and provides assistance in remote parts of the world where health care does not exist. In addition to humanitarian assistance, MSF promotes awareness of health crises and human rights violations (MSF 2008).

The development of Oxfam International can be traced back to a group called the Oxford Committee for Famine Relief, which was established in England in 1942 by a group of British social activists and intellectuals. The organization was formed in response to the plight of Greek refugees during World War II. Over time, other national Oxfam organizations became established in industrialized states such as the United States, Canada, Japan, France, and Germany, and in 1995 these national organizations joined together to create Oxfam International. Oxfam has moved beyond its original mandate of famine relief: it has promoted access to medicines and humanitarian relief work, and has lobbied governments on a number of policy issues related to health, trade, education, climate change, and human rights.

The influence of NGOs was evident during the TRIPS controversy and the Doha declaration addressing the protection of patented medicines. They have sought to lower prices on pharmaceuticals by lobbying MNCs, and they assisted developing states by providing them with the expertise to challenge the TRIPS provisions in the WTO. NGOs were active in the lawsuit filed by the pharmaceutical companies against the South African government in 1998. Oxfam and MSF encouraged developing states to make or import generics even if the practice violated TRIPS. Oxfam also argued that health professionals should be included on WTO panels deciding health-related disputes, and interested parties such as Oxfam should be permitted to submit briefs to the panel (Lanoszka 2003).

NGOs may also substitute for national governments in providing basic health services in some poorer states. Sub-Saharan Africa, in particular, has a major need for NGOs to provide services. In Tanzania, for example, hospitals administered by NGOs account for 43 percent of all medical services. While their role is not as prominent in Asia, 13 percent of medical services in Bangladesh and 12 percent of services in Indonesia are provided by NGOs (Bartsch and Kohlmorgen 2007).

NGOs play an important, yet largely indirect, role in global health governance. It is indirect because much of their influence on global health policy results from their advocacy and information sharing with other actors, mostly states. They can be a significant force, as the campaign against patented medicines and the negotiations around the Doha declaration demonstrate. However they also face obstacles because of their relative lack of financial resources and their competition with one another to influence policy-makers. As Sonja Bartsch and Lars Kohlmorgen (2007) argue, these organizations view themselves as welfare-oriented mechanisms to address the market failures of neoliberalism promoted by MNCs, the WTO and the Washington Consensus. But their moral authority is limited owing to questions about the extent of their representation and their accountability to constituencies as a result of their narrow mandates and the wide discretion their leaderships have in determining the means and ends of pursuing particular policies. In some cases, however, they have empowered themselves by linking with other NGOs and IGOs that serve a greater representation, such as the WHO.

Summary

While the state is the most prominent and powerful actor in global health governance, other actors have emerged with a greater role as the world has become more globalized.

The WHO continues to play a leading role in global health, but has recently seen its role challenged by other IGOs, primarily the World Bank. It has therefore reinvented itself to collaborate more with other IGOs and NGOs in promoting the role of health in economic development. The World Bank, IMF, and WTO have also come to a greater realization of the effects of neoliberal economic policies on health issues.

MNCs have been important actors in the governance process. While their influence has increased as a result of globalization, they have also struggled with some of the market failures associated with health, such as inequalities regarding access to medicines and health services. NGOs have been strengthened following enhancements in communications technology and the general decline in state regulation. While they have experienced some successes in promoting health policy change, they do face constraints on their influence, since they are largely challenging the neoliberal ideology which has become the norm of both states and IGOs in global economic policy in the most recent wave of globalization.

Although all actors benefit from healthy populations, as with any such endeavor, achieving cooperation to reach a common goal can be problematic with a large number of diverse actors. This problem of cooperation and coordination in achieving "health for all" in global health governance will be explored in the next chapter.

7

Global Health Governance: Public Goods and Collective Action

The acceleration of globalization at the end of the Cold War enhanced linkages between states and people in a number of areas, including health. The increased interconnections created a growing number of public health concerns about disease threats that transcended national boundaries. In order to reduce these concerns, achievement of the goal of "health for all," as stated in the 1978 Alma Ata declaration, was intended to guide efforts to establish a healthier human society on a global basis. In September 2000, the United Nations General Assembly built upon this idea in its adoption of the Millennium declaration. This declaration incorporated eight development goals that the UN member states agreed to achieve by 2015, among them to halt the spread of HIV/AIDS, malaria, tuberculosis, and other major diseases, thus reducing health risks to people around the world and increasing the economic efficiency of states with the resulting healthier and more productive workers. Once a norm of good health becomes a universal standard, health care costs should be greatly reduced, with fewer people requiring expensive medicines and treatment. And, of course, the human condition would be improved with a longer and better quality of life.

Although this goal is in the best interest of everyone, its achievement remains problematic. Different levels of socioeconomic development among people and states, limitations on resources, distribution problems, conflicts of interest among relevant actors, and other issues all pose significant obstacles that still need to be overcome. Nevertheless, the goal remains health for all people on a global scale – thus mandating that countries cooperate to achieve this outcome.

National governments still maintain a significant amount of control over health policy and the responsibility of providing for the welfare of their citizens. Globalization, however, has subjected these policies to international forces to a greater degree. As a result, states increasingly need assistance to offer adequate health care and protection. This assistance is particularly important for developing states. Since there is no authority above the state to provide quality global health, global governance can act as the closest substitute. As discussed in the previous chapter, however, global governance in the area of health is composed of a number of different actors that have various degrees of influence on policy. Coordination among these actors, as well as overcoming potential conflicts of interest, poses difficulties in achieving the "health for all" standard.

This chapter will analyze this situation by first examining the concept of health as a global public good. Secondly, it will consider the problem of collective action and how it affects global health governance in providing for adequate health. The remainder of the chapter will look at the problems of collective action in the areas of infectious diseases, focusing on polio and HIV/AIDS and non-communicable diseases, and also examine the regulation of the harmful effects of tobacco and poor diet.

Health as a Global Public Good

Before considering whether health and governance can be considered as global public goods, it is important first to consider the questions What exactly is a public good? and How can a public good be global? A public good is a good that can be considered "non-excludable" and "non-rivalrous." This definition stands in contrast to private goods, which are "excludable" and "rivalrous." The term non-excludable means that the good is available to all and its use cannot be restricted. The term non-rivalrous means that consumption of the good by one individual does not limit the consumption of the same good by others. An example of such a good would be a public highway. The highway is built and maintained by the government, and anyone can use it, regardless of whether or not they pay taxes to the government. Also, the use of the highway by one individual does not limit another individual's ability to use it. The vast majority of goods, however, are private. The primary reason why so few public goods are available has to do with the lack of incentive to provide them. Since these goods are not restricted in any way, the provider does not receive an economic benefit for providing them while it does absorb the cost of creating or maintaining the good. The market provides goods that are limited in supply and restricted in some manner, generally by setting a price that an individual must pay. Since no price can be enforced with public goods, there is a concern that individuals will "free-ride" or use the good without contributing anything. Because of this lack of economic incentive, public goods need to be provided by the state since the market is unwilling to do so.

What is a global public good? The United Nations Development Program (UNDP) defines it as "a public good with benefits that are strongly universal in terms of countries (covering more than one group of countries), people (accruing to several, preferably all, population groups) and generations (extending to both current and future generations, or at least meeting the needs of current generations without foreclosing development options for future generations)" (Kaul et al. 1999: 509–10). An alternative definition proposed by Woodward and Smith (2003: 9) states that a global public good is "a good which it is rational, from the perspective of a group of nations collectively, to produce for universal consumption, and for which it is irrational to exclude an individual nation from its consumption, irrespective of whether that nation contributes to its financing." In considering these definitions, it is apparent that global public goods should be considered as non-excludable goods that are open to everyone, regardless of the state or region in which they happen to reside.

On account of its large scale of availability, the global public goods concept appears to be rather abstract. National security, for example, clearly qualifies as a public good. The government provides security for all of its citizens without exclusions. The security for one individual does not detract from the security of others. Although citizens may have to pay taxes to the government that are used for security, it is still provided for all regardless of their level of payment, or even for individuals who do not pay. Assessing the concept of security as a global public good, however, is more problematic. There is no global defense force above the level of the state that provides security for everyone in the world, the closest mechanism for global security being the UN Security Council. The objective of the UN is to maintain peace and security. In order to provide an institutional basis for this objective, the UN charter provides that states shall refrain from threatening and using force, as well as seek to settle disputes by peaceful means.

Additionally, the UN Security Council has the authority to identify states that have used aggressive force in violation of the charter, and it can call on all UN members to use economic sanctions or even military force against the aggressor. While, owing to politics and cooperation issues, the collective security provisions in the charter have proven to be weak and often ineffective in practice, it does fit as a global public good at least as a concept. If the UN charter functioned ideally, then all states would receive protection from the Security Council regardless of their contribution to the UN. The environment is another example of a global public good. Reducing CFCs put into the atmosphere and protecting the ozone layer benefits everyone around the world.

The environment and security are examples of public goods that can be found at the global level. The next question is whether health is also a global public good. Zacher (1999) argues that disease surveillance is a global public good. In terms of non-excludability, modern technology and the global media make it difficult for a state to conceal a significant outbreak of a disease. It is also non-rivalrous in that all states benefit from disease surveillance, since they take measures to protect against the possibility of any outbreak affecting their citizens. Woodward and Smith (2003), however, argue that, while preventing and containing communicable diseases may constitute a global public good, health in general is not such a good. Health is considered excludable in that it benefits principally an individual or a state rather than the global public as a whole. While this is an arguable point, Woodward and Smith point out that access to adequate health care is not available to all and that health is consumed (used) primarily at the individual and state level. They do suggest that, despite these limitations, interventions to improve health provide potential global public goods in such areas as communicable diseases and trade in goods that affect health, such as food, tobacco, and drugs. Chen et al. (1999) make a similar argument in that health has both public and private aspects. They indicate, however, that globalization may be moving health into the position of a global public good. This shift is the result of two different forces. The first force has to do with the increased international linkages, such as trade and migration, which have led to a greater incidence of cross-border infectious diseases as well as a rise in the number of goods that pose health risks, such as tobacco and illicit drugs. The second force is environmental. As the world has become more globalized, pollution, the depletion of the ozone layer, and global warming, as well as their effects on health, have emerged as larger issues.

In assessing health as a global public good, it seems that the concept does have merit. The application is particularly clear in the case of communicable diseases. Globalization has contributed to an upturn in international cooperation. A by-product of these interactions is the spread of disease across borders. If this spread is prevented, or at least contained, the entire global population will benefit because the risk of infection will be reduced. In terms of non-communicable diseases, the application of the concept is not quite so clear. Globalization, however, has promoted non-communicable disease as more of a global public good by increased linkages among states and people. As global economies become more interdependent, health burdens in certain states can spill over into the global economy. If the global proliferation of goods related to health risks, such as tobacco, alcohol, and processed foods enriched with sugar and saturated fats, contributes to a decline in health, economic productivity may suffer at the national and global level. As a result, it would seem that regulating the spread of the products that are potentially hazardous to health would qualify as a global public good, as both the economy and the quality of life would improve for all.

Global Health and Collective Action

The key issue with public goods is who will provide them? As discussed earlier, the market does not have an incentive to provide them because of their non-excludable and non-rivalrous nature. Because of this lack of incentive, public goods usually need to be provided by the state. The provision of public goods becomes more problematic at the global level, however, since there is no world government. The actors involved in global governance, namely states, IGOs, MNCs, and NGOs, have the potential to act as substitutes to provide global public goods. This system of organization, however, is much weaker than that of a national government on account of the lack of a structured hierarchy and possible conflicts of interest among the actors.

Providing a global public good creates a collective action problem – meaning that common goods must be provided by more than one actor. Global health, for example, requires the contribution of multiple actors in order for it to be provided effectively. Different theoretical models have been used to examine the dynamics of collective action in providing a common good. These models include "The Logic of Collective Action," "The Prisoner's Dilemma," and "New Institutionalism." The Logic of Collective Action was developed by Mancur Olson (1971) in a book of the same name. Olson argued that, just because all members of a group would benefit from a collective good, it does not mean that all members will contribute to that good. With the exception of very small groups and a mechanism that is coercive, rational individuals will not act to achieve a common good. The basis of this behavior has to do with "free-riding." Actors have an incentive to free-ride because they cannot be excluded from the benefits of a common good once it has been produced. If all participants choose to free-ride, then a common or public good will come about. If only some of the actors contribute, then a good will be produced that is sub-optimal and will yield only limited benefits. As a result, it would be expected that public goods, such as health, would be undersupplied.

The Prisoner's Dilemma refers to a situation where individuals have complete information but they cannot communicate with one another. In this game two prisoners (Joe and Tom) are put in separate cells so that they cannot confer. Each prisoner must decide whether to keep quiet or confess to the crime. The prosecutors know that they will have a much stronger case if the prisoners confess, so they want to keep them apart to encourage such a confession. If the prisoners both decide to keep quiet, they will each get two years in prison on a lesser charge. If one confesses while the other keeps quiet, the one who confesses will get only one year while the one who keeps quiet will get seven years. If they both confess, then they will both be sentenced to three years. The "dilemma" in this situation is that both would be better off cooperating, by keeping quiet, rather than confessing, as they would serve two years rather than three. Since they cannot communicate, however, they cannot make an agreement to keep quiet. They also cannot trust their partner, who might be tempted to confess and receive the lighter sentence. It is therefore rational for each prisoner to confess, as the worst sentence that each will receive will be three years, with the possibility of one year if their partner keeps quiet. The Prisoner's Dilemma is depicted in table 7.1.

New Institutionalism focuses on the interaction of institutions to resolve the collective action problem. Elinor Ostrom's (1990) approach to collective action provides an example. While her analysis looked at common pool resources, this is analogous to a public good and involves a collective action problem. Ostrom considers whether the government or the private sector can solve the dilemma. The government solution involves coercive power to regulate the use of common goods. Ostrom argues that this solution is inadequate because complete information about the activities of individuals is required

Table 7.1 *The Prisoner's Dilemma*

		Joe	
		Keep quiet	*Confess*
Tom	*Keep quiet*	Joe and Tom get 2 years	Joe gets 1 year Tom gets 7 years
	Confess	Joe gets 7 years Tom gets 1 year	Joe and Tom get 3 years

in order effectively to sanction non-compliance and avoid the free-rider problem. The private sector is also an inadequate solution because some goods are common by their nature, and establishing individual property rights might prove to be too costly or simply impractical. Ostrom offers an alternative solution in which individuals negotiate and implement a binding commitment to cooperate. This agreement means they do not have to depend on the government to monitor their behavior and decide appropriate sanctions. The government still provides enforcement power, but the individuals agree to the terms of the contract and what is to be enforced. This approach brings private, non-profit organizations into the provision of common goods – a solution that can potentially deter free-riding by allowing individuals to have more of a stake in the cooperative strategy by participating in the agreement, plus it still offers the enforcement power of government. Additionally, monitoring can be improved, since the individuals themselves, rather than the government, will watch for non-compliance. This solution brings monitoring and information sharing to a more local level.

The logic of the Prisoner's Dilemma is similar to that of collective action. In both cases, there is a rational incentive not to cooperate, even though the parties, collectively, would be better off by cooperating. While the main problem with the collective action situation is free-riding, the Prisoner's Dilemma represents problems with lack of communication as well as lack of trust. If an actor believes that other actors will not contribute to a public good, then they will be less likely to contribute to the good, either because they believe their contribution will lead only to a suboptimal good or because they do not wish to assume the costs for a good that will benefit free-riders. Either way, it represents how self-interest conflicts with the provision of public goods. The New Institutionalism approach offers a solution to the problems of free-riding and incomplete information other than relying solely on the power of government to resolve these problems. However, it does still depend on government enforcement for its effectiveness. Global public goods, such as health, lack any centralized enforcement agency through the absence of a government at the global level. The question, then, is does global health governance provide an adequate substitute in providing for global health? This question will be analyzed by looking at both infectious diseases and health-risk factors associated with non-communicable diseases.

Polio Eradication

Poliomyelitis provides an interesting case for global health governance in that it is a disease that has largely been eradicated, thus serving as an example where a global health good has been provided successfully. Polio is caused by three known viruses. It is transmitted primarily via the fecal–oral route, most commonly through eating or drinking food or liquids infected with the virus or touching objects that have been contaminated and then placing a hand in the mouth. It is especially common in sewage water. Most individuals affected by polio do not exhibit symptoms. It is estimated that one in 100 to one in 850 infected persons develop symptomatic polio, which can lead to restricted mobility, paralysis, or even death (Reingold and Phares 2006). The response to the polio epidemic began in the United States in the 1930s. Polio was a major concern of the Americans in the pre- and post-World War II period, and public opinion polls in the early 1950s listed the disease only behind nuclear war as the most important concern (Seavey et al. 1998). Fears of polio in the US, however, soon were alleviated with the inactivated polio virus vaccine (IPV) developed by Jonas Salk in 1952. Mass immunization with the IPV vaccine reduced polio cases in developed states by 86 percent between 1955 and 1957 (Ahrin-Tenkorang and Conceicao 2003). The further development of the oral polio vaccine (OPV) by Albert Sabin in 1962 virtually eliminated the disease in developed states on account of its lower cost and easier administration.

Although polio had largely been eradicated in the developed part of the world, it was still a major problem in developing countries. Brazil was the first developing state to make its elimination a priority, and in 1980 it pursued a program of OPV immunization. This policy soon spread to other Latin American states, and by 1987 polio had almost been eliminated in the region (de Quadros et al. 1992). The success of this program spurred the World Health Assembly the following year to endorse a resolution that called for the global eradication of polio by 2005. In addition to routine vaccinations, developing states relied on national immunization days to eradicate the disease. This was quite ambitious as it required the immunization of very large numbers of people in a short period of time. Because of the concern of polio being transmitted across borders, many governments decided to coordinate their immunization days. In 1995, eighteen states in the eastern Mediterranean, Middle East, and former Soviet republics organized a joint immunization day. The global polio eradication initiative proved to be very successful: the incidence of the disease around the world declined from 350,000 cases in 125 states in 1988 to only 500 cases by 2001 (Ahrin-Tenkorang and Conceicao 2003). Currently, polio is only endemic to Nigeria, India, Pakistan, and Afghanistan.

Although national governments in polio-infected states played a substantial role in the success of the eradication initiative, IGOs and NGOs also made significant contributions to the effort. UN agencies such as the UNDP and the Office of the High Commissioner for Refugees have helped provide transportation and resources for immunization programs. The International Federation of the Red Cross and Red Crescent Movement and MSF have participated in the training, surveillance, and administration of immunizations. Rotary International, in particular, has played an important role by providing thousands of volunteers to assist with immunization activities. By the end of 2007, it had contributed almost $700 million of its own resources to the eradication of polio, in addition to its advocacy of financial resources from national governments. In November of that year Rotary announced a partnership with the Bill and Melinda Gates Foundation to put an additional $200 million into new polio funding from 2008 to 2012 (WHO 2008a).

The global campaign to eradicate polio has seen the number of cases drop by 99 percent since its initiation in 1988 (WHO 2008a). The campaign, however, continues to face some challenges. Polio is still endemic in Afghanistan, India, Pakistan, and Nigeria, and the possibility remains that the disease could spread and infect other states. Between 2003 and 2007, several states reported infections from the virus stemming from Nigeria and India. By the end of 2007, Somalia and Myanmar announced that they had stopped their outbreaks. Chad and the Democratic Republic of Congo experienced the largest number of new cases in 2007, with twenty-one and forty-one cases, respectively (WHO 2008a). As a result, despite the success of the campaign, the global polio eradication initiative still needs support.

A study by Aylward et al. (2003) suggests that a number of lessons can be learned from the polio eradication initiative that could be useful for other campaigns attempting to provide a global public good for health. These include the decision-making process, the collective action issue in providing the good, and financing involved with the good. In terms of decision-making, leadership played a key role. The International Health Regulations (IHR) adopted by the WHA in 2005 formed an important step in improving the global surveillance of polio by requiring that it would be one of four diseases that must immediately be reported to the WHO. Although the WHA also provided the political forum for discussion and debate of the eradication initiative, financial support was necessary from the US Centers of Disease Control and Rotary International, as many other major donors made only limited contributions until 1995. Much of this lack of support had to do with the uncertainty concerning the resources necessary to accomplish the initiative.

In terms of collective action, a major problem with the initiative is that polio had already been eradicated from high-income states by the time the WHA resolution was passed in 1988. Because some states therefore do not necessarily view polio eradication as a global public good, their incentive to support the initiative is reduced. Financing also continues to be a problem. Rotary International determined "fair shares" of the polio eradication budget, a calculation based on member contributions to the WHO's regular budget. But the "fair share" concept has proven to be of limited value, as only sixteen of the twenty-two WHO member states, who are also members of the Organization of Economic Cooperation and Development's Development Assistance Committee, have made contributions to the initiative (Aylward et al. 2003: 48). The global polio eradication initiative has received $6 billion since 1988, the largest contributor being the United States, with over $1 billion in funding over this time. Rotary International and the United Kingdom follow, with over $500 million in funds, and then Japan and the World Bank, with over $250 million (WHO 2008b). Despite some shortfalls in funding, many states do contribute to the initiative, even though they do not face a foreseeable threat from polio. The G8 Research Group found at the 2006 summit in St Petersburg that Italy was the state among the major industrialized countries which did not comply with its commitment to eradicate polio. Canada, Germany, Russia, the United Kingdom, and the United States were found to be in full compliance, while France and Japan were found to be in partial compliance (G8 Research Group 2007).

The most significant issue in the global eradication of polio has to do with whether it is a global public good, since it does not pose a threat to most of the world. One possible alternative would be a less aggressive approach by maintaining a low number of cases, which would be less costly than eradication. Recent studies, however, suggest that such an approach would not be cost-effective. Aylward et al. (2003: 44) suggest that, between 2010 and 2040, there would be 10.6 million new cases of polio worldwide if eradication did not take place. Thompson and Tebbens (2007) came up with similar findings, in that controlling polio would cost significantly more in the long term than eradication. Their study considered that thousands of new cases would arise under a control strategy, which would cost billions of dollars on outbreak response and treatment.

Despite a few glitches, the success of global governance in addressing the global transmission of polio has been demonstrated by the small number of cases that have occurred in the world over the last twenty years. Additionally, the eradication program has arguably produced the WHO's largest and best prepared disease immunization and response team (Garwood 2007). The campaign has involved a number of actors in global governance that have worked together to promote a common cause. Developed states (especially the United States and United Kingdom) have made large contributions despite being free from polio for a number of years. IGOs such as the WHO and the United Nations Children's Fund (UNICEF) have played important roles in terms of both leadership and advocacy, and NGOs, particularly Rotary International, have provided a large number of financial and human resources to combat the disease. Although polio eradication represents a case where global health governance was able to overcome the collective action problem and provide a world largely free of the disease, it does have some limitations in application to other areas of global health governance. First of all, many states had already eradicated polio based upon national campaigns before the global initiative began in 1988. Secondly, effective vaccinations were developed in the 1950s and 1960s, and so distributional issues rather than advances in medical technology have been the primary concern. In other areas of global health governance, these problems have yet to be resolved to the same extent.

The Control of HIV/AIDS

The Acquired Immune Deficiency Syndrome (AIDS) and the Human Immunodeficiency Virus (HIV), which causes AIDS, present a different challenge for global health governance. There are at least three major areas of concern about HIV/AIDS that involve governance issues. One is controlling a disease that lacks a cure. Unlike polio, a vaccine for AIDS has yet to be developed. As a result, an eradication strategy is not possible. The objective for global governance in addressing HIV/AIDS is control by prevention programs and treatment. New advances in antiretroviral (ARV) treatment have allowed people who have acquired HIV to live longer lives, but the global growth of HIV is greater than the distribution of ARV drugs. The disease also has different mutations that complicate issues in treatment. One mutation, HIV-1, has a global distribution, while HIV-2 is confined mostly to West Africa. Consequently, the control of HIV remains a global problem. The second issue has to do with the political conflict of interests surrounding the treatment of HIV/AIDS. ARVs are produced by pharmaceutical companies that seek profits from their sale, and the development of these drugs is legally protected as intellectual property. This situation creates a problem for their acquisition by developing states, which have difficulty affording the cost. The third issue has to do with the global scope and seriousness of the disease. HIV/AIDS is not confined to any particular regions of the world. It was the first health issue debated by the UN Security Council: Resolution 1308 was passed in July 2000 and recognized that the disease posed a threat to stability and security.

HIV/AIDS was first identified in 1981 among male homosexuals in the United States, where its initial spread was attributed to unprotected sexual intercourse among homosexual and bisexual men. The virus, however, was also spread by heterosexual intercourse, blood transfusions, and injections using infected equipment. It was estimated that, in 2007, 33.2 million people had been infected with HIV worldwide and 2.1 million deaths had been attributed to AIDS. HIV/AIDS is particularly prevalent in sub-Saharan Africa, which had 68 percent of the world's HIV infections and 76 percent of the total AIDS-related deaths in 2007. Developed states, however, are certainly not isolated from the epidemic, with approximately 2.1 million people in North America and Western and Central Europe living with HIV and 33,000 deaths (UNAIDS 2007a).

Neither national nor international policy-makers responded quickly to the identification of HIV/AIDS in the early 1980s, as it was associated with certain risk groups – especially homosexuals and intravenous drug users – that were considered to be immoral and at the margins of society. The disease, however, spread quickly around the world. The first International AIDS conference, held at Atlanta, Georgia, in 1985, was organized by the US Centers for Disease Control and Prevention and recognized AIDS as a global issue. It also presented an overview of knowledge about HIV/AIDS and discussions regarding treatment and prevention.

International actors became more involved with the AIDS issue in 1987. The WHO established the Global Program on AIDS (GPA), designed to facilitate collaboration regarding the knowledge of AIDS as well as information gathering and monitoring of AIDS cases globally. The UN General Assembly conducted its first discussion of the issue, and in Resolution 42/8 it called upon the UN system to mobilize against AIDS. Around the same time, the organization ACT UP (the AIDS Coalition to Unleash Power) was established to draw the attention of policy-makers to the issue through demonstrations. The GPA sought connections to ACT UP and other AIDS advocacy groups to assist its purpose. These events were soon followed by a World Summit of Heath Ministers in 1988 to discuss a common AIDS strategy. This meeting produced the London declaration, which emphasized the importance of education and information in national AIDS programs as well as the protection of human rights of affected groups. The increased international attention towards AIDS was indicated in GPA funding, which increased from $30 million in 1987 to $109 million in 1990 (Lee and Zwi 2003).

The 1980s witnessed both the emergence of HIV/AIDS and the beginning of global governance to address the issue. Despite the efforts of the GPA to develop national AIDS control programs as well as establish linkages with NGOs that advocated a more aggressive national response towards the disease, global governance was relatively weak until the mid-1990s. Patterson (2007) suggests two reasons for this weakness. First, international institutions had different views on developing a global response to HIV/AIDS. The WHO and policy-makers in developed states focused on a biomedical approach which emphasized the importance of developing new technologies to control the disease, as well as a vaccine to eradicate it. In the interim, this approach also highlighted the screening of blood products, education and information campaigns to warn of risk factors, and the marketing of condoms (Lee and Zwi 2003). The GPA promoted a more political and social response to the disease, focusing on the human rights aspects. This approach emphasized how discrimination and the marginalization of individuals and groups affected by HIV/AIDS would hinder an effective response to the disease.

Lee and Zwi (2003) point out that neoliberalism was also an approach to the problem. Neoliberalism stressed the importance of market forces in health care services. In the case of HIV/AIDS the particular focus was on financial contributions. The rise of neoliberalism in international health policy is associated with the increased role of the World Bank, which, in the 1980s, became the largest source of external health care funding for developing states. Its lending for AIDS projects, which began in 1986 and reached $500 million by 1993 (World Bank 1994), gave it influence in policy development. The bank has tended to emphasize the cost-effectiveness of AIDS interventions, in particular prevention among high-risk groups, as the basis of policy (Lee and Zwi 2003).

Secondly, according to Patterson (2007), a weakness of the first fifteen years of global governance was a lack of commitment by states. Although the United States was the largest donor to HIV/AIDS programs, it exhibited a lack of political leadership in addressing the issue, as President Ronald Reagan made his only speech on AIDS in 1987. Neither did developing states demonstrate a significant commitment to combating the disease, as they tended to view it as a Western homosexual problem. As a result, many governments in the developing world tended either to remain inactive in developing a national response to HIV/AIDS or to be in denial, even as the number of cases in those countries increased (Seckinelgin 2008).

In order to address the weaknesses in the global HIV/AIDS regime, the UN Economic and Social Council passed a resolution to establish the Joint United Nations Programme on HIV/AIDS (UNAIDS), which became operational in January 1996. UNAIDS replaced the GPA as the lead organization in developing an effective international response to the disease. It is headquartered in Geneva and is governed by a programme coordinating board, which is composed of twenty-two governmental representatives and also includes five representatives from NGOs. In addition to extensive surveillance and data gathering, UNAIDS has developed partnerships with NGOS, has brought together ten organizations of the UN system around a common agenda on the issue, and has become the leading advocate in the global response against HIV/AIDS. Another important step in the development of AIDS governance took place at the eleventh international AIDS conference, held in Vancouver in July 1996. During this conference, it was announced that aggressive treatment through the use of multiple drugs could make AIDS a manageable disease. Although this news created a lot of optimism regarding the fight against the disease, the high costs of the drugs created a problem in that therapy would be a viable option only in developed states. This result created a situation where treatment could be incorporated into medical programs of developed states, while developing states would have to continue to rely on prevention.

Needless to say, the high cost of the drugs created political conflicts between large pharmaceutical companies, which wanted to protect their patent rights in producing the drugs, and socially oriented NGOs, which wanted to see widespread distribution of ARVs. In addition, intergovernmental conflict emerged between the United States, which sought to protect the rights of the pharmaceutical industry, and developing states such as Thailand, Brazil, and South Africa, which wanted to produce and use much cheaper generic drugs (Seckinelgin 2008).

The new millennium brought some major changes to global health governance and the global response to HIV/AIDS, led by three key events in 2001 and 2002, in particular. The first of these was the resolution of the lawsuit by several pharmaceutical companies against the South African government, which was originally filed in 1997. The claim was that South Africa's Medicines and Related Substances Control Amendment Act violated the TRIPS agreement. This legislation allowed compulsory licensing of patent protected drugs. Pressure from NGOs, social activists, and the public in general convinced the pharmaceutical companies to withdraw the suit in April 2001. The salience of the issue involving access to medicines and TRIPS was addressed in November 2001 at the WTO ministerial conference in Doha, Qatar. This meeting produced the Doha declaration, which clarified the scope of TRIPS and allowed the issuance of compulsory licenses by states to protect public health. Following the declaration and mounting public pressure, the multinational pharmaceutical companies became more willing to reduce their prices. With supplemental international aid, this reduction allowed much greater access to ARVs. The number of people receiving treatment increased from 240,000 in 2002 to well over 1 million by 2005 (UNAIDS 2006). Despite these improvements, access to ARVs remains a costly proposition, especially for developing states. The problem has been exacerbated by the growth in drug-resistant variants of the virus. As a result, yet more drugs will have to be produced to deal with these variants until a vaccine is developed. It is not clear whether new lines of drugs will have the same pricing patterns as the first generation (Seckinelgin 2008).

The second key event was the 2001 UN General Assembly special session on HIV/AIDS. This meeting led to the declaration of commitment on HIV and AIDS, which acknowledged that the epidemic constituted a global emergency. Among the actions that the resolution called for were leadership at the global, regional, and national levels; the establishment of global prevention targets; to make treatment a fundamental element of a response to the disease; and human rights protection for those suffering from HIV/AIDS. This resolution went beyond biomedical responses to the disease and recognized its connection to social and economic development. It also stated a number of national goals, such as to make significant progress in implementing comprehensive health care strategies, to increase ARV treatment by 2005, and to eliminate discrimination against people with HIV/AIDS by 2003, and it called for $7 to $10 billion per year to fight AIDS in low- and middle-income countries. Although the document did not provide specific details on how these goals were to be reached, it did have some political influence. In particular, it led to a greater emphasis on treatment than just on prevention activities.

The third key event was the establishment of the Global Fund to Fight AIDS, Tuberculosis, and Malaria (Global Fund). In order to further the goals of the declaration of commitment on HIV and AIDS, it was considered by political leaders that a funding mechanism needed to be put into place to make the goals more of a reality. The Global Fund became functional with the meeting of the board for the first time in 2002. Since the Global Fund operates as a funding mechanism, it works closely with national governments, IGOs, NGOs, and public and private sector actors through a country coordinating mechanism in affected countries. This is responsible for developing proposals for funding, and those in receipt of the grant, typically the national government, implement the funding programs. The implementation is monitored by the Global Fund's secretariat. It is a public–private partnership with three representatives of NGOs on the executive board. In addition to the need for additional money to combat AIDS, tuberculosis, and malaria globally, Bartsch (2007) identifies three reasons why the fund was successfully established. The first was a stronger political commitment by powerful states. The second was the realization that the spread of infectious disease was a threat to both national and international security. This realization involved a broader conceptualization of security after the Cold War to include non-military threats such as the environment and poverty in addition to health. The third reason had to do with the desire of some powerful states, especially the US and Japan, to circumvent the UN system and have more control over the new institution. The Global Fund has made significant contributions to the treatment of HIV/AIDS in developing countries. Overall, 64 percent of the grants go to low-income countries (Bartsch 2007: 168).

As Patterson (2007) suggests, the strengthening of global governance in response to HIV/AIDS can be attributed primarily to two factors – the greater interest and involvement of powerful states in combating the disease and a greater role for non-state actors in governance. Increased interest by the United States was exhibited by the first national AIDS strategy, announced by President Bill Clinton in 1996. This strategy was aimed both at a biomedical response, to research a cure and a vaccine, and a social response, to ensure access to health services and the prevention of discrimination against those suffering from HIV/AIDS. Clinton then strengthened his commitment to the AIDS strategy in 1997 by announcing a greater need for international collaboration among both state and non-state actors to find a vaccine. He also announced the establishment of a research center at the National Institute of Health to accomplish this purpose. During the Clinton administration, AIDS-related spending by the Department of Health and Human Services increased from $2.1 billion in 1993 to $4.6 billion by 2000 (US DHHS 2000).

The administration of President George W. Bush also recognized the interest of the US in fighting AIDS. In 2003, he announced the President's Emergency Plan for AIDS Relief (PEPFAR), a funding program directed at countries with high levels of HIV/AIDS, mostly in Africa and the Caribbean. This program was the largest by any state directed at an international health initiative. Since it was announced, American spending on the global HIV/AIDS crisis increased from $840 million in 2001 to $6 billion in fiscal year 2008 (PEPFAR 2008). China has also recently taken a much more active role in combating HIV/AIDS. China was compelled to confront the AIDS epidemic publicly in 2001, when its senior AIDS researcher announced that it could soon have the highest number of AIDS infections in the world, which could lose the economy somewhere between $56 and $93 billion (Beach 2001). Since 2001, the Chinese government has increased funding substantially, and in 2006 alone it doubled its spending from the previous year, to $185 million (Ahmad 2006).

The increased role of non-state actors in global governance after 2000 was demonstrated by the institutional role provided for NGOs in both UNAIDS and the Global Fund, both of which have representatives from NGOs serving on their respective governing boards. PEPFAR provides a prominent role for NGOs as well. Almost 25 percent of all PEPFAR money is channeled through faith-based organizations (FBOs) (Bartsch and Kohlmorgen 2007). FBOs are seen as important partners in the plan and provide prevention messages as well as counseling and health services. These examples indicate how non-state actors have moved beyond advocacy and monitoring activities to participate in the decision-making and the implementation of policies by states and IGOs.

Despite the improvements in global governance in addressing and containing the HIV/AIDS epidemic, some significant collective action problems remain. One problem has to do with funding. A very large funding gap remains for universal access to HIV prevention. UNAIDS estimates that global funding would have to quadruple from its 2007 level of approximately $10 billion to reach the total necessary for global access in 2010, which would be approximately $42.2 billion. Funding would need to increase yet further, to $54 billion, to establish this standard by 2015 (UNAIDS 2007b). UNAIDS, which coordinates global AIDS-related activities among UN agencies, the WHO, and the World Bank, has an annual budget of only $60 million and a staff of about 130, which limits its capacity to function effectively (Boone and Batsell 2007; Kohlmorgen 2007). The Global Fund also has some funding difficulties, and in 2005 it found itself unable to provide funds for a sixth round of grants in early 2006. Although donations from Europe late in the year made a sixth round of grants possible, financing has been a challenge (Patterson 2007). While PEPFAR provides another avenue of funding outside the UN, it limits the financial contributions of the US to the Global Fund. PEPFAR funds come with some conditions attached, stipulating, for example, that a third of funds for education and prevention have to be spent on abstinence-promoting programs, that recipient countries have to renounce prostitution, and that FBOs should receive priority in obtaining care and treatment funds. These conditions have contributed to the politicization of the funds, as some states, such as Brazil, have expressed their objection on the basis that it would difficult to promote safe sex practices among prostitutes while simultaneously morally renouncing their activities (Garrett 2005).

A second problem has to with intellectual property protection. Although the Doha declaration led to a reduction in prices by pharmaceutical companies, some issues remain.

India, for example, is leading producer of generic ARVs, and many developing states rely on the affordability of these drugs. Indian generics account for about half of ARVs used in these states (Shadlen 2007: 575). India, however, moved towards compliance with the TRIPS agreement in 2005 with its Patents Act. This change has led some Indian firms to spend more money on research and development, with the expectation that increased production development will be protected by patents. Indian firms could then move away from producing generics to more specialized drugs. The resulting outcome could lead to an undersupply of generics globally and an increase in price (Shadlen 2007). This situation could become even more problematic if future generations of ARVs are needed to combat drug resistance. Another issue has to do with the continued support by the United States of patent protection. Since the Doha declaration, the US has sought to address this issue through multilateral and bilateral agreements rather than via the WTO and has sought to negotiate intellectual property standards that are more stringent than those stipulated by the WTO. The free trade agreement between the US and Singapore, for example, places limits on Singapore's imports of generic drugs (Russell 2007). With these developments, it is certainly unclear whether the Doha declaration will be successful in moving toward universal treatment of HIV/AIDs or if it will be overcome by the market incentives of pharmaceutical companies. Although prevention and treatment of HIV/AIDS would be a global public good, a lack of cooperation among the primary actors in this area makes it difficult for global governance to provide.

The Regulation of Tobacco

In addition to infectious diseases, global governance has addressed risk factors for non-communicable diseases, especially tobacco. The WHO has acknowledged that tobacco is the most preventable cause of death in the world. It estimated that, in 2008, tobacco would cause more deaths than tuberculosis, malaria, and AIDS combined (WHO 2008c). Limiting tobacco use would certainly improve health as a global public good. Despite these findings, however, smoking continues to be prevalent on a global scale. The addictive qualities of tobacco and a lack of knowledge regarding the health hazards it causes have made its use difficult to deter. This problem is exacerbated by the economic power of the tobacco industry, which can market the product extensively as well as provide jobs and income by promoting its consumption.

The dilemma regarding tobacco has been around ever since Europeans began expeditions to the Americas over 500 years ago. The European explorers brought tobacco back to Europe and introduced the practice of smoking. Unlike the Native Americans, who used the drug for medicinal and ceremonial reasons, the Europeans used it primarily for recreational purposes (Kiernann 1991). Its negative health effects were soon realized, and by 1640 it was prohibited in Japan, China, and New Amsterdam (later New York) (Borio 2003). Its addictive properties, however, also encouraged states to realize that tobacco was a profitable product that could be taxed to increase national income. In fact, the movement for American independence was partially financed by tobacco production in the colonies (Yach et al. 2007).

While states have taxed tobacco to raise revenue, the primary beneficiaries and advocates of its use have been those in the tobacco industry. The lobbying efforts by tobacco companies have had quite a bit of influence on regulation of the product. For example, after tobacco was included in the US Pharmacopoeia – the official US government listing of drugs – tobacco companies said that tobacco-growing states would not support the 1906 Food and Drug Act, which would create the Food and Drug Administration (FDA). As a result of this protest the listing of tobacco as a drug was dropped (Fritschler 1989), leaving the FDA unable to regulate tobacco use, despite legal challenges. In 2000, in the case of *FDA* vs. *Brown and Williamson Tobacco Corporation*, the US Supreme Court ruled that the FDA did not have jurisdiction over tobacco products without congressional approval.

However, in 2009, President Barack Obama reversed this decision by signing legislation that provided the FDA with the authority to regulate the manufacturing, marketing, and sale of tobacco products. The Family Smoking Prevention and Tobacco Control Act passed by Congress allows the FDA to set standards for nicotine levels and regulate chemicals in tobacco smoke, further restrict advertising and ban the use of terms such as "light," "mild," and "low tar," force tobacco companies to disclose details about ingredients, approve or ban new tobacco products, and require larger graphic warnings about smoking on cigarette packs. For the first time in history, the federal government has placed controls on tobacco products.

The previous lack of regulation over tobacco has had a global effect. The American Tobacco Company was the dominant influence in global tobacco production and distribution until the early twentieth century, when it was broken up by the US government on account of antitrust violations. The tobacco industry, however, has continued oligarchic in nature. Just four corporations – Philip Morris, British American Tobacco (BAT), Japan Tobacco/R. J. Reynolds, and the China National Tobacco Corporation – control most of the global tobacco market (Crescenti 1999). With the exception of the China National Tobacco Corporation, these companies have a strong base in the United States, whence they have extended their activities worldwide. Strong lobbying efforts by these MNCs have proven successful against national attempts at regulation in Latin America, the Middle East, and Africa. These companies have a significant amount of power, as demonstrated by the amount of income that they produce: Philip Morris, BAT, and Japan Tobacco/R. J. Reynolds combined had more in the way of revenue in 2002 than the combined gross national products of Albania, Bahrain, Belize, Bolivia, Botswana, Cambodia, Estonia, Georgia, Ghana, Honduras, Jamaica, Jordan, Macedonia, Malawi, Malta, Moldova, Mongolia, Namibia, Nepal, Paraguay, Senegal, Tajikistan, Togo, Uganda, Zambia, and Zimbabwe (Yach et al. 2007). As a result, less developed countries have experienced great difficulty in regulating tobacco use.

Globalization has had a significant effect on tobacco use and distribution. Before the 1980s, most tobacco facilities were in the United States and Western Europe. Since the start of the latest wave of globalization, the major tobacco companies have expanded their operations worldwide. Hammond (1998) suggests that expansion of the global tobacco industry followed pressure by the IMF and the World Bank on countries to open their markets to foreign investment and to privatize state-owned tobacco companies. These international institutions believed that market liberalization and privatization would provide the optimal path for economic development and help states remedy balance of payments deficits. This change in policy has led many developing countries to seek investment by tobacco companies, so that their investment can assist them with their financial difficulties. The move to privatization has allowed the major tobacco companies to buy assets of state-owned firms and consolidate their power in the global market. These pressures were accompanied by the movement in the 1990s towards a liberal market economy in China, Russia, and Eastern Europe. The multinational tobacco corporations have been very successful in penetrating these markets since the end of the Cold War. Philip Morris and BAT are two of the largest foreign investors in Russia and Moldova. In fact, BAT saw the former Soviet Union as a great place to invest on account of the shortage of tobacco products in the region and the lack of regulation during the early post-communist transition period (Gilmore and McKee 2004b).

Since the late 1990s, multinational tobacco companies have made several agreements with Chinese tobacco companies to improve manufacturing and processing tobacco products in China (Yach et al. 2007). The result of this change in policy and corporate tactics has led the prevalence of smoking in communist and former communist states to be the highest in the world. The World Bank found that, between 2000 and 2005, China, in addition to having the world's largest population, had the second highest smoking rate of adult males in the world, at 67 percent. Mongolia had a slightly higher percentage, at 68 percent. Other states with percentages in the 60s are the post-communist states of Albania, Kazakhstan, and Russia. Female adults, however, had much lower smoking rates in the vast majority of countries. Only 4 percent of the female population in China and only 16 percent in Russia smoked. The highest rates for female smokers during this period were 37 percent in Chile and 34 percent in Serbia and Montenegro (World Bank 2007).

In addition to investments and the movement toward market openness in China and the former Soviet Union, the international movement to liberalize trade had a major effect on the global distribution of tobacco products. The WTO agreements that went into effect in the 1990s reduced both tariff and non-tariff barriers in the trade of goods, including tobacco.

Liberalization in the tobacco trade has been further facilitated by regional arrangements such as the European Union, the North American Free Trade Agreement, and the Association of South East Asian Nations. Bilateral trade agreements have had an effect as well. In response to trade pressures by the United States, Japan, Taiwan, South Korea, and Thailand opened up their markets to American cigarettes in the mid-1980s. According to the World Bank (1999), smoking rates in these countries increased by 10 percent as result of this change in policy. The relationship between trade and smoking was also examined in a study by Taylor et al. (2000), which found that trade liberalization has had an impact on cigarette consumption, particularly in low-income states, and to a lesser extent in middle-income states.

Globalization has also facilitated the illicit trade in tobacco through the opening of borders and global trade. The smuggling of tobacco products is very lucrative business, since tobacco tends to be a heavily taxed good, which increases its price to the consumer. It is estimated that, in 2002, a quarter of all internationally traded cigarettes were smuggled (WHO 2002). It is also estimated that national governments lose about $25 to $30 billion each year in tax revenue from cigarette smuggling (Jha and Chaloupka 2000). As a result, even as states are suffering from the negative health effects of tobacco use, they are also losing some of the economic benefits of trade and sale of tobacco products. Interestingly, tobacco companies are not experiencing the same kind of losses. These companies make their profit before the product becomes traded on the market. Smuggling actually helps increase demand for their products because the increased supply results in lower prices (Yach et al. 2007).

The movement for government regulation of tobacco use on account of its impact on health began in the 1950s. Some American states adopted laws restricting cigarettes and smoking during the late nineteenth and early twentieth century, though they were seldom enforced. They were also aimed at prohibiting cigarette smoking primarily because it was a bad social behavior, rather than because of its risk to health. After World War I, tobacco use was largely unregulated in the US (Studlar 2008). During the 1950s, scientific research began to find a significant relationship between smoking and lung cancer, but the tobacco industry countered these reports in 1954 by putting together its own research committee. Tobacco companies maintained that their products were not harmful to health, though they did begin to market cigarettes that were lighter, with low amounts of tar, in response to the negative health reports.

Through successful political lobbying, the tobacco industry was largely able to avoid national regulation of tobacco until the 1970s. The first countries effectively to curb tobacco use through regulations were Finland, Canada, Singapore, and Norway. Both Finland and Norway, for example, passed comprehensive advertising bans. Finland and Singapore also placed health warnings on packages and prohibited smoking indoors (Yach et al. 2007). The United States took a different approach in response to the scientific findings, favoring the promotion of health education and individual responsibility. It did approve health warnings and banned broadcast advertising, but did not impose a federal tax increase on cigarettes (Studlar 2008). In the 1980s, however, the US became increasingly restrictive toward tobacco. This change in policy was based on further scientific evidence regarding its dangers and the growing influence of anti-tobacco NGOs. Tobacco companies have, however, been successful at avoiding some regulations, such as the US Supreme Court's 2000 decision that the FDA could not regulate tobacco products. While national regulations have been effective in some, mostly developed states, overall national regulations have been ineffective on account of the lack of anti-tobacco legislation or the weak implementation and enforcement of existing legislation (Yach et al. 2007).

Measures to regulate tobacco at the international level did not fully emerge until the late 1990s. Three key events spurred this movement: the Minnesota lawsuit settlement, the WHO's Tobacco Free Initiative (TFI), and the World Bank's 1999 report on the tobacco epidemic. The Minnesota settlement involved an agreement in 1998 between several tobacco companies and the state of Minnesota and Blue Cross/Blue Shield of Minnesota, in which the companies agreed to pay the costs arising from tobacco-related illnesses that the state had paid in Medicaid funds. Additionally, they agreed to make confidential documents available to the public. These documents revealed that the tobacco industry had known about the harmful effects of tobacco since the mid-1950s, and had attempted to conceal this information and obfuscate scientific research on tobacco use (Yach et al. 2007). This finding lent fuel to anti-tobacco NGOs in their lobbying efforts.

The TFI began in 1998 after Gro Harlem Brundtland became the WHO's director general. Its goal was to draw international attention and develop an international response to the negative health, social, environmental, and economic effects that tobacco use had on the global community. The TFI sought to address this issue through global information sharing, grassroots actions at the national and local level, and partnerships among governments, IGOs and non-state actors, as well as global regulation and international law (Yach and Bettcher 2000). The first step was for the WHO to establish partnerships with other IGOs. The UN agreed with the WHO to create an international task force on tobacco, which would include the UN as well as the World Bank, the IMF, and the WTO. One of the results of this collaboration was the World Bank's report on the tobacco "epidemic" in 1999. The findings of this report had an effect on how states should view tobacco policy. It suggested a number of interventions, especially tax increases on tobacco products, that could save lives, improve public health, and be cost-effective for national economies. Evidence was provided in the report that demonstrated the direct costs for public health expenditures and the loss of income that could be attributed to tobacco consumption and showed that developing states were overly concerned that the tobacco industry was too important for their economic growth to provide for effective regulations (Collin 2004).

The progressive movement for tobacco regulation generated enough support to develop the Framework Convention on Tobacco Control (FCTC), which came into force in February 2005. The idea for a comprehensive international agreement on tobacco control began at the WHA in 1995. The WHA agreed that Director-General Brundtland should initiate the development of a WHO-sponsored treaty on tobacco control. After receiving the Director-General's report, it facilitated the treaty development process in May 1999 by passing a resolution to establish a WHO working group on the treaty, as well as an intergovernmental negotiating body to allow member states to negotiate the FCTC. The negotiation process involved public hearings in October 2000, the first time that the WHO had included such a practice. These hearings gave the chance for both public health advocacy groups and the tobacco companies to express their views on the proposed convention. Over 144 organizations and institutions provided verbal testimony (WHO 2000). After the continuation of negotiations, the FCTC was adopted by the WHA on 21 May 2003 and went into effect in February 2005 after it had been ratified by forty states, the first treaty ever adopted by the WHO under its constitution. By August 2008, 160 states had ratified the treaty, making it largely universal in application.

The FCTC contained a number of regulations against tobacco that states were obligated to follow. Some of the key regulations are a comprehensive ban on tobacco advertising, subject to constitutional free speech limitations; the adoption of measures to promote public awareness regarding the health risks of tobacco use; the regulation of the contents of tobacco products; and an encouragement to promote smoke-free workplace laws, take enforcement measures against tobacco smuggling, and raise taxes on tobacco. The negotiation and final text of the FCTC was influenced quite significantly by developing states, many of which had participated in the negotiation process. The WHO's African region became the first to take part in the negotiations as a regional bloc (Collin 2004). NGOs also had an influence, as they encouraged domestic political debates about the convention. Among developed states, Canada, Australia, and New Zealand emerged as strong supporters (Yach et al. 2007).

Although the global movement to regulate tobacco has been successful, as evidenced by the large acceptance of the FCTC, the provision of tobacco regulations as a global public good has experienced some lack of commitment and conflicts of interest among the actors of global governance. The role of the United States, representing the most powerful actor in the international system, provides an example. The US has demonstrated inconsistency in regard to its commitment to the global tobacco regime and has developed a relatively restrictive domestic policy on tobacco consumption since the 1980s. A comparative study by Wilensky (2002) found that, along with the United Kingdom, Canada, Australia, and New Zealand, it has among the strongest national regulations regarding tobacco consumption as well as the greatest enforcement of those regulations. The US, however, was the most prominent advocate of a treaty with a minimal application that would favor more a declaration of goals than binding obligations (Collin 2004). During negotiations the US was successful in changing some the text of the final agreement, such as including the accordance with constitution limitation clause regarding the ban on advertising. It also pushed for changes to the treaty that were rejected, for example eliminating the clauses in Article 11 regarding the minimum size of health warnings on tobacco products and the clause regarding a prohibition of misleading advertising such as "low tar." The US was critical of the final text (American Journal of International Law 2003) but despite its reservations signed the FCTC in May 2004. As of November 2008, however, it was the only major state not to have ratified the treaty.

The primary conflict of interest with the global tobacco regime has been the multinational tobacco corporations, which have been effective in the past through their political lobbying in circumventing national legislation. In the United States, they have successfully avoided regulation by the FDA. They have actually increased marketing expenditures, despite the master settlement agreement between the four largest tobacco companies and the attorney generals of most American states, which posed more marketing restriction (Yach et al. 2007). Even with the FCTC, the wealth, power, and legal expertise of the tobacco industry will make it difficult for states with relatively weak legal infrastructures to regulate tobacco. The WHO has found that only 5 per cent of countries in the world have imposed a complete ban on advertising. It has also found that, where a partial ban has been adopted, the restrictions have often not been enforced. Also, forty-five countries lack a tobacco control agency and, of those that do have one, most are substantially understaffed (WHO 2008c). Furthermore, tobacco companies have attempted to reimage themselves as socially responsible actors. Phillip Morris, for example, has been supportive of international and domestic regulations. Support for regulations, however, can still be good for business. As Yach et al. (2007) suggest, Phillip Morris is the industry leader and can gain an advantage over its competitors through stronger regulations. In order to address successfully the global health problems posed by tobacco, states and NGOs need to cooperate to constrain the reach of the multinational tobacco industry.

Diet

Another significant risk factor associated with non-communicable disease is diet. Foods that are high in saturated fat, sugar, and salt have been linked to high blood pressure, high cholesterol, and obesity, conditions that are associated with such illnesses as stroke, heart disease, cancer, and diabetes. These diet-related diseases have usually been connected with developed states in the West. For example, it is estimated that almost a quarter of American adults are obese. While there is a lower level of obesity among adults in Europe than in the US, obesity rates have increased significantly in European countries (Chopra 2002). Drewnowski and Popkin (1997) have suggested that these diet-related illnesses have now spread to developing states. The global diet has shifted from grains and vegetables to one dominated by processed foods and a much heavier intake of dairy, eggs, and meat products (Popkin 2006). The WHO has reported that rapid increases in body mass index in developing countries have emerged since the 1980s. Globally, it is estimated that 300 million adults are clinically obese (WHO 2002).

This trend toward obesity coincides with the process of globalization. The opening of global trade through the WTO has facilitated the spread of processed foods as well as the global marketing of these products. Most of US agricultural exports between 1976 and 2002 were high-value processed foods (meat, frozen food, and dairy), and much of the increase in these exports during the 1990s was on account of the depreciation in the US dollar and trade agreements such as NAFTA (Whitton 2004). It has been suggested that imports of inexpensive processed food has led to a major change in the diet of citizens of developing countries (Popkin et al. 2001). While national income has increased with globalization, so has fat consumption through animal sources and vegetable oils, such as soybean and sunflower. The use of caloric sweeteners, mostly sugar, has also increased as a result of rising income, especially in urban areas. At same time, however, obesity rates have risen in low-income and rural areas of developing countries (Popkin and Mendez 2007)

Food processing has been significant for foreign direct investment (FDI) as well. American FDI in food processing increased from $9 billion in 1982 to $36 billion in 2000. This trend has led FDI to become a key component in bringing highly processed foods and soft drinks into developing states by lowering prices and increasing availability through supermarkets and restaurants (Hawkes 2004). For example, Coca-Cola is sold in over 200 countries, and McDonald's makes more than half of its sales through its activities outside the United States (Popkin 2006). Kentucky Fried Chicken and Pizza Hut, while not as globally prevalent as McDonald's, also have locations in many countries around the world.

While poor diet is similar to smoking in that it is a global risk factor for non-communicable disease, the regulation of the two are very different for global health governance. First of all, unlike tobacco, food is not directly harmful to human health. The risks associated with processed foods and sweetened soft drinks can be mitigated by a moderate intake of these products and by undertaking physical activity. Secondly, the scientific evidence linking diet and health is not as clear and convincing as that for tobacco. Because of a lack of scientific clarity on the relationship between diet and health, the policy approach to this issue is much more complex (Lee 2006).

Despite the gaps in scientific knowledge, the WHO has been concerned over the increasing rates of obesity and diet-related illness around the world. Its response was to develop the Global Strategy on Diet, Physical Activity, and Health (GSDPAH), which was approved by a WHA resolution in 2004. In drafting the strategy the WHO secretariat consulted with member states, NGOs, and the food industry. The GSDPAH has four main objectives:

1 reduce risk factors for non-communicable diseases that stem from unhealthy diet and physical inactivity;
2 increase awareness and understanding of the impact of diet and physical activity on health;
3 encourage the development and implementation of global, regional, national, and local policies to improve diet and increase physical activity; and
4 monitor scientific data on diet and physical activity.

The GSDPAH suggests roles for states, civil society, and the private sector to play in achieving these objectives, and that these actors should support a reduction in the intake of sugar, fat, and salt in food and promote consumption of fruits, vegetables, and whole grains.

The approach taken by the WHO through the GSDPAH is very different from that of the FCTC. The strategy, basically a series of policy recommendations for the relevant global actors, is largely declaratory and does not pose any binding obligations upon WHO member states. Nevertheless, it has not been free from political conflict. The United States, after lobbying by sugar producers, expressed objections to regulation over diet. The American sugar industry requested that the US Congress cut funding to the WHO unless the latter revised its 2003 guidelines on nutrition and healthy eating. The industry also made it clear to the WHO that its findings were questionable and that it would continue to lobby Congress to reduce funding (Ashraf 2003). In regard to the WHO's earlier draft of the GSDPAH, the US cited concerns regarding scientific evidence and the need for individual responsibility rather than regulation of dietary choices. Additionally, the sugar industry is influential in countries where the production and exportation of sugar is an important part of the economy. As a result, the final draft that was approved by the WHO was a milder version that was designed to be politically acceptable (Zarcostas 2004).

In addition to political constraints, the WHO faces a significant financial issue in implementing the GSDPAH. Before the resolution adopting the strategy, the WHO spent only 3 percent of its budget on non-communicable diseases (Tukuitonga and Keller 2005). This lack of funding poses a major limitation on the organization's ability to promote the objectives of the resolution. Since the policy options of the GSDPAH function largely as recommendations, the WHO encourages states to adopt some, if not all, of its policies. The WHO has also provided technical assistance to member states in developing marketing codes and guidance in dealing with the private sector (Tukuitonga and Keller 2005). Nevertheless, the response of global health governance is much weaker in the area of diet. Despite globalization's effect on diet, it remains an area that is largely regulated by national governments, which, so far, have not embraced the policies advocated by the GSDPAH. A progress report indicated that only twenty-five states had implemented them (WHO 2007). It is also the case that much of the private sector has not modified its activities in response to the strategy. The food and beverage companies face a problem with the policy recommendations because they are directed at the foods which are high in fat, sugar, and salt. Although the companies are concerned about their reputations, such foods are their most profitable commodities (Magnusson 2007). Until a more legalized approach is taken by the WHO, and supported by other organizations such as the UN and the World Bank, it seems that global health governance will have little impact on the global diet.

Global Health Governance and the Provision of Good Health

Although there is certainly a private aspect to health, in that health benefits may be excluded at both the individual and the state level, there is also a public dimension. Globalization has made individuals and states more interdependent than ever before. Providing for good health for the world population can lead to many benefits to the global community. Economically, states will be productive and generate more national income. Socially, quality of life will improve. Politically, improved economic and social conditions will enhance peaceful relations and cooperation. Morally, such a goal would be profoundly just. The global community has taken steps, albeit mostly aspirational, to achieve this goal. The Alma Ata declaration's "health for all" objective and the UN General Assembly's Millennium Development Goals demonstrate a political desire toward this end.

It appears, however, that, although efforts at promoting good health have been gaining ground, especially in the 2000s, the goal of "health for all" is a long way from becoming a reality. The UN's 2008 report on halting the spread of infectious diseases such as HIV/AIDS and malaria reveals that, while some progress has been made, much improvement is still necessary. The report says that, in terms of progress, the number of deaths due to AIDS has been declining and significant gains have been made in preventing new HIV infections in heavily infected countries. It also mentions the success of the polio initiative in the decline of polio transmission. But it mentions that funding remains a problem in combating infectious diseases, especially in providing for adequate health care and the research and development of essential drugs for treating these diseases.

The main issue that needs to be overcome for global health governance to provide good health is the collective action problem. The Logic of Collective Action, the Prisoner's Dilemma, and the New Institutionalism provide perspectives on collective action and how the problem may be overcome. The Logic of Collective Action emphasizes the difficulty in achieving cooperation among a large number of actors, which is certainly the case in providing a global public good such as global health. With the large number of actors involved, the participants in global governance have an incentive to free-ride and not contribute to global health, since they will benefit from it regardless of their contribution. The Prisoner's Dilemma demonstrates that lack of communication and trust makes cooperation difficult even in the case of mutual benefit. The New Institutionalism approach suggests the inefficiency of coercive regulation in providing a common good. The lack of information by the sanctioning authority will limit its effectiveness.

Although these approaches highlight the problems that need to be resolved to provide a common good, their explanations also provide guidance in overcoming these problems. Both the Logic of Collective Action and the Prisoner's Dilemma point out how the self-interests of actors conflict with the provision of a common good. An international institution can assist in reducing the incentive not to cooperate by monitoring and exposing non-compliance as well as providing potential sanctions. The New Institutionalism approach suggests that a partnership between private actors and the regulatory authority will improve monitoring and sanctioning for non-compliance. Global governance is a mechanism that can help overcome collective action problems for global public goods. It can provide regulatory power through states, and it can monitor and encourage compliance through collaborative relationships among states, IGOs, NGOs, MNCs, and influential individuals in the private sector.

The cases of global health governance in this chapter reveal that the response to polio has been by far the most successful. The WHO played a key leadership role in this effort by its global eradication initiative and its strengthening of the IHR. It also provided a funding mechanism for the program, a forum for discussion and debate about the eradication initiative, and an advocacy role in supporting it. In order to help implement the initiative, UN agencies and NGOs assisted states in administering immunization programs. Funding by states was supplemented by non-state actors such as Rotary International and the Bill and Melinda Gates Foundation. Through the collaborative efforts of these actors, polio is now endemic in only four states in the world. Despite its success, however, polio eradication is still affected by collective action problems. Free-riding is an issue in regard to funding the initiative. Some high-income states which had already eradicated polio before the initiative have been very limited in their contributions, as they have been less inclined to view it as a public good.

Although polio eradication demonstrates, for the most part, a successful resolution of collective action by global health governance, its application to the other cases examined in this chapter is very limited. One reason has to do with the fact that many countries had already eradicated polio by the time of the WHO's resolution in 1988. A second reason is that the technology to eradicate the disease already exists. As a result, the private sector does not have as much stake financially as it does in other areas of health, such as the production of drugs for HIV/AIDS. There is a relatively low conflict of interest among the actors in global health governance in regard to polio because, morally, it is seen as the right thing to do and, in this case, the moral objective is compatible with economic interests. Free-riding is the more significant issue.

The case of HIV/AIDS is a much more complicated matter. First of all, the social perception of HIV/AIDS as a product of immoral behavior means that the moral objective to combat the disease is not as clear among some actors. Secondly, HIV/AIDS represents a significant conflict between, on the one hand, providing the public good and, on the other, the economic interests of individual actors. Pharmaceutical companies, with the support of developed states – and in particular the United States – have resisted attempts to lower prices and compete with generic drugs, and they have international organizations such as the WTO to support their claim. Developing states and NGOs have challenged their actions to provide cheaper drugs to enhance treatment of HIV/AIDS in poorer countries, but funding for the disease remains a problem. Despite international mechanisms such as UNAIDS and the Global Fund, a large funding gap remains to achieve universal access to treatment. HIV/AIDS illustrates an area where the collective action problem has not been resolved.

The collective action problem also remains in the cases of tobacco and diet. In both these cases conflict between individual economic interests and global public health limits the ability of global health governance to reduce non-communicable disease. A global consensus seems to be emerging that smoking is morally wrong because of its deleterious effects on health. The WHO, working with various countries, managed to develop the FCTC. In this regard, global health governance has been successful in establishing legal obligations to promote better health. Implementation of the agreement, however, remains a problem. The global tobacco industry is well financed and has a lot of power, particularly in regard to developing states, and trade in tobacco falls under the constraining rules of the WTO. The decision of the United States to not ratify the FCTC also contributes to a weakness in the efforts of global health governance to control tobacco.

The case of diet represents the weakest and least effective instance of global governance and health. The moral objective of regulating diet is the least compelling of these cases because the link between diet and health is not as clear, and poor diet is not inherently harmful in the same way as is tobacco. This results in even greater leverage for the economic interests of the private sector. Global health governance, led by the WHO, has addressed this issue and has been successful in convincing member states to adopt a global strategy to promote better diet. The compromise, however, as exhibited in the GSDPAH, represents largely a series of voluntary guidelines, with a much weaker commitment than the FCTC and the tobacco regulations.

Much of the influence of globalization on health is related to the influence of neoliberal ideology and the globalization process. Neoliberalism advocates the importance of the market, and how the market functions more effectively without state regulation. As more countries have adopted neoliberal economic policies since the end of the Cold War, the trend has been for the state to become less influential in global affairs.

One problem with neoliberalism, and correspondingly with globalization, is that of market failure. An unregulated market may generate more income, but it will also fail to account for its effects on inequality, the environment, and health. As a result, state intervention is necessary to address these failures. Neoliberal ideology, coupled with self-interest, however, makes states more reluctant to intervene. As a proponent of neoliberalism, the United States is a very important actor in that it has the greatest voting power in the IMF and World Bank, as well as a tremendous amount of informal political power. The US has demonstrated much inconsistency in its commitment to global health. On one hand, it is the largest donor to both polio eradication and HIV/AIDS. It also has some of the most stringent anti-tobacco measures in the world. At the same time, however, it has consistently been siding with corporate interests in limiting the influence of global health governance.

Despite ideology and conflict, globalization has created greater opportunities for other actors, such as IGOs and NGOs, to become involved in the process and to address market failure. Much progress has been made since the late 1990s in cooperation in global health. The Doha declaration, the FCTC, and the GSDPAH all represent important international political steps in addressing the collective action problems in HIV/AIDS, tobacco control, and improving diet. It appears that global governance is moving closer to providing better global health rather than moving away from it.

Concluding Remarks

One image suggested by the term "health and globalization" is a vision of good health sweeping the world, improving economic productivity, quality of life, and social relationships. Morally such a goal would be profoundly just. The global community has taken steps, albeit mostly aspirational, to achieve this goal. The Alma Ata declaration's "health for all" objective and the UN General Assembly's Millennium Development Goals demonstrate a political desire toward this end. But, as noted in the last chapter, this goal is far from being met. Life expectancy has generally risen in the world, except in Africa south of the Sahara, where AIDS has taken a heavy toll, and in Belarus, Russia, Ukraine, and Kazakhstan, where longevity has yet to recover from the nearly forty-five-year downward slide that started under communism. Other countries, such as North Korea and Haiti, have likewise seen reversals in life expectancy, reflecting an adverse health situation. Despite these major exceptions, the health of the world's population has generally been improving, though the overall outcome to date is uneven, with life expectancy improving in most countries, slowing in others, and reversing in some; as of yet, there is no guarantee of "any general deterministic process of convergence" (McMichael et al. 2004: 1158).

However, there is also another, darker image associated with the relationship between health and globalization: the threat of pandemic disease. As discussed in chapter 3, there is a long history of epidemics being introduced into communities by infected travelers. The proliferation of previously unknown infectious diseases, such as HIV/AIDS, or diseases common only to specific geographical areas, such as West Nile disease, is evidence of how easily modern international transportation systems assist the spread of deadly infections from continent to continent. The problem of emerging infectious diseases is so serious that their containment is the WHO's leading priority. So, while the world is moving closer to health for all, there is much work yet to be done.

States remain the most prominent and powerful actors in global health governance, since they maintain sovereignty over what happens within their borders, but other actors have joined WHO to have influence on health issues as the world becomes more globalized. The WHO continues to play the leading role in global health, but the World Bank and IMF have assumed highly prominent roles in promoting health through economic development. The World Bank is now the largest source of funding worldwide for health-related projects, having lent some $2.5 billion annually since 2000 (Labonté et al. 2008). Various NGOs, such as the Red Cross, have assumed roles in global health matters as well, and MNCs have been important actors in the governance process as the providers of medical products, drugs, and services. While their influence has increased as a result of globalization, they have also struggled with some of the market failures associated with health in poor nations, such as inequalities regarding access to medicines and health services largely because of high costs to consumers (Labonté et al. 2008). Efforts at cost recovery by governments have been a mixed success and, in the final analysis, make it harder for those in extreme poverty to obtain health care.

Although all actors benefit from healthy populations, as with any endeavor involving a large number of diverse actors, achieving cooperation to reach a common goal can be problematic. There is no single worldwide authority in health matters, so any intervention or participation in international efforts to solve health problems requires negotiation and cooperation. Different levels of socioeconomic development among people and states, limitations on resources, distribution problems, and conflicts of interest between relevant actors, among other issues, all pose significant obstacles that still need to be overcome. Nevertheless, the goal remains health for all people on a global scale – thus mandating that countries cooperate to achieve this outcome.

When it comes to health care, American medicine has contributed significantly to solving health problems around the world through its technology, high level of medical science, and storehouse of health knowledge. Although the United States has played a major role in the development of medicine, its health care delivery system is not the envy of the world and is currently subject to reform. This is both because it is costly and because part of the population lacks the insurance which would give them equal access to the health care delivery system. Practically all advanced countries have universal health coverage, but the US to date does not. Instead, it has a fee-for-service system that reduces access for those unable to pay the fees directly or who lack the necessary health insurance. These persons – some 16.4 percent of the population in 2005 – typically go without services or receive care in welfare facilities. Their situation, rather than globalization, is the catalyst for current efforts at health reform. Moreover, in various low-income countries with limited resources and a lack of presence in international trade, the influence of globalization on health care is likely to be minimal.

Nevertheless, globalization, through the diffusion of medical information, the emergence of health services to an international clientele, the migration of health care personnel, medical tourism, the promotion of world markets for medical products and drugs, the influence on health policies, and the establishment of international controls on pandemics is a major influence on the world's health. This situation is likely to intensify as globalization itself intensifies. The critical factor in this development is upholding the benefits and reducing the risks to health that accompany globalization.

References

Abbott, Frederick M. (2002) "The TRIPS Agreement, Access to Medicines, and the WTO Doha Ministerial Conference," *Journal of World Intellectual Property* 5: 15–52.

—— (2005) "The WTO Medicines Decision: World Pharmaceutical Trade and the Protection of Public Health," *American Journal of International Law* 99: 317–58.

Adlung, Rudolf, and Antonia Carzaniga (2001) "Health Services under the General Agreement on Trade Services," *Bulletin of the World Health Organization* 79: 352–64.

Ahmad, Khabir (2006) "China Set to Double Annual Spending on HIV/AIDS," *Lancet Infectious Diseases* 6: 79.

Ahrin-Tenkorang, Dyna, and Pedro Conceicao (2003) "Beyond Communicable Disease Control: Health in the Age of Globalization," pp. 484–515 in I. Kaul, P. Conceicao, K. Le Goulven, and R. Mendoza (eds), *Providing Global Public Goods: Managing Globalization*. New York: Oxford University Press.

American Journal of International Law (2003) "Adoption of the Framework Convention on Tobacco Control," *American Journal of International Law* 97: 689–91.

American Medical Association, Organized Medical Staff Section (2007) *Medical Travel Outside the US, Report B*. Chicago: AMA.

Anesaki, Masahira, and Tsunetsugu Munakata (2005) "Health, Illness, and Health Policy in Japan," pp. 441–55 in W. Cockerham (ed.), *The Blackwell Companion to Medical Sociology*. Oxford: Blackwell.

Annandale, Ellen C., and David Field (2005) "Medical Sociology in Britain," pp. 180–98 in W. Cockerham (ed.), *The Blackwell Companion to Medical Sociology*. Oxford: Blackwell.

Asher, Robert E., and Edward S. Mason (1973) *The World Bank since Bretton Woods*. Washington, DC: Brookings Institution.

Ashraf, Haroon (2003) "WHO's Diet Report Prompts Food Industry Backlash," *The Lancet* 361: 1442.

Aylward, Bruce R., Arnab Acharya, Sarah England, Mary Agnocs, and Jennifer Linkins (2003) "Polio Eradication," pp. 33–53 in R. Smith, R. Beaglehole, D. Woodward, and N. Drager (eds), *Global Public Goods for Health: Health Economic and Public Health Perspectives*. New York: Oxford University Press.

Bartsch, Sonja (2007) "The Global Fund to Fight AIDS, Tuberculosis and Malaria," pp. 146–71 in W. Hein, S. Bartsch, and L. Kohlmorgen (eds), *Global Health Governance and the Fight against HIV/AIDS*. Basingstoke and New York: Palgrave Macmillan.

Bartsch, Sonja, and Lars Kohlmorgen (2007) "The Role of Civil Society Organizations in Global Health Governance," pp. 92–118 in W. Hein, S. Bartsch, and L. Kohlmorgen (eds), *Global Health Governance and the Fight against HIV/AIDS*. Basingstoke and New York: Palgrave Macmillan.

Bauman, Zygmunt (1992) *Intimations of Postmodernity*. London: Routledge.

Beach, Marilyn V. (2001) "Blood Heads and AIDS Confront China's Countryside," *The Lancet* 357: 49.

Beck, Ulrich (1992) *The Risk Society: Towards a New Modernity*, trans. Mark Ritter. London: Sage.

—— (1999) *World Risk Society*. Cambridge: Polity.

Becker, Jasper (2000) *The Chinese*. New York: Free Press.

Belsky, Leah, Reidar Lie, Aaditya Mattoo, Ezekiei J. Emanuei, and Gopai Sreenivasan (2004) "The General Agreement on Trade in Services: Implications for Health Policy-Makers," *Health Affairs* 23: 137–45.

Bhagwati, Jagdish (2004) *In Defense of Globalization*. New York: Oxford University Press.

Biehl, Joao (2007) "Pharmaceuticalization: AIDS Treatment and Global Health Politics," *Anthropological Quarterly* 80 (4): 1083–126.

Blaxter, Mildred (2004) *Health*. Cambridge: Polity.

Bloche, M. Gregg, and Elizabeth R. Jungman (2007) "Health Policy and the World Trade Organization," pp. 250–67 in I. Kawachi and S. Wamala (eds), *Globalization and Health*. New York: Oxford University Press.

Bloom, Gerald, and Shengian Tang (1999) "Rural Health Prepayment Schemes in China: Towards a More Active Role of Government," *Social Science & Medicine* 48: 951–60.

Blumenthal, David, and William Hsiao (2005) "Privatization and its Discontents: The Evolving Chinese Health Care System," *New England Journal of Medicine* 353: 1165–170.

Boone, Catherine, and Jake Batsell (2007) "Politics and AIDS in Africa: Research Agendas in Political Science and International Relations," pp. 3–35 in R. Ostergard (ed.), *HIV/AIDS and the Threat to National and International Security*. Basingstoke and New York: Palgrave Macmillan.

Borio, Gene (2003) *Tobacco Timeline: The Seventeenth Century – The Great Age of the Pipe*, at www.tobacco.org/resources/history/Tobacco_History17.html (21 October 2008).

Breman, Anna, and Carolyn Shelton (2007) "Structural Adjustment Programs and Health," pp. 219–33 in I. Kawachi and S. Wamala (eds), *Globalization and Health*. New York: Oxford University Press.

Brown, Theodore M., Marcos Cueto, and Elizabeth Fee (2006) "The World Health Organization and the Transition from 'International' to 'Global Health,'" *American Journal of Public Health* 96: 62–72.

Budrys, Grace (2001) *Our Unsystematic Health Care System*. Lanham, MD: Rowman & Littlefield.

—— (2003) *Unequal Health*. Lanham, MD: Rowman & Littlefield.

Cantor, Norman F. (2001) *In the Wake of the Plague: The Black Death and the World it Made*. New York: Free Press.

Cassileth, Barrie R., Vasily V. Vlassov, and Christopher C. Chapman (1995) "Health Care, Medical Practice, and Medical Ethics in Russia," *Journal of the American Medical Association* 273: 1562–9.

Castells, Manuel (1998) *End of Millennium*, Vol. 3: *The Information Age: Economy, Society, and Culture*. Oxford: Blackwell.

CGD (Center for Global Development) (2007) *Does the IMF Constrain Health Spending in Poor Countries: Evidence and an Agenda for Action*, at www.cgdev.org/doc/IMF/IMF_Report.pdf.

Chandola, Tarani (2000) "Social Class Differences in Mortality using the New UK National Statistics Socioeconomic Classification," *Social Science & Medicine* 50: 641–9.

Chen, Lincoln, and Vasant Narasimhan (2003) "A Human Security Agenda for Global Health," pp. 3–12 in L. Chen, J. Leaning, and V. Narasimhan (eds), *Global Health Challenges for Human Security*. Cambridge, MA: Harvard University Press.

Chen, Lincoln C., Tim G. Evans, and Richard Cash (1999) "Health as a Global Public Good," pp. 284–305 in I. Kaul, I. Grunberg, and M. Stein (eds), *Global Public Goods: International Cooperation in the 21st Century*. New York: Oxford University Press.

Chen, Meei-Shia (2005) "The Great Reversal: Transformation of Health Care in the People's Republic of China," pp. 456–82 in W.

Cockerham (ed.), *The Blackwell Companion to Medical Sociology*. Oxford: Blackwell.

Chopra, Mickey (2002) "Globalization and Food: Implications for the Promotion of 'Healthy' Diets," pp. 1–16 in World Health Organization (ed.), *Globalization, Diets, and Noncommunicable Diseases*. Geneva: World Health Organization.

Clark, Gregory (2007) *A Farewell to Alms: A Brief Economic History of the World*. Princeton, NJ: Princeton University Press.

Cockerham, William C. (1997) "The Social Determinants of the Decline in Life Expectancy in Russia and Eastern Europe: A Lifestyle Explanation," *Journal of Health and Social Behavior* 38: 131–48.

—— (1999) *Health and Social Change in Russia and Eastern Europe*. London: Routledge.

—— (2000) "Health Lifestyles in Russia," *Social Science & Medicine* 51: 1313–24.

—— (2006) "Class Matters: Health Lifestyles in Post-Soviet Russia," *Harvard International Review* 28: 64–7.

—— (2007) "Health Lifestyles and the Absence of the Russian Middle Class," *Sociology of Health and Illness* 29: 457–73.

—— (2010) *Medical Sociology*, 11th edn. Upper Saddle River, NJ: Pearson Prentice-Hall.

Cockerham, William C., Hiroyuki Hattori, and Yukio Yamori (2000) "The Social Gradient in Life Expectancy: The Contrary Case of Okinawa in Japan," *Social Science and Medicine* 51: 115–22.

Cockerham, William C., M. Christine Snead, and Derek F. DeWaal (2002) "Health Lifestyles in Russia and the Socialist Heritage," *Journal of Health and Social Behavior* 43: 131–48.

Cohen, Jillian Clare, and Lybecker, Kristina M. (2005) "AIDS Policy and Pharmaceutical Patents: Brazil's Strategy to Safeguard Public Health," *World Economy* 28: 211–30.

Coleman, Fred (1996) *The Decline and Fall of the Soviet Empire*. New York: St Martin's Press.

Collier, Paul, and David Dollar (2001) *Globalization, Growth, and Poverty: Building an Inclusive World Economy*. Washington, DC: World Bank.

Collin, Jeff (2004) "Tobacco Politics," *Development* 47: 91–6.

Commission on Global Governance (1995) *Our Global Neighborhood: Report on the Commission on Global Governance*. Oxford: Oxford University Press.

Commission on Human Security (2003) *Human Security Now*. New York: Commission on Human Security.

Cornia, Giovanni Andrea, Stefano Rosignoli, and Luca Tiberti (2008) "An Empirical Investigation of the Relation between Globalization and Health," pp. 34–62 in R. Labonté, T. Schrecker, C. Packer, and V. Runnels (eds), *Globalization and Health*. New York: Routledge.

Cornman, Deborah H., Sarah J. Schmiege, Angela Bryan, T. Joseph Benziger, and Jeffrey D. Fisher (2007) "An Information–Motivation–Behavioral Skills (IMB) Model-Based Prevention Intervention for Truck Drivers in India," *Social Science & Medicine* 64: 1572–84.

Crescenti, Marcelo G. (1999) "The New Tobacco World," *Tobacco Journal International* March: 51–3.

Cueto, Marcos (2004) "The Origins of Primary Health Care and Selective Primary Health Care," *American Journal of Public Health* 94: 1864–74.

Danishevski, K., A. Gilmore, and M. McKee (2008) "Public Attitudes towards Smoking and Tobacco Control Policy in Russia," *Tobacco Control* 17: 276–83.

de Beyer, Joy A., Alexander S. Preker, and Richard G. A. Feacham (2000) "The Role of the World Bank in International Health: Renewed Commitment and Partnership," *Social Science & Medicine* 50: 169–76.

de Quadros, Ciro A., Jon K. Andrus, Jean-Marc Olive, and Carlyle Guerra de Macedo (1992) "Polio Eradication from the Western Hemisphere," *Annual Review of Public Health* 13: 239–52.

Deng, Rui, Jianghong Li, Luechai Sringernyuang, and Kaining Zhang (2007) "Drug Abuse, HIV/AIDS and Stigmatization in a Dai Community in Yunnan, China," *Social Science & Medicine* 64: 1560–71.

Dmitrieva, Elena (2005) "The Russian Health Care Experiment: Transition of the Health Care System and Rethinking the Sociology of Medicine," pp. 320–33 in W. Cockerham (ed.), *The Blackwell Companion to Medical Sociology*. Oxford: Blackwell.

Dodoo, F. Nii-Amoo, Eliya M. Zulu, and Alex C. Ezeh (2007) "Urban–Rural Differences in the Socioeconomic Deprivation–Sexual Behavior Link in Kenya," *Social Science & Medicine* 64: 1019–31.

Douglas, Mary (1992) *Risk and Blame: Essays in Cultural Theory*. London: Routledge.

Drewnowski, Adam, and Barry M. Popkin (1997) "The Nutrition Transition: Trends in the Global Diet," *Nutrition Review* 55: 31–43.

Drucker, Peter (1993) *Post-Capitalist Society*. New York: Harper Business.

DuBos, René (1969) *Man, Medicine, and Environment*. New York: Mentor.

Engel, George L. (1977) "The Need for a New Medical School Model: A Challenge for Biomedicine," *Science* 196: 129–35.

Fahey, David W. (2006) "Twenty Questions and Answers about the Ozone Layer: 2006 Update," at http://ozone.unep.org/Assessment_Panels/SAP/Scientific_Assessment_2006/Twenty_Questions.pdf (29 December 2008).

Featherstone, Mike (ed.) (1990) *Global Culture*. London: Sage.

Fidler, David P. (1999) *International Law and Infectious Disease*. Oxford: Clarendon Press.

—— (2004) *SARS, Governance and the Globalization of Disease*. Basingstoke and New York: Palgrave Macmillan.

Field, Mark G. (1993) "The Physician in the Commonwealth of Independent States: The Difficult Passage from Bureaucrat to Professsional," pp. 162–83 in F. Hafferty and J. McKinley (eds), *The Changing Medical Profession*. New York: Oxford University Press.

—— (2000) "The Health and Demographic Crisis in Post-Soviet Russia: A Two-Phase Development," pp. 11–42 in M. Field and J. Twigg (eds), *Russia's Torn Safety Nets*. New York: St Martin's Press.

Frankel, Jeffrey (2000) "Globalization of the Economy," pp. 45–71 in J. Nye and J. Donahue (eds), *Governance in a Globalizing World*. Washington, DC: Brookings Institution.

Frieden, Jeffery A. (2006) *Global Capitalism*. New York: W. W. Norton.

Friedman, Thomas L. (2000) *The Lexus and the Olive Tree*. New York: Anchor Books.

—— (2005) *The World is Flat: A Brief History of the Twenty-First Century*. New York: Farrar, Straus & Giroux.

Fritschler, A. Lee (1989) *Smoking and Politics: Policy-Making and the Federal Bureaucracy*, 4th edn. Englewood Cliffs, NJ: Prentice-Hall.

G8 Research Group (2007) *2006 St Petersburg Final Compliance Report, 20 July 2006 to 15 May 2007*, at www.g7.utoronto.ca/evaluations/2006compliance_final/2006_g8compliance_final.pdf (23 August 2008).

Garrett, Geoffrey, and Peter Lange (1996) "Internationalization, Instititutions and Political Change," pp. 48–75 in R. Keohane and H. Milner (eds), *Internationalization and Domestic Politics*. New York: Cambridge University Press.

Garrett, Laurie (1994) *The Coming Plague*. New York: Farrar, Straus & Giroux.

—— (2005) "The Lessons of HIV/AIDS," *Foreign Affairs* 84: 51–64.

Garwood, Paul (2007) "What Will Become of the Polio Network?" *Bulletin of the World Health Organization* 85: 87–8.

Giddens, Anthony (1990) *The Consequences of Modernity*. Stanford, CA: Stanford University Press.

—— (2000) *Runaway World*. New York: Routledge.

—— (2002) "The Globalizing of Modernity," pp. 60–6 in D. Held and A McGrew (eds), *The Global Transformations Reader: An Introduction to the Globalization Debate*. Cambridge: Polity.

Gilmore, Anna B., and Martin McKee (2004a) "Tobacco and Transition: An Overview of Industry Investments, Impact and Influence in the Former Soviet Union," *Tobacco Control* 13: 136–42.

—— (2004b) "Moving East: How the Transnational Tobacco Industry Gained Entry to the Emerging Markets of the Former Soviet Union, Part I: Establishing Cigarette Imports," *Tobacco Control* 13: 143–50.

—— (2005) "Exploring the Impact of Foreign Direct Investment on Tobacco Consumption in the Former Soviet Union," *Tobacco Control* 14: 13–21.

Gilpin, R. (2002) *The Challenge of Global Capitalism*. Princeton, NJ: Princeton University Press.

Global Carbon Project (2007) "Carbon Trends 2007," at www.globalcarbonproject.org/carbontrends/index.htm (30 December 2008).

Global Fund to Fight AIDS, Tuberculosis, and Malaria (2008) *How the Global Fund Works*, at http://www.theglobalfund.org/en/how/.

Godlee, Fiona (1994) "WHO in Retreat: Is it Losing its Influence?" *British Medical Journal* 309: 1491–5.

Gold, Marsha R. (1999) "The Changing US Health Care System: Challenges for Responsible Public Policy," *Milbank Quarterly* 77: 3–37.

Goldman, Merle (1998) "The Post-Mao Reform Era," pp. 406–51 in John King Fairbank and Merle Goldman, *China: A New History*. Cambridge, MA: Belknap Press of Harvard University Press.

Hale, Victoria G., Katherine Woo, and Helene Levens Lipton (2005) "Oxymoron No More: The Potential of Nonprofit Drug Companies to Deliver on the Promise of Medicines for the Developing World," *Health Affairs* 24: 1057–63.

Hammond, Ross (1998) "Consolidation in the Tobacco Control Industry," *Tobacco Control* 7: 426–8.

Hannerz, Ulf (1990) "Cosmopolitans and Locals in World Culture," pp. 237–51 in M. Featherstone (ed.), *Global Culture*. London: Sage.

Hawkes, Corinna (2004) "The Role of Foreign Direct Investment in the Nutrition Transition," *Public Health Nutrition* 8: 357–65.

Hein, Wolfgang (2007) "Global Health Governance and WTO/TRIPS: Conflicts between 'Global Market-Creation' and 'Global Social Rights'," pp. 38–66 in W. Hein, S. Bartsch, and L. Kohlmorgen (eds), *Global Health Governance and the Fight against HIV/AIDS*. Basingstoke and New York: Palgrave Macmillan.

Held, David, and Andrew McGrew (2002) "The Great Globalization Debate," pp. 1–50 in D. Held and A. McGrew (eds), *The Global Transformations Reader: An Introduction to the Globalization Debate*. Cambridge: Polity.

Hesketh, Therese, and Weixing Zu (1997) "Health in China: Traditional Chinese Medicine: One Country, Two Systems," *British Medical Journal* 314: 115–17.

Heymann, David L. (2003) "Evolving Infectious Disease Threats to National and Global Security," pp. 105–24 in L. Chen, J. Leaning, and V. Narasimhan (eds), *Global Health Challenges for Human Security*. Cambridge, MA: Harvard University Press.

Hirst, Paul, and Grahame Thompson (2002) "The Limits of Economic Globalization," pp. 98–105 in D. Held and A. McGrew (eds), *The Global Transformations Reader: An Introduction to the Globalization Debate*. Cambridge: Polity.

Homedes, Nuria, and Antonio Ugalde (2005) "Why Neoliberal Health Reforms Have Failed in Latin America," *Health Policy* 71: 83–96.

Hosegood, Victoria, Eleanor Preston-Whyte, Joanna Busza, Sindile Moitse, and Ian M. Timaeus (2007) "Revealing the Full Extent of Households' Experiences of HIV and AIDS in Rural South Africa," *Social Science & Medicine* 65: 1249–59.

Howard-Jones, Norman (1975) *The Scientific Background of the International Sanitary Conferences, 1851–1938*. Geneva: World Health Organization.

Hunter, Mark (2007) "The Changing Political Economy of Sex in South Africa: The Significance of Unemployment and Inequalities for the Scale of the AIDS Epidemic," *Social Science and Medicine* 64: 689–700.

IHR (International Health Regulations) (2005) at www.who.int/csr/ihr/WHA58-en.pdf (27 June 2008).

Ikegami, Naoki, and John C. Campbell (1995) "Medical Care in Japan," *New England Journal of Medicine* 333: 1295–9.

IPCC (Intergovernmental Panel on Climate Change) (2001) *Climate Change 2001: Impacts, Adaptation and Vulnerability*. Cambridge: Cambridge University Press.

Jarvis, Martin J., and Jane Wardle (1999) "Social Patterning of Individual Health Behaviours: The Case of Cigarette Smoking," pp. 240–55 in M. Marmot and R. Wilkinson (eds), *The Social Determinants of Health*. Oxford: Oxford University Press.

Jasso-Aguilar, Rebecca, Howard Waitzkin, and Angela Landwehr (2004) "Multinational Corporations and Health Care in the United States and Latin America," *Journal of Health and Social Behavior* 45: 136–57.

Jewkes, Rachel K., Jonathan B. Levin, and Loveday A. Penn-Kekana (2003) "Gender Inequalities, Intimate Partner Violence and HIV Preventive Practices: Findings of a South African Cross-Sectional Study," *Social Science & Medicine* 56: 125–34.

Jha, Prabhat, and Frank L. Chaloupka (eds) (2000) *Tobacco Control Policies in Developing Countries*. Oxford: Oxford University Press.

Kapstein, Ethan (1999) *Sharing the Wealth*. New York: W.W. Norton.

Kapur, Devesh, John P. Lewis, and Richard Webb (1997) *The World Bank: Its First Half Century*, Volume 1. Washington, DC: Brookings Institution.

Karns, Margaret P., and Karen A. Mingst (2004) *International Organizations: The Politics and Processes of Global Governance*. Boulder, CO: Lynne Rienner.

Kaul, Inge, Isabelle Grunberg, and Marc A. Stein (1999) *Global Public Goods: International Cooperation in the 21st Century*. New York: Oxford University Press.

Kawachi, Ichiro, and Sarah Wamala (2007) "Poverty and Inequality in a Globalizing World," pp. 122–37 in I. Kawachi and S. Wamala (eds), *Globalization and Health*. New York: Oxford University Press.

Keohane, Robert O., and Joseph S. Nye (2000) "Introduction," pp. 1–41 in J. Nye and J. Donahue (eds), *Governance in a Globalizing World*. Cambridge, MA: Brookings Institution.

Kiernann, V. G. (1991) *Tobacco: A History*. London: Hutchinson Radius.

King, Anthony D. (1990) "Architecture, Capital and the Globalization of Culture," pp. 397–411 in M. Featherstone (ed.), *Global Culture*. London: Sage.

Knaus, William A. (1981) *Inside Russian Medicine*. Boston: Beacon Press.

Kohlmorgen, Lars (2007) "International Governmental Organizations and Global Health Governance: The Role of the World Health Organization, World Bank and UNAIDS," pp. 119–45 in Wolfgang Hein, Sonja Bartsch, and Lars Kohlmorgen (eds), *Global Health Governance and the Fight against HIV/AIDS*. Basingstoke and New York: Palgrave Macmillan.

Koivusalo, Meri (2003) "Assessing Health Policy Implications of WTO Agreements," pp. 161–76 in K. Lee (ed.), *Health Impacts of Globalization*. New York: Palgrave Macmillan.

Kornai, János (2008) *From Socialism to Capitalism*. Budapest: Central European University Press.

Labonté, Ronald, Ted Schrecker, Corinne Packer, and Vivien Runnels (eds) (2008) *Globalization and Health*. New York: Routledge.

Lahelma, Eero, Sara Arber, Katarina Kivela, and Eva Roos (2002) "Multiple Roles and Health among British and Finnish Women: The Influence of Socioeconomic Circumstances," *Social Science & Medicine* 54: 727–40.

Lanoszka, Anna (2003) "The Global Politics of Intellectual Property Rights and Pharmaceutical Drug Policies in Developing Countries," *International Political Science Review* 24 (2): 181–97.

Lassey, Marie L., William R. Lassey, and Martin J. Jinks (1997) *Health Care Systems around the World*. Upper Saddle River, NJ: Prentice-Hall.

Lee, Kelley (2006) "Health Promotion: How Can We Strengthen Governance and Build Effective Strategies?" *Health Promotion International* 21: 42–50.

Lee, Kelley, and Anthony Zwi (2003) "A Global Political Economy Approach to AIDS," pp. 13–32 in K. Lee (ed.), *Health Impacts of Globalization*. Basingstoke and New York: Palgrave Macmillan.

Light, Donald W. (1997) "From Managed Competition to Managed Cooperation: Theory and Lessons from the British Experience," *Milbank Quarterly* 75: 297–341.

—— (2004) "Introduction: Ironies of Success – A New History of the American Health Care System," *Journal of Health and Social Behavior* 45 (extra issue): 1–24.

Livi Bacci, Massimo (2008) *Conquest: The Destruction of the American Indios*. Cambridge: Polity.

Lopez, Alan D. (1998) "Smoking and Death in Russia," *Tobacco Control* 7: 3–4.

Lupton, Deborah (1999) *Risk*. London: Routledge.

Maddison, Angus (2001) *The World Economy: A Millennial Perspective*. Paris: Organization for Economic Cooperation and Development.

Magnusson, Roger S. (2007) "Non-Communicable Diseases and Global Health Governance: Enhancing Global Processes to Improve Health Development," *Globalization and Health* 3: 2; www.globalizationandhealth.com/content/3/1/2 (13 November 2008).

Malia, Martin (1994) *The Soviet Tragedy: A History of Socialism in Russia, 1917–1991*. New York: Free Press.

Marmot, Michael (2004) *The Status Syndrome*. New York: Times Books.

Matthews, Jessica T. (1997) "Power Shift," *Foreign Affairs* 76: 50–66.

Mbugua, J. Karanja, Gerald Bloom, and Malcolm Segal (1995) "Impact on User Charges on Vulnerable Groups: The Case of Kibwezi in Rural Lenya," *Social Science and Medicine* 41: 829–35.

McIntosh, William Alex, and John K. Thomas (2004) "Economic and Other Social Determinants of the Prevalence of HIV: A Test of Competing Hypotheses," *Sociological Quarterly* 45: 303–24.

McMichael, Anthony J., and G. Ranmuthugala (2007) "Global Climate Change and Human Health," pp. 81–97 in I. Kawachi and S. Wamala (eds), *Globalization and Health*. New York: Oxford University Press.

McMichael, Anthony J., Martin McKee, Vladimir Shkolnikov, and Tapani Valkonen (2004) "Mortality Trends and Setbacks: Global Governance or Divergence?" *The Lancet* 363: 1155–9.

Mechanic, David (2004) "The Rise and Fall of Managed Care," *Journal of Health and Social Behavior* 45 (extra issue): 76–86.

Medvedev, Roy (2000) *Post-Soviet Russia: A Journey through the Yeltsin Era*, ed. and trans. G. Shriver. New York: Columbia University Press.

Mezentseva, Elena, and Natalia Rimachevskaya (1992) "The Health of the Populations in the Republics of the Former Soviet Union: An Analysis of the Situation in the 1970s and 1980s," *International Journal of the Health Sciences* 3: 127–42.

Moran, Mary, Anne-Laure Roper, Javier Guzman, Jose Diaz, and Christopher Garrison (2005) *The New Landscape of Neglected Disease Drug Development*. London: London School of Economics and Political Science.

Morse, Stephen S. (1995) "Factors in the Emergence of Infectious Diseases," *Emerging Infectious Diseases* 1: 17–15.

MSF (Médecins Sans Frontières) (2008) "About MSF," www.msf.org/msfinternational/aboutmsf/ (5 August 2008).

Mtika, Mike Mathambo (2007) "Political Economy, Labor Migration, and the AIDS Epidemic in Rural Malawi," *Social Science & Medicine* 64: 2454–63.

Munakata, Tsunetsugu, and Kazoo Tajima (1996) "Japanese Risk Behaviors and their HIV/AIDS-Preventive Behavior," *AIDS Education and Prevention* 8: 115–33.

Nemstov, Alexander (2002) "Alcohol-Related Human Losses in Russia in the 1980s and 1990s," *Addiction* 97: 1413–25.

Nettleton, Sarah (2006) *The Sociology of Health and Illness*, 2nd edn. Cambridge: Polity.

Nishi, Nobuo, Kae Makino, Hidebi Fukuda, and Kozo Tatarra (2004) "Effects of Socioeconomic Indicators on Coronary Risk Factors, Self-Rated Health, and Psychological Well-Being among Urban Japanese Civil Servants," *Social Science & Medicine* 58: 1159–70.

Norris, Pippa (2000) "Global Governance and Cosmopolitan Citizens," pp. 155–77 in J. Nye and J. Donahue (eds), *Governance in a Globalizing World*. Washington, DC: Brookings Institution.

Nye, Joseph S. (2002) *Paradox of American Power: Why the World's Only Superpower Can't Go it Alone*. New York: Oxford University Press.

Oglobin, C., and G. Brock (2003) "Smoking in Russia: The 'Marlboro Man' Rides but without 'Virginia Slims' for Now," *Comparative Economic Studies* 45: 87–103.

Olson, Mancur (1971) *The Logic of Collective Action.* Cambridge, MA: Harvard University Press.

Ostrom, Elinor (1990) *Governing the Commons: The Evolution of Institutions for Collective Action.* Cambridge: Cambridge University Press.

Packard, Randall M. (1997) "Malaria Dreams: Postwar Visions of Health and Development in the Third World," *Medical Anthropology* 17: 279–96.

Palosuo, Hannele (2000) "Health-Related Lifestyles and Alienation in Moscow and Helsinki," *Social Science & Medicine* 51: 1325–41.

Patterson, Amy S. (2007) "The UN and the Fight against HIV/AIDS," pp. 203–25 in Paul G. Harris and Patricia D. Siplon (eds), *The Global Politics of AIDS.* Boulder, CO: Lynne Rienner.

PEPFAR (President's Emergency Plan for AIDS Relief) (2008) "PEPFAR Overview," September, at www.pepfar.gov/press/81352. htm (18 September 2008).

Perlman, Francesca, Martin Bobak, Anna Gilmore, and Martin McKee (2007) "Trends in the Prevalence of Smoking in Russia during the Transition to a Market Economy," *Tobacco Control* 16: 299–305.

Pescosolido, Bernice A., and Carol A. Boyer (2005) "The American Health Care System: Entering the 21st Century with High Risk, Major Challenges, and Great Opportunities," pp. 180–98 in W. Cockerham (ed.), *The Blackwell Companion to Medical Sociology.* Oxford: Blackwell.

Pescosolido, Bernice A., Steven A. Tuch, and Jack K. Martin (2001) "The Profession of Medicine and the Public: Examining Americans' Changing Confidence in Physician Authority from the Beginning of the 'Health Care Crisis' to the Era of Health Care Reform," *Journal of Health and Social Behavior* 42: 1–16.

PhRMA (Pharmaceutical Research and Manufacturers of America) (2008) "R&D Spending by US Pharmaceutical Companies Reaches Record $58 Billion in 2007," press release, 24 March, at www. phrma.org/news_room/press_releases/us_biopharmaceutical_ companies_r%26d_spending_reaches_record_%2458.8_billion_ in_2007 (11 July 2008).

Popkin, Barry M. (2006) "Technology, Transport, Globalization and the Nutrition Transition Food Policy," *Food Policy* 31: 554–69.

Popkin, Barry M., and Michelle Mendez (2007) "The Rapid Shifts in Stages of the Nutrition Transition: The Global Obesity Epidemic," pp. 68–80 in I. Kawachi and S. Wamala (eds), *Globalization and Health.* New York: Oxford University Press.

Popkin, Barry M., Sue Horton, and Soowon Kim (2001) "The Nutrition Transition and Prevention of Diet-Related Diseases in Asia and the Pacific," *Food and Nutrition Bulletin* 22 (supplement 4): 1–58.

Popkin, Barry, Namvar Zohoori, Lenore Kohlmeier, Alexander Baturin, Arseni Martinchik, and Alexander Deev (1997) "Nutritional Risk Factors in the Former Soviet Union," pp. 314–34 in J. Bobadilla, C. Costello, and F. Mitchell (eds), *Premature Death in the New Independent States*. Washington, DC: National Academy Press.

Porter, Roy (1997) *The Greatest Benefit to Mankind: A Medical History of Humanity*. New York: W. W. Norton.

Powell, Margaret, and Masashira Anesaki (1990) *Health Care in Japan*. London: Routledge.

Preston, Richard (1999) *The Hot Zone*. New York: Anchor Books.

Quadagno, Jill (2004) "Why the United States Has No National Health Insurance: Stakeholder Mobilization against the Welfare State, 1945–1996," *Journal of Health and Social Behavior* 45 (extra issue): 25–44.

—— (2005) *One Nation, Uninsured: Why the US Has No National Health Insurance*. New York: Oxford University Press.

Ray, Larry (2007a) "Globalization," pp. 1956–60 in G. Ritzer (ed.), *The Blackwell Encyclopedia of Sociology*, Volume IV. Oxford: Blackwell.

—— (2007b) *Globalization and Everyday Life*. London: Routledge.

Reid, Ivan (1998) *Social Class Differences in Britain*. Cambridge: Polity.

Reingold, Arthur L., and Christina R. Phares (2006) "Infectious Diseases," pp. 139–206 in M. Merson, R. Black, and A. Mills (eds), *International Public Health: Diseases, Programs, Systems, and Policies*, 2nd edn. Sudbury, MA: Jones & Bartlett.

Rensburg, Dingie van, Irwin F. Friedman, Charles Ngwena, André Pelser, François Steyn, Frederik Booysen, and Elizabeth Adendorff (2002) *Strengthening Local Government and Civic Responses to the HIV/AIDS Epidemic in South Africa*. Bloemfontein, South Africa: Centre for Health Systems Research & Development.

Rensberg, H. C. J. van (ed.) (2004) *Health and Health Care in South Africa*. Hatfield, Pretoria: Van Shaik.

Rensberg, H. C. J. van, and Charles Ngwena (2005) "Health and Health Care in South Africa against an African Background," pp. 365–91 in W. Cockerham (ed.), *The Blackwell Companion to Medical Sociology*. Oxford: Blackwell.

Reznik, David L., John W. Murphy, and Linda Liska Belgrave (2007) "Globalisation and Medicine in Thailand," *Sociology of Health and Illness* 29: 536–50.

Robertson, Roland (1992) *Globalization*. London: Sage.

Ruger, Jennifer Prah (2005) "The Changing Role of the World Bank in Global Health," *American Journal of Public Health* 95: 50–70.

Russell, Asia (2007) "Trading Life and Death: AIDS and the Global Economy," pp. 225–46 in P. Harris and P. Siplon (eds), *The Global Politics of AIDS*. Boulder, CO: Lynne Rienner.

Seavey, Nina Gilden, Jane S. Smith, and Paul Wagner (1998) *A Paralyzing Fear: The Triumph over Polio in America*. New York: TV Books.

Seckinelgin, Hakan (2008) *International Politics of HIV/AIDS*. New York: Routledge.

Sengupta, Amit (2003) "Health in the Age of Globalization," *Social Scientist* 31: 66–85.

Shadlen, Kenneth C. (2007) "The Political Economy of AIDS Treatment: Intellectual Property and the Transformation of Generic Supply," *International Studies Quarterly* 51: 559–81.

Shapiro, Judith (1995) "The Russian Mortality Crisis and its Causes," pp. 149–78 in A. Åslund (ed.), *Russian Economic Reform at Risk*. London: Pinter.

Shaw, Mary, Danny Dorling, and George Davey Smith (1999) "Poverty, Social Exclusion, and Minorities," pp. 211–39 in M. Marmot and R. Wilkinson (eds), *The Social Determinants of Health*. Oxford: Oxford University Press.

Shibuya, Kenji (2003) "Health Problems as Security Risks: Global Burden of Disease Assessments," pp. 209–332 in L. Chen, J. Leaning, and V. Narasimhan (eds), *Global Health Challenges for Human Security*. Cambridge, MA: Harvard University Press.

Shisana, Olive, Nompumelelo Zunga-Dirwayi, and William Shisana (2003) "AIDS: A Threat to Human Security," pp. 141–60 in L. Chen, J. Leaning, and V. Narasimhan (eds), *Global Health Challenges for Human Security*. Cambridge, MA: Harvard University Press.

Shkolnikov, Vladimir M., and Alexander V. Nemstov (1997) "The Anti-Alcohol Campaign and Variations in Russian Mortality," pp. 239–61 in J. Bohadilla, C. Costello, and E. Mitchell (eds), *Premature Mortality in the New Independent States*. Washington, DC: National Academy Press.

Shkolnikov, Vladimir, Martin McKee, and David Leon (2001) "Changes in Life Expectancy in Russia in the Mid-1990s," *The Lancet* 357: 917–27.

Slaper, Harry, Guus J. M. Velders, John S. Daniel, Frank R. De Gruijl, and Jan C. Van Der Leun (1996) "Estimates of Ozone Depletion and Skin Cancer Incidence to Examine the Vienna Convention Achievements," *Nature* 384: 256–8.

Smith, Anthony D. (1990) "Towards a Global Culture," pp. 171–91 in M. Featherstone (ed.), *Global Culture*. London: Sage.

Stevens, Fred (2005) "The Convergence and Divergence of Modern Health Care Systems," pp. 139–76 in W. Cockerham (ed.), *The Blackwell Companion to Medical Sociology*. Oxford: Blackwell.

Stevens, Rosemary (1971) *American Medicine and the Public Interest*. New Haven, CT: Yale University Press.

Stiglitz, Joseph E. (2003) *Globalization and its Discontents*. New York: W. W. Norton.

Stocker, Karen, Howard Waitzkin, and Celia Iriart (2008) "The Exportation of Managed Care to Latin America," *Health Policy Report* 340: 1131–6.

Strange, Susan (2002) "The Declining Authority of States," pp. 127–34 in D. Held and A. McGrew (eds), *The Global Transformations Reader: An Introduction to the Globalization Debate*. Cambridge: Polity.

Studlar, Donley T. (2008) "US Tobacco Control: Public Health, Political Economy, or Morality Policy?" *Review of Policy Research* 25: 393–410.

Tawfik, Linda, and Susan Cotts Watkins (2007) "Sex in Geneva, Sex in Lilongwe, and Sex in Balaka," *Social Science & Medicine* 64: 1090–101.

Taylor, Allyn, Frank J. Chaloupka, Emmanuel Guindon, and Michaelyn Corbett (2000) "Trade Policy and Tobacco Control," pp. 343–64 in P. Jha and F. Chaloupka (eds), *Tobacco Control Policies in Developing Countries*. Oxford: Oxford University Press.

Thomas, Caroline (2003) "Trade Policy, the Politics of Access to Drugs and Global Governance for Health," pp. 177–91 in K. Lee (ed.), *Health Impacts of Globalization*. Basingstoke and New York: Palgrave Macmillan.

Thomas, Caroline, and Martin Weber (2004) "The Politics of Global Governance: Whatever Happened to 'Health for All by the Year 2000'?" *Global Governance* 10: 187–205.

Thompson, John B. (2002) "The Globalization of Communication," pp. 246–59 in D. Held and A. McGrew (eds), *The Global Transformations Reader: An Introduction to the Globalization Debate*. Cambridge: Polity.

Thompson, Kimberly M., and Radboud J. Duintjer Tebbens (2007) "Eradication versus Control of Poliomyelitis: An Economic Analysis," *The Lancet* 369: 1363–71.

Tomlinson, John (2003) "Globalization and Cultural Identity," pp. 269–77 in D. Held and A. McGrew (eds), *The Global Transformations Reader: An Introduction to the Globalization Debate*. Cambridge: Polity.

Trouiller, Patrice, Piero Olliaro, Els Torreele, James Orbinski, Richard Laing, and Nathan Ford (2002) "Drug Development for Neglected Diseases: A Deficient Market and a Public-Health Policy Failure," *The Lancet* 359: 2188–94.

Tukuitonga, Colin, and Ingrid Keller (2005) "Implementing the World Health Organization Global Strategy on Diet, Physical Activity, and Health," *Scandinavian Journal of Nutrition* 49: 122–6.

Turner, Bryan (2004) *The New Medical Sociology: Social Forms of Health and Illness.* New York: W. W. Norton.

Turner, Leigh (2007) "Medical Tourism," *Canadian Family Physician* 53: 1639–41.

Twigg, Judith L. (2002) "Health Care Reform in Russia: A Survey of Head Doctors and Insurance Administrators," *Social Science & Medicine* 55: 2253–65.

UNAIDS (2006) *2006 Report on the Global AIDS Epidemic.* Geneva: UNAIDS.

—— (2007a) *AIDS Epidemic Update 2007.* Geneva: UNAIDS.

—— (2007b) *Financial Resources Required to Achieve Universal Access to HIV Prevention, Treatment, Care, and Support.* Geneva: UNAIDS; http://data.unaids.org/pub/Report/2007/20070925_advocacy_grne2_en.pdf (29 September 2008).

UNDP (United Nations Development Program) (2002) *Human Development Report 2002.* New York: Oxford University Press.

—— (1994) *Human Development Report 1994: New Dimensions of Human Security.* New York: Oxford University Press.

—— (2007) *Human Development Report 2007.* New York: Oxford University Press.

US DHHS (Department of Health and Human Services) (2000) *Clinton Administration Record on HIV/AIDS,* 1 December, at www.hhs.gov/news/press/2000pres/00fsaids.html (18 September 2008).

Vitousek, Peter M., Harold A. Mooney, Jane Lubchenco, and Jerry M. Melillo (1997) "Human Domination of Earth's Ecosystems," *Science* 277: 494–9.

Wapner, Jessica (2008) "American Medical Association Provides Guidance on Medical Tourism," *British Medical Journal* 337: 575.

Warren, Mary Guptill, Rose Weitz, and Stephen Kulin (1998) "Physician Satisfaction in a Changing Health Care Environment: The Impact of Challenges to Professional Autonomy, Authority, and Dominance," *Journal of Health and Social Behavior* 39: 356–67.

Weber, Max ([1922] 1978) *Economy and Society,* ed. and trans. G. Roth and C. Wittick, 2 vols. Berkeley: University of California Press.

Williams, Simon J., Jonathan Gabe, and Peter Davis (eds) (2009) *Pharmaceuticals and Society: Critical Discourses and Debates.* Oxford: Wiley-Blackwell.

Whitton, Carol (2004) *Processed Agricultural Exports Led Gains in US Agricultural Exports between 1976 and 2002* (Electronic Output Report FAU-85–01). Washington, DC: US Department of Agriculture.

WHO (World Health Organization) (2000) "Public Hearings on the WHO Framework Convention on Tobacco Control," 12–13 October, at www.who.int/fctc/public_hearings/en/ (30 October 2008).

—— (2002) *World Health Report 2002: Reducing Risks, Promoting Healthy Life*. Geneva: World Health Organization.

—— (2004) *Heat Waves: Risks and Responses*. Copenhagen: WHO Regional Office for Europe.

—— (2007) *Report by the Former Acting Director-General to the Executive Board at its 120th Session* (EB120/40). Geneva: World Health Organization.

—— (2008a) *Global Polio Eradication Initiative: Annual Report 2007*. Geneva: World Health Organization.

—— (2008b) *Global Polio Eradication Initiative: Financial Resource Requirements, 2008–2012*. Geneva: World Health Organization.

—— (2008c) *WHO Report on the Global Tobacco Epidemic, 2008: The MPOWER Package*. Geneva: World Health Organization.

Wilensky, Harold L. (2002) *Rich Democracies: Political Economy, Public Policy, and Performance*. Berkeley: University of California Press.

WMO (World Meteorological Organization) (2003) "According to the World Meteorological Organization, Extreme Weather Events Might Increase," at www.wmo.ch/web/Press/Press695.doc (30 December 2008).

Wogart, Jan Peter (2007) "From Conflict over Compromise to Cooperation? Big Pharma, the HIV/AIDS Crisis and the Rise of Countervailing Power in the South," pp. 38–66 in Wolfgang Hein, Sonja Bartsch, and Lars Kohlmorgen (eds), *Global Health Governance and the Fight against HIV/AIDS*. Basingstoke and New York: Palgrave Macmillan.

Woodward, David (2005) "The GATS and Trade in Health Services: Implications for Health Care in Developing Countries," *Review of International Political Economy* 12: 511–34.

Woodward, David, and Richard D. Smith (2003) "Global Public Goods and Health: Concepts and Issues," pp. 3–29 in R. Smith, R. Beaglehole, D. Woodward, and N. Drager (eds), *Global Public Goods for Health: Health Economic and Public Health Perspectives*. New York: Oxford University Press.

World Bank (1987) *Financing Health Services in Developing Countries: An Agenda for Reform*. Washington, DC: World Bank.

—— (1993) *World Development Report 1993: Investing in Health.* Washington, DC: World Bank.

—— (1994) *World Bank HIV/AIDS Activities.* Washington, DC: World Bank.

—— (1999) *Curbing the Epidemic: Governments and the Economics of Tobacco Control.* Washington, DC: World Bank.

WTO (World Trade Organization) (2001) *Declaration on TRIPS Agreement and Public Health,* at www.wto.org/english/thewto_e/minist_e/min01_e/mindecl_trips_e.htm.

Xiao, Yan, Sibylle Kristensen, Jiangping Sun, Lin Lu, and Sten H. Vermund (2007) "Expansion of HIV/AIDS in China: Lessons from Yunnan Province," *Social Science & Medicine* 64: 665–75.

Yach, Derek, and Douglas W. Bettcher (2000) "Globalization of the Tobacco Industry: Influence and Responses," *Tobacco Control* 9: 206–16.

Yach, Derek, Heather Wipfli, Ross Hammond, and Stanton Glantz (2007) "Health Policy and the World Trade Organization," pp. 39–67 in I. Kawachi and S. Wamala (eds), *Globalization and Health.* New York: Oxford University Press.

York, Diane (2008) "Medical Tourism: The Trend toward Outsourcing Medical Procedures to Foreign Countries," *Journal of Continuing Education in the Health Professions* 28: 99–102.

Zacher, Mark W. (1999) "Global Epidemiological Surveillance: International Cooperation to Monitor Infectious Diseases," pp. 266–83 in I. Kaul, I. Grunberg, and M. Stein (eds), *Global Public Goods: International Cooperation in the 21st Century.* New York: Oxford University Press.

Zakaria, Fareed (2009) *The Post-American World.* New York: W. W. Norton.

Zarcostas, John (2004) "WHO Waters Down Draft Strategy on Diet and Health," *The Lancet* 363: 1373.

Zhou, Yanqui Rachel (2007) "'If You Get AIDS…You Have to Endure it Alone': Understanding the Social Construction of AIDS in China," *Social Science & Medicine* 65: 284–95.

Zurek, Laylah (2007) "The European Communities Biotech Dispute: How the WTO Fails to Consider Cultural Factors in the Genetically Modified Food Debate," *Texas International Law Journal* 42: 345–68.

Author Index

Abbott, Frederick M., 135, 137
Acharya, Arnab, 158–9
Adendorff, Elizabeth, 54
Adlung, Rudolf, 138
Agnocs, Mary, 158–9
Ahmad, Khabir, 166
Ahrin-Tenkorang, Dyna, 156–7
Andrus, Jon K., 156
Anesaki, Masahira, 93–6
Annandale, Ellen C., 90
Arber, Sara, 92
Asher, Robert E., 128
Ashraf, Haroon, 179
Aylward, Bruce R., 158–9

Bartsch, Sonja, 145–6, 165, 167
Batsell, Jake, 167
Baturin, Alexander, 113
Bauman, Zygmunt, 105
Beach, Marilyn V., 166
Beck, Ulrich, 33
Becker, Jasper, 98
Belgrave, Linda Liska, 114–15
Belsky, Leah, 137
Benziger, T. Joseph, 57
Bettcher, Douglas W., 174
Bhagwati, Jagdish, 37, 140
Biehl, Joao, 140

Blaxter, Mildred, 21
Bloche, M. Gregg, 133–4
Bloom, Gerald, 102, 117
Blumenthal, David, 97, 102
Bobak, Martin, 114
Boone, Catherine, 167
Booysen, Frederik, 54
Borio, Gene, 169
Boyer, Carol A., 77–8
Breman, Anna, 131
Brock, G., 113
Brown, Theodore M., 123–5
Bryan, Angela, 57
Budrys, Grace, 77
Busza, Joanna, 54

Campbell, John C., 94–5
Cantor, Norman F., 43
Carzaniga, Antonia, 138
Cash, Richard, 152
Cassileth, Barrie R., 107
Castells, Manuel, 106
Chaloupka, Frank J., 172
Chandola, Tarani, 92
Chapman, Christopher C., 107
Chen, Lincoln C., 35, 152
Chen, Meei-Shia, 97, 99, 102
Chopra, Mickey, 177

Clark, Gregory, 7
Cockerham, William C., 68, 96, 110, 112
Cohen, Jillian Clare, 140
Coleman, Fred, 106
Collier, Paul, 12–14
Collin, Jeff, 174–6
Conceicao, Pedro, 156–7
Corbett, Michaelyn, 172
Cornia, Giovanni Andrea, 37
Cornman, Deborah H., 57
Crescenti, Marcelo G., 170
Cueto, Marcos, 123–5

Daniel, John S., 38
Danishevski, K., 114
Davis, Peter, 139
de Beyer, Joy A., 129, 131–2
De Gruijl, Frank R., 38
de Quadros, Ciro A., 156
Deev, Alexander, 113
Deng, Rui, 56
DeWaal, Derek F., 112
Diaz, Jose, 141–2
Dmitrieva, Elena, 113
Dodoo, F. Nii-Amoo, 55
Dollar, David, 12–14
Dorling, Danny, 92
Douglas, Mary, 33
Drewnowski, Adam, 177
Drucker, Peter, 65
DuBos, René, 27

Emanuei, Ezekiei J., 137
Engel, George L., 27
England, Sarah, 158–9
Evans, Tim G., 152
Ezeh, Alex C., 55

Fahey, David W., 39
Feacham, Richard G. A., 129, 131–2
Featherstone, Mike, 9
Fee, Elizabeth, 123–5
Fidler, David P., 48–9, 98, 121, 123–4, 126

Field, David, 90
Field, Mark G., 108, 112
Fisher, Jeffrey D., 57
Ford, Nathan, 141
Frankel, Jeffrey, 18
Frieden, Jeffery A., 3, 7
Friedman, Irwin F., 54
Friedman, Thomas L., 4–6, 15
Fritschler, A. Lee, 169
Fukuda, Hidebi, 96

Gabe, Jonathan, 139
Garrett, Geoffrey, 16
Garrett, Laurie, 61–2, 167
Garrison, Christopher, 141–2
Garwood, Paul, 159
Giddens, Anthony, 4, 7, 34
Gilmore, Anna B., 113–14, 171
Gilpin, R., 3
Glantz, Stanton, 169–76
Godlee, Fiona, 125
Gold, Marsha R., 72, 79
Goldman, Merle, 100–1
Grunberg, Isabelle, 150
Guerra de Macedo, Carlyle, 156
Guindon, Emmanuel, 172
Guzman, Javier, 141–2

Hale, Victoria G., 141
Hammond, Ross, 169–76
Hannerz, Ulf, 9
Hattori, Hiroyuki, 96
Hawkes, Corinna, 178
Hein, Wolfgang, 136
Held, David, 11
Hesketh, Therese, 99, 103
Heymann, David L., 36
Hirst, Paul, 12
Homedes, Nuria, 130–1
Horton, Sue, 177
Hosegood, Victoria, 54
Howard-Jones, Norman, 120
Hsiao, William, 97, 102
Hunter, Mark, 55

Ikegami, Naoki, 94–5
Iriart, Celia, 80

Jarvis, Martin J., 92
Jasso-Aguilar, Rebecca, 80, 142
Jewkes, Rachel K., 55
Jha, Prabhat, 172
Jinks, Martin J., 80, 83
Jungman, Elizabeth R., 133–4

Kapstein, Ethan, 4
Kapur, Devesh, 129
Karns, Margaret P., 138, 143–4
Kaul, Inge, 150
Kawachi, Ichiro, 36
Keller, Ingrid, 179
Keohane, Robert O., 9, 15, 17, 22–3
Kiernann, V. G., 169
Kim, Soowon, 177
King, Anthony D., 9
Kivela, Katarina, 92
Knaus, William A., 107
Kohlmeier, Lenore, 113
Kohlmorgen, Lars, 145–6, 167
Koivusalo, Meri, 133–5
Kornai, János, 104–5
Kristensen, Sibylle, 56
Kulin, Stephen, 79

Labonté, Ronald, 22, 37, 186
Lahelma, Eero, 92
Laing, Richard, 141
Landwehr, Angela, 80, 142
Lange, Peter, 16
Lanoszka, Anna, 135, 145
Lassey, Marie L., 80, 83
Lassey, William R., 80, 83
Lee, Kelley, 162, 178
Leon, David, 111
Levin, Jonathan B., 55
Lewis, John P., 129
Li, Jianghong, 56
Lie, Reidar, 137
Light, Donald W., 73, 78, 90

Linkins, Jennifer, 158–9
Lipton, Helene Levens, 141
Livi Bacci, Massimo, 43–4
Lopez, Alan D., 113
Lu, Lin, 56
Lubchenco, Jane, 38
Lupton, Deborah, 33
Lybecker, Kristina M., 140

Maddison, Angus, 12
Magnusson, Roger S., 180
Makino, Kae, 96
Malia, Martin, 105
Marmot, Michael, 92
Martin, Jack K., 77
Martinchik, Arseni, 113
Mason, Edward S., 128
Matthews, Jessica T., 19
Mattoo, Aaditya, 137
Mbugua, J. Karanja, 117
McGrew, Andrew, 11
McIntosh, William Alex, 55
McKee, Martin, 85–6, 111, 113–14, 171, 185
McMichael, Anthony J., 38, 85–6, 185
Mechanic, David, 78–80
Medvedev, Roy, 112
Melillo, Jerry M., 38
Mendez, Michelle, 177
Mezentseva, Elena, 107
Mingst, Karen A., 138, 143–4
Moitse, Sindile, 54
Mooney, Harold A., 38
Moran, Mary, 141–2
Morse, Stephen S., 44
Mtika, Mike Mathambo, 54
Munakata, Tsunetsugu, 56, 93, 95–6
Murphy, John W., 114–15

Narasimhan, Vasant, 35
Nemstov, Alexander V., 111, 113
Nettleton, Sarah, 92
Ngwena, Charles, 54, 116
Nishi, Nobuo, 96

Norris, Pippa, 17
Nye, Joseph S., 9, 15, 17, 22–3

Oglobin, C., 113
Olive, Jean-Marc, 156
Olliaro, Piero, 141
Olson, Mancur, 153
Orbinski, James, 141
Ostrom, Elinor, 154–5

Packard, Randall M., 123
Packer, Corinne, 22, 37, 186
Palosuo, Hannele, 113
Patterson, Amy S., 162, 165, 167
Pelser, André, 54
Penn-Kekana, Loveday A., 55
Perlman, Francesca, 114
Pescosolido, Bernice A., 77–8
Phares, Christina R., 156
Popkin, Barry M., 113, 177–8
Porter, Roy, 25, 28–9, 54
Powell, Margaret, 94, 96
Preker, Alexander S., 129, 131–2
Preston, Richard, 1, 51–2
Preston-Whyte, Eleanor, 54

Quadagno, Jill, 69, 82

Ranmuthugala, G., 38
Ray, Larry, 2
Reid, Ivan, 92
Reingold, Arthur L., 156
Rensberg, H. C. J. van, 54, 116
Reznik, David L., 114–15
Rimachevskaya, Natalia, 107
Robertson, Roland, 3
Roos, Eva, 92
Roper, Anne-Laure, 141–2
Rosignoli, Stefano, 37
Ruger, Jennifer Prah, 129–31
Runnels, Vivien, 22, 37, 186
Russell, Asia, 168

Schmiege, Sarah J., 57
Schrecker, Ted, 22, 37, 186
Seavey, Nina Gilden, 156

Seckinelgin, Hakan, 163–4
Segal, Malcolm, 117
Sengupta, Amit, 131
Shadlen, Kenneth C., 168
Shapiro, Judith, 113
Shaw, Mary, 92
Shelton, Carolyn, 131
Shibuya, Kenji, 36
Shisana, Olive, 36
Shisana, William, 36
Shkolnikov, Vladimir M., 85–6,
    111, 185
Slaper, Harry, 38
Smith, Anthony D., 7–8
Smith, George Davey, 92
Smith, Jane S., 156
Smith, Richard D., 150–2
Snead, M. Christine, 112
Sreenivasan, Gopai, 137
Sringernyuang, Luechai, 56
Stein, Marc A., 150
Stevens, Fred, 77
Stevens, Rosemary, 63
Steyn, François, 54
Stiglitz, Joseph E., 3, 14
Stocker, Karen, 80
Strange, Susan, 6
Studlar, Donley T., 172–3
Sun, Jiangping, 56

Tajima, Kazoo, 56
Tang, Shengian, 102
Tatarra, Kozo, 96
Tawfik, Linda, 55
Taylor, Allyn, 172
Tebbens, Radboud J. Duintjer, 159
Thomas, Caroline, 124, 135, 141
Thomas, John K., 55
Thompson, Grahame, 12
Thompson, John B., 12
Thompson, Kimberly M., 159
Tiberti, Luca, 37
Timaeus, Ian M., 54
Tomlinson, John, 17
Torreele, Els, 141
Trouiller, Patrice, 141

Tuch, Steven A., 77
Tukuitonga, Colin, 179
Turner, Bryan, 11, 22
Turner, Leigh, 30
Twigg, Judith L., 108

Ugalde, Antonio, 130–1

Valkonen, Tapani, 85–6, 185
Van Der Leun, Jan C., 38
Velders, Guus J. M., 38
Vermund, Sten H., 56
Vitousek, Peter M., 38
Vlassov, Vasily V., 107

Wagner, Paul, 156
Waitzkin, Howard, 80, 142
Wamala, Sarah, 36
Wapner, Jessica, 31
Wardle, Jane, 92
Warren, Mary Guptill, 79
Watkins, Susan Cotts, 55
Webb, Richard, 129
Weber, Martin, 124
Weber, Max, 25–6

Weitz, Rose, 79
Whitton, Carol, 177
Williams, Simon J., 139
Wipfi, Heather, 169–76
Wogart, Jan Peter, 139
Woo, Katherine, 141
Woodward, David, 137–8, 150–2

Xiao, Yan, 56

Yach, Derek, 169–76
Yamori, Yukio, 96
York, Diane, 31–2

Zacher, Mark W., 151
Zakaria, Fareed, 7–9, 66
Zarcostas, John, 179
Zhang, Kaining, 56
Zhou, Yanqui Rachel, 56
Zohoori, Namvar, 113
Zu, Weixing, 99, 103
Zulu, Eliya M., 55
Zunga-Dirwayi, Nompumelelo, 36
Zurek, Laylah, 134
Zwi, Anthony, 162

Subject Index

Affordable Health Care for America Act, 81
Agreement on Sanitary and Phytosanitary Measures (SPS), 133–4, 138
Agreement on Trade-Related Aspects of Intellectual Property Rights (TRIPS), 132–9, 145, 164, 168
alcohol consumption, 37, 85, 96, 110–13, 133, 152
allied health enterprises, 70–1
Alma Ata declaration, 124, 148, 180, 185
American exceptionalism, 69, 76
American Journal of International Law, 176
American Medical Association, 31, 82–3
Americanization, 17, 64, 66
antiretroviral drugs (ARVs), 53, 140, 160, 163–5, 168

bioterrorism, 45, 51
Bretton Woods, 13, 128, 132, 144
Britain, *see* United Kingdom

British Medical Association (BMA), 89
bubonic plague, 22, 43, 120, 123
Bush, George W., 40, 82, 140, 166

capitalism, 2, 4, 7, 15, 25–6, 66
capitation financing, 71, 77, 79–80, 88, 90
Centers for Disease Control and Prevention (CDC), 21–2, 51, 58–9, 70, 158, 161
China
    barefoot doctors movement, 99, 102
    health care system, 97–104
    health reform, 102
    level of globalization, 97–8
    uninsured, 104
Chinese medicine, 93, 98–9
cholera, 22, 28, 120, 123, 126
chronic diseases, 110, 112
    see also heart disease; obesity
cigarette use, *see* smoking
climate change, 10–11, 34, 38–42, 145, 152
Clinton, Bill, 40, 77, 82–3, 140, 166

Cold War, end of, 2, 4, 10, 14, 17, 19, 34, 119, 123, 125, 127, 142, 148, 171, 183
collective action, 149, 153–5, 158–9, 167, 181–4, 186
    free-riding, 153, 155, 182
compulsory licensing, 135–6, 139–40, 164
convergence of health, 85–6
cosmopolitans, 9, 17

diagnostic related groups (DRGs), 75, 80
diet, 95–6, 110, 112–13, 149, 177–80, 183–4
diphtheria, 28, 44
disease patterns, 95, 110
Doctors Without Borders, *see* Médecins Sans Frontières (MSF)
Doha declaration, 136–8, 145, 164, 167–8, 184

Ebola, 1, 22, 45
employer-sponsored health insurance, 72, 83
European Union, 40, 83–4, 172
exercise, *see* physical activity

fee-for-service health care, 68–73, 77, 87, 94, 97, 103–4, 118, 187
foreign direct investment (FDI), 177–8
Foreign Policy, 15–16
formal rationality, 25–6
Framework Convention on Tobacco Control (FCTC), 126, 174–6, 179, 183–4

Gates Foundation, 142, 157, 182
General Agreement on Tariffs and Trade (GATT), 13, 132–4
General Agreement on Trade in Services (GATS), 132–3, 137–8

general practitioner (GP), 88, 90–1
    as gatekeeper, 78–9, 88
generic drugs, 135, 139–41, 145, 163, 168, 182
genetically modified (GM) foods, 134
global culture, 7–9, 65, 67, 84, 97, 101
Global Fund to Fight AIDS, Tuberculosis, and Malaria, 126, 144, 165–7, 183
global governance, 23, 67–8, 149, 155–6, 159–60, 162–8, 175, 178–84, 186
    actors in, 19–21, 23, 29, 119–24, 127, 129, 131, 138–9, 141–6, 153
    defined, 18
global interconnections, 10, 29, 42, 64–6, 84, 86, 92, 97, 104, 106, 116, 148, 152
global pandemics, 29, 42, 45–7, 62, 185, 187
Global Program on AIDS (GPA), 161–3
global public good, 23, 149–56, 158–9, 168, 175, 181–2
Global Strategy on Diet, Physical Activity, and Health (GSDPAH), 178–9, 183–4
global warming, *see* climate change
globalization, 2, 24
    and environment, 37–9
    and risk, 32–4, 42
    barriers to, 10
    defined, 2–10
    historical context, 10–15
    homogenization, 7, 9, 64–5, 67, 83–4, 86, 92, 97–8, 104, 116
    inequality, 15
    level of, 16
    periods of, 5
    political aspects, 4
    regulated, 18
    social aspects, 4

health, defined, 21
health maintenance organizations
    (HMOs), 70–3, 77, 82
Health Organization of the
    League of Nations, 121–2
heart disease, 92, 95–6, 103, 110,
    112, 177
HIV/AIDS, 22, 35–6, 42, 44–5,
    52–62, 85, 117–18, 127, 135,
    140–1, 148–9, 160–8, 180,
    182–6
human security, 34–6

immunization, 44, 125, 129,
    156–7, 159, 182
infectious diseases, 1, 22, 28, 35,
    38, 42, 44–5, 85, 103, 110,
    112, 129, 141, 149, 152,
    156, 168, 181, 186
  spread of, 11, 19, 36, 42–5,
    119–20, 123, 148, 152, 165,
    180, 186
  surveillance of, 35, 126–7, 151,
    158, 163
  see also bubonic plague; cholera;
    diphtheria; Ebola; HIV/AIDS;
    influenza; malaria; Marburg
    virus; polio; severe acute
    respiratory syndrome;
    smallpox; tuberculosis; West
    Nile virus; yellow fever
influenza, 22, 45–7
intellectual property protection,
    134, 137, 139, 141, 160,
    167–8
intergovernmental organizations
    (IGOs), 18–20, 65, 67, 84,
    120–1, 127, 131–2, 143–4,
    146, 153, 157, 159, 165,
    167, 174, 181, 184
International AIDS Conference,
    161, 163
International Health Regulations
    (IHR), 123–4, 126–7, 158,
    181
international law, 19–20, 121,
    126, 174

International Monetary Fund
    (IMF), 13–14, 19, 37, 114,
    120, 125, 127–32, 142, 146,
    170, 174, 184, 186
International Trade Organization
    (ITO), 13, 132
Internet, 6, 14–16, 22, 29, 48, 64,
    92, 98, 101

Japan
  health care system, 92–6
  level of globalization, 92
Joint United Nations and World
    Health Organization
    Programme on HIV/AIDS, 53

Kenya
  barriers to care, 117
  health care system, 115–18
Kyoto Protocol, 40

League of Nations, 13, 121, 144
life expectancy, 54, 85–6, 92, 95,
    99, 103, 108–12, 114, 117,
    185
Logic of Collective Action, 153, 181

malaria, 28, 38, 118, 123–4, 126,
    148, 165, 168, 180
malnutrition, 36, 39
managed care, 70–2, 77–80, 83–4,
    142–3
Marburg virus, 22, 45
Médecins Sans Frontières (MSF),
    21–2, 144–5, 157
Medicaid, 72–6, 81–2, 84, 142,
    173
medical research, 28, 63, 66, 71,
    100
medical schools, 28–9, 91, 93,
    100, 107, 117
medical tourism, 24, 29–32, 88
Medicare, 72–6, 81–2, 84, 142
migrant labor system, 54, 56,
    61–2
migration, 10–14, 29, 43, 45, 54,
    101, 152

modernization, 2, 26, 33–4, 92–3, 96–7, 101, 106, 110, 114
Montreal Protocol, 39–40
multinational corporations (MNCs), 5–8, 20–1, 29, 63, 65, 67, 80, 84, 115, 120, 138–46, 153, 170–1, 176, 181, 186

national health insurance, 69, 81–2, 87, 89, 93–4, 117
neoliberalism, 14, 37, 125, 130, 133, 146, 162, 183–4
New Institutionalism, 153–5, 181
non-governmental organizations (NGOs), 18–21, 65, 67, 84, 120, 126–7, 132, 135, 143–6, 153, 157, 159, 162–6, 173–6, 178, 181–2, 184, 186
non-state actors, 119, 129, 166–7, 174, 182
authority of, 64–5, 67, 84, 86, 92, 98, 104
North American Free Trade Agreement (NAFTA), 10, 172, 177

Obama, Barack, 41, 68, 80, 83, 169
obesity, 141, 177–8
Organization for Economic Cooperation and Development, 21, 142, 158
Oxfam International, 20, 144–5

pharmaceutical industry, 21–2, 65–6, 72, 120, 125, 127, 135–6, 139–41, 143, 145, 160, 163–4, 167–8, 182
physical activity, 110, 112–13, 178
polio, 149, 156–60, 180–2, 184
pollution, 2, 41, 112, 152
poverty, 35–7, 41, 55, 74–5, 89, 92, 117, 165, 186
preferred provider organizations (PPOs), 71–3, 77

President's Emergency Plan for AIDS Relief (PEPFAR), 166–7
Prisoner's Dilemma, 153–5, 181
private health insurance, 70, 72, 80–1, 87, 131
public–private partnerships (PPPs), 126, 141–2, 144, 165

quarantine procedures, 43, 45, 50, 120

rationality, 25–6
Red Cross, 20–1, 65, 67, 144, 157, 186
responsibility for health, 35
Rotary International, 157–9, 182
Russia
health care system, 104–14
level of globalization, 104

sanitation, 36, 43, 99, 121
severe acute respiratory syndrome (SARS), 22, 34, 44–5, 47–50, 98, 103
sexually transmitted diseases (STDs), 61–2
smallpox, 11, 22, 43–4, 123–4, 126
smoking, 21, 36–7, 85, 96, 103–4, 110, 112–14, 126, 133, 149, 152, 168–76, 178, 183–4
Social Security, 69, 73–4
socialism, 2, 82, 97, 100, 105, 107
state sovereignty, 11, 17, 19, 121–2, 186
structural adjustment program (SAP), 128, 130–2
substantive rationality, 26

technological change, 2–3, 5–6, 11, 14–15, 17, 106, 110, 119, 143, 146
tobacco use *see* smoking

traditional/folk medicine, 114,
116–17
Trinidad, health care system,
114–15
tuberculosis, 28, 141, 148, 165,
168

unhealthy lifestyles, 85, 92, 110,
112–13
United Kingdom
health care system, 86–92
level of globalization, 86
United Nations (UN), 13, 19, 35,
55–7, 61, 65, 67, 92, 120–3,
128, 157, 165, 167, 174,
180, 182
Children's Fund (UNICEF),
159
Development Program
(UNDP), 15, 150, 157
Economic and Social Council,
144, 163
Framework Convention on
Climate Change, 40
General Assembly, 122, 148,
161, 164
Human Development Report, 36
Intergovernmental Panel on
Climate Change (IPCC), 38
Millennium Development
Goals, 36, 148, 180, 185
Office for the Coordination of
Humanitarian Affairs, 35
Program on AIDS (UNAIDS),
140, 163–4, 166–7, 183
Security Council, 19, 122, 127,
151, 160
United States
Department of Health and
Human Services, 70, 74, 166
Food and Drug Administration
(FDA), 70, 169, 173, 176
health care system, 63, 68–84
health reform, 77, 80–3

level of globalization, 64–8
Pharmacopoeia, 169
Public Health Service, 70
uninsured, 68, 80, 82–4, 187
universal health coverage, 68, 76,
81–3, 102–3, 108, 187

Washington Consensus, 125, 146
West Nile virus, 22, 45, 50–2,
186
Western medicine, 24–9, 63, 67,
93, 98–9, 114–16, 187
Westernization, 64, 66–7
World Bank, 13–14, 19, 21, 37,
65, 86, 114, 120, 125,
127–32, 138, 142, 146, 158,
162, 167, 170–4, 180, 184,
186
*World Bank Development Report
1993*, 129
World Health Assembly (WHA),
21, 39, 122–5, 127, 156,
158, 174–5
World Health Organization
(WHO), 19, 21–2, 24, 29,
39, 42, 44, 47–50, 55–7, 61,
66, 86, 92, 98, 120–9,
131–2, 144, 146, 157–9,
161–2, 167–8, 172, 174–83,
186
Commission on Social
Determinants of Health, 37
Tobacco Free Initiative (TFI),
173–4
World Summit of Health
Ministers, 161
World Trade Organization
(WTO), 10, 13–14, 19, 21,
120, 127, 132–8, 140, 145–6,
164, 168, 171, 174, 177,
182–3
World Values Survey, 17

yellow fever, 123, 126

Lightning Source UK Ltd.
Milton Keynes UK
UKOW06f2231130515

251461UK00001B/54/P